Tramping to Jerusalem

TRAMPING TO JERUSALEM

The End Game of All or Nothing at All

A Memoir

Antonio Cammarata

SUNSTONE PRESS
SANTA FE

© 2015 by Antonio Cammarata
All Rights Reserved.

No part of this book may be reproduced in any form or by any electronic or mechanical means including information storage and retrieval systems without permission in writing from the publisher, except by a reviewer who may quote brief passages in a review.

Sunstone books may be purchased for educational, business, or sales promotional use. For information please write: Special Markets Department, Sunstone Press, P.O. Box 2321, Santa Fe, New Mexico 87504-2321.

Book and cover design › Vicki Ahl
Body typeface › Adobe Hebrew
Printed on acid-free paper
∞
eBook 978-1-61139-359-0

Library of Congress Cataloging-in-Publication Data

Cammarata, Antonio, author.
 Tramping to Jerusalem : the end game of all or nothing at all / a memoir by Antonio Cammarata.
  pages cm
 ISBN 978-1-63293-051-4 (softcover : alk. paper)
 1. Israel--Description and travel. 2. Cammarata, Antonio. I. Title.
 DS107.5.C35 2015
 307.77'6092--dc23
 [B]
                         2014047922

WWW.SUNSTONEPRESS.COM
SUNSTONE PRESS / POST OFFICE BOX 2321 / SANTA FE, NM 87504-2321 /USA
(505) 988-4418 / ORDERS ONLY (800) 243-5644 / FAX (505) 988-1025

To my father Cateno
and
oppressed people everywhere.

Foreword

In 1986 I thought it was time to realize my wife Mona's long deferred dream of working on a kibbutz, (a collective community in Israel traditionally based on agriculture)—"a right of return," a kind of passage or pilgrimage akin to the Muslims' journey to Mecca.

When it came to Israel, despite our past travels we were the perennial innocents abroad, like most Americans regarding Palestinians as "terrorists" trespassing on the Land God gave to Israel. Our awakening, especially difficult for Mona, led to this book, a highly personal account which has become the road to Gaza for me. A primer for today.

Our day by day working and traveling "kibbutz hopping" is an incidental but interesting bearing-witness to the how and why of an apparent unconditional support of Israel illustrated by a literal fusion of America's stars and stripes and a Star of David. This "flag," this fusion is about confusing the issue—the Palestinians' decades-long struggle for the freedom that eventually came to South Africa. In such a situation a "terrorist," can be seen as a freedom fighter.

To speak honestly about Israel, like the late Gore Vidal or Noam Chomsky, is to be dismissed as anti-Semitic, or engaging in the rant of a self-hating Jew, when righteous anger is a resonable response to "genocidal" and suicidal policy of occupation. The literal wall that now cuts across the land has only widened the division between Arab and Jew and the rest of the civilized world.

To make the unacceptable understandable to the uninformed or misinformed reader, it is necessary to know what followed Israel's independence in 1948. Most Palestinian villages were left in ruins and as in ancient times these ruins formed actual foundations for kibbutzim. I saw one such kibbutz at Gilgal. Also, grave-sized holes just beyond. Yet Theodore Herzl, Viennese founder of Zionism and advocating Jewish emigration to Palestine, claimed that a people without a land would be going to a land without people. Not only was the land inhabited, the people who did not flee the zionist invasion came under an occupation that has led to a series of wars.

I think that it has been well established that the 1967 war, blamed on Egypt, was started by Israel. An American warship monitoring Israel's preparation for an invasion was actually attacked by Israel. The Israel Defense Forces (IDF) is efficient, but Israel's major battles, in my opinion are won on American soil. Our response to the attack was a slap on the wrist as Israel's enemies became ours.

Nothing brought home more the demonization of the Palestinian than an incident that occurred one brisk morning at the kibbutz Sde Boker bus stop, south of Beersheba. I sat next to a lone Palestinian workman, a gentle but salt of the earth soul who smelled of fire and the cold night. Such was the contrast between him and the arrogant kibbutzniks, that I couldn't help speaking to him, to the consternation of the standoffish Israelis—as much victims of this apartheid as the Palestinians.

The following day the personnel director chastised me: I was not in America. The implication was that I was consorting with the enemy, cause for dismissal—on Christmas Eve. A couple of weeks later, hiking about kibbutz Gilgal on the West Bank where I worked with Mona, an Israeli soldier in the valley fired a shot at me. Either he thought I was a Palestinian, or I was that Palestinian sympathizer who had worked in Sde Boker and was speaking out. The soldier said later he was hunting. (Palestinians would have been blamed for my demise.)

Real or imagined "terrorists" (freedom fighters) deflect from the universally condemned illegal settlements of Israel that preclude a peace settlement. And yet, decades down the road, accepted as gospel is the dismissive fiction that Palestinian resistance to the occupation and provocation is the manifestation of an ancient blood feud when for much of history, until Israel drove Palestinians from their land, Muslims regarded Jews as people of the book, recognizing the same prophets. And except for Palestinians about to lose their land, they more than any other group, assisted Jews at the risk of losing their own lives during the Nazi occupation of Europe and North Africa.

Ignoring what the American Israel Political Action Committee (original meaning of AIPAC) knows to be true is not to be real about the greatest travesty, tragedy, since the Holocaust. And so obfuscation remains the response to "occupation"—a word strangely absent in standard explications of resistance to oppression.

In *The New York Times* of September 16, 2014 "An Open Letter to President Barack Obama" (full page) endorsed by such organizations as Deir Yassin Remembered, Americans for a Just Peace in the Middle East, Jewish Witnesses for Peace and Friends, If Americans Knew, and several others makes a powerful support of what I am saying in this book. Several days later, September 20, 2014, a related full-page article in *The New York Times* by Michael Laitman, "Who Are You, People of Israel?" makes a plea for peace that fits well with the sentiments in the September 16th piece.

And interestingly, the opera presented at the Metropolitan Opera in New York, "The Death of Klinghoffer," based on actual events in 1984, in which a Palestinian "terrorist" murders Leon Klinghoffer, has been met with protesting groups demanding that the production be scrapped, "contending that this opera is anti-Semitic" as *The New York Times* reports in an editorial of September 20, 2014. Such is the sensitivity over the Israel/Palestine situation.

Israel will not know peace until the Palestinians know justice and Americans understand that treating people as terrorists, who yearn to be free, is to create them—often crazed, homicidal as well as suicidal. The threat to the U.S. will be less if there is a valid peace in Israel.

Our first introduction to kibbutz life was Snir, in the Golan Heights. Like a concentration camp it was surrounded by barbed wire. It was the saddest irony, that in the Jewish about-face, wearing the jack boots, becoming the oppressor, it became a prisoner.

The tragedy of Israel/Palestine was made possible by the negation, the "invisibility" of a people who never left their land. This indifference of the Israelis borne by the inconvenience of the suffering of others was not unlike their own fate in World War II and throughout much of history. Though it warrants repeating, Muslims, ironically, were their greatest benefactors during World War II—an inconvenient fact.

Hitchhiking lends itself to communion, confessions of strangers passing in the night (often at night in our case). Responding to my point about Israel breaking its biblical covenant with God and being essentially a Godless country, one benefactor in the driver's seat said: Jews no longer need God, they have Israel.

My focus on Israel may be misleading in that this book is basically a travel journal, the last leg on many levels, of a journey that took me through Turkey, Cyprus and Greece, which informs my book. I am less an "expert" (if such a thing exists on Israel) than a seeker of old, but the situation in the Middle East at this time is so dire that I've allowed myself to be sidetracked with what I know and feel to be true.

—Los Alamos/Taos, New Mexico, September 2014

1

Where the Grapes of Wrath are Stored

It's not yet ten and Europe is in the grip of an Arctic winter but a hot sun has already awakened the man-biting fleas and is beginning to bake the West Bank. I look longingly through the grapevines I am pruning with my wife Mona, beyond the even rows of date palms to the cooler hills and the feathery cirrus clouds swirling in out of the north. Mount Hermon covered with snow on the Syrian border comes to mind and I think of our Druse friends huddled around their electric heater.

The clouds promised relief. Another broken promise in the Promised Land, but recent rains have left in their wake a vast undulating sea of wildflowers that have breached the barbed-wire perimeter of our kibbutz and even spring up, poppy and posy, in and around the wadis winding their way to the River Jordan. Just a few miles north of the Dead Sea patches of remaining marshes spared by the merciless military are alive with waterfowl and you can almost block out the machinegun fire.

I came this way a couple of days ago trying to catch a glimpse of the river, beyond bulldozer and bunkers, almost up to the red and white oil barrels that lined what was supposed to be a wired fence running parallel to the border road. I couldn't have been very far from the Gilgal of Moses, those stones which to him represented the tribes of Israel he was leading to the Promised Land, crossing the Jordan, just beneath our kibbutz of the same name. Gilgal (Kibbutzniks considered this journey as part of the Moses "myth").

I hoped the area wasn't mined. Kibbutz members knew of my intention to wander about the lower wadis, or did they think I would be driven here.

Israelis had a somewhat cavalier approach to death. In 1982 on the Golan Heights, across the road from Kibbutz Snir where we worked in early November, two young Americans were blown away in the unmarked minefield—cow field which remains unlabeled. Their deaths occurred opposite the kiosk the kibbutz operated (in season) above the Banyas Falls.

Snir was just below Banyas, where Christ is thought to have said "on this rock I will build my church." The altar to Pan, Herod's Palace, the spring that is one of the sources of the Jordan River or at least the Sea of Galilee (or Kinneret as the Israelis call that lovely but now near toxic lake) is in the bosom of encircling mine fields—identified as such with little metal triangles.

The practical way to approach the river is by the bus that runs the length of the Jordan valley, between Gilgal's tangle of grapevines, by February pruned head-high and the ghoulish gray corn we left rotting on their stalks those last days of December (an effect of Europe's nuclear accident). The bus would pass the civilian road that could then take me the remaining six miles or so to the Allenby Bridge. But it is already ano 1987, and Mona, who had been sitting out most of my misadventures these past few months, and I could not bear to board another Egged, other than the one that would take us into Jerusalem for a grand finale.

Of course, I could hitchhike, as we did around much of Turkey and miniscule Israel, but that was no picnic either and you could say the party or the moveable feast was over. At least the Turks were hospitable and didn't I see the handwriting on the wall of the shelter outside the Ein Gedi Youth Hostel. It is designed for hitchhikers, as well as bus riders, who sometimes left a little message for those who might follow in their footsteps.

Suffice it to say that at this stage of the game nothing was more appealing to me than a lone trek along some deserted goat trail a thousand feet below sea level. There was even a breeze keeping the fleas at bay and I meditated upon a desert pine of respectable height.

Reaching the narrow tarmac that led to the border road, I was met head on by an army jeep. It struck me if this was a military zone, the best defense was an offense, an Israeli stratagem. Quixotically, I asked the lone driver where I might be able to command a good view of the river.

"Do you know where you are?" the officer asked.

"Yes."

"Where are you coming from?"

I replied, "New York." Where else, but the borough of La Mancha.

A quizzical look crossed his face that seemed to say that explains everything. "You aren't permitted to be here."

Like most of the Israelis we'd met, the army captain said he had recently been to New York and the Big Apple was my ticket to ride. Without being asked for my passport or visa, I was allowed to ride shotgun while he interrogated me ever so smoothly. As laid back as an Israeli soldier hitchhiking sans Uzi.

"Kibbutz?" The stocky young man with the rumpled bars on his shoulders and a little blonde hair on his head eyed my gray-streaked beard. The average age of a kibbutz "volunteer" was about 21. By the time my guide had driven me to the "fish pond," he had surmised I was a "hobo." As hitchhiking was referred to as "tramping," I could not take too much offense. And weren't Mona and I unpaid workers, migrant workers without a home to return to? Those lyrics we'd heard at the Turkish officers' club on the Black Sea near the Russian border after one raki too many played in my head, "Sometimes I feel like a motherless child a long way from home."

In the canal, ducks, maybe baby mallards, were paddling peacefully by. Encouraged by the bucolic scene to push my luck with the young captain, I said, "I really would like a view of the river." That almost mythical Jordan, rolling on. Gateway to that promised land that is only in the pure of heart.

"Impossible. I will take you back to Gilgal to keep you out of trouble."

Lift that bar, tote that bale, get a little drunk on the idea of liberation and you land in jail. As we neared the main road, the territory occupied by the moshov to the south of Gilgal's farmland was being worked by mostly black stoop laborers, segregated Palestinians picking eggplants for about a third of what an Israeli might earn if he stooped so low. The freshly picked vegetables went into the Legumbres Selectiones boxes ("produce of Israel") piled on the side of the road.

Some of these workers lived down the main road in the Ein Sultan Refugee Camp, north of Jericho, where many of the Palestinians were indistinguishable from their African ancestors. Here, women and children in ancient dress labored in the fields beneath the Mount of Temptation. A black boy from this area assisted Mona and me in pulling away the vines we were pruning in the vineyards, before we went to work with the young Zionists from Chile and Argentina. These 16- and 17-year-old innocents, with rats in their kibbutz accommodations (for which they paid), were unaware that Jacobo Timerman had left Israel to return to Argentina an embittered man.

Mona, making a kind of proxy pilgrimage for her ailing mother, was also torn apart by the numbing disparity between the Israeli dream and the Madison Avenue whitewash of a reality as black as the hat of the hated Hassidim. Oh, they were good PR for the Holy Land image, but they refused to bear arms as they awaited the arrival of the Messiah on the back of a white ass. Both Mona's parents are Jewish and have invested a small fortune in the future of Israel, and even Mona bought a tree or two as a child, maybe one of those ecologically incorrect eucalyptus trees that are a mixed blessing.

Planes screamed up the valley towards Lebanon, one of them veering off to the west as if in salute of Massu's Sarraba above the road to Tel Aviv. The day after Christmas or the first Hanukkah eve (we spent Christmas eve in the town of Bethlehem, where I almost went to jail because I refused to give up my metal detected penknife), a kibbutznik drove us up to the base of the pyramidal peak—the windswept saddle above the archaeological site I never saw. A small turnout was on hand to watch auto tires go up in smoke, billowing towards Lebanon, lit up in commemoration of the Maccabee victory over the Greeks.

In antiquity, the flames could be seen beyond these Biblical Bethel hills, the Jerusalem Hills and in the Holy City itself; but now out of convenience or fear the tires were torched before the sun had set. A Gilgalite bearing a flaming torch took off down the mountain accompanied by a couple of members. Soon they were on the main road, taking turns keeping their symbol of liberation aloft. David, the New Yorker, was carrying the torch for several minutes before it resembled a smoking revolver. His fire had gone out. The torch was relit and they were heading back to Gilgal to light the Menorah—after we had chow in the dining hall. Again, just a handful of members turned out for the lighting of the huge Hebrew candelabra—the desired shape of a pruned grapevine.

David is a nice kid and looked for all the world like the young Mark Spitz sprinting down the highway in the direction of his beloved banana grove, hedged in between the picked cotton and the radiated corn with those grotesque marble-sized kernels distorted beyond recognition. A couple of days later, Dave was teaching us how to poison the young banana shoots. We kidded him about his mother having paid us to take him back to the States, and he retorted that Mona actually looked like his mother and I looked like her boyfriend. We are a hodgepodge of farmhands as different as the crops we pruned and picked, and some required more irrigation.

Dave completed his opan months ago and had made his mother's Zionist dream come true—up to a point. She didn't want her son going into the army to serve his mandatory time, but running alongside that highway Hanukkah eve as if proclaiming the West Bank to be Israeli seemed like the next best thing. I thought what a tempting target David would make for any armed Palestinian on either side of the border. But I looked at the young runner jogging down that road of no return with mixed feelings. Was the muscular Jew running tall and proud a phoenix or a peacock, if not a sitting duck. And then his fire expired. Dave has already said, "My mom should be doing what you guys are doing."

The army jeep turned right on the main road, and I looked down an exquisite expanse of scallions, as green as any emerald isle, swallowed up by the wadis from which we had emerged.

"Are you having any trouble down there?"

My military friend—and by now we were on a first name basis—simply glanced at me, "What do you think?" All of the artillery fire and machinegun bursts that punctured life the length of this long "island" (replete with those pre-fab Levittowns) wasn't all military exercises.

"Do you expect any trouble here...someday?" I qualified my question. A Palestinian bent over the seedlings he was planting in a patch of desert straightened up as if in defiance of the passing army vehicle. There was no mistaking the expression in his dark face.

"I'm sure," Rom replied, without a trace of an accent. He'd used those words too often.

"Well, thanks for the ride old boy, I think I'll take the bus to the Allenby Bridge."

He motioned to the inviting mountains rolling down from Ramallah. Rom smiled and said, "Climb the mountains." The one Israeli I had encountered in those canyons had greeted my distant approach with a

15

burst of gunfire. Soldier and settler, soldier/settler, didn't know me from a Palestinian without his permissible flock of sheep or goats. A few weeks ago we heard over our transistor radio that a settler in the Ramallah or Nablus area had responded to a recent protest by shooting a Palestinian from the car in which he was riding with soldiers/settlers. Many soldiers are actually stationed at a kibbutz or moshavs, the latter being the station of the soldier I ran into "hunting" with his Uzi.

But I felt safer in those verdant hills and cave pocked canyons than I did in the New York subway. It was either my mountain greenery with the patch quilt flowers or the kibbutz.

The first thing that hit us when we drove up the Gilgal road was the heavy air that surrounded the "33 litre a day" computer-controlled cows, though it wasn't milk we smelled. These poor beasts were confined to the kibbutz where they were milked to an early but "more profitable" death.

I said hello to Mona, filled my canteen and, with six miles of walking under my belt (the food in my pouch would be eaten on the first grassy plateau I scaled) and a half day stretching before me, I ran the gauntlet of Shabbat or Sabbath sharpshooters outside the back gate. One youth was enjoying his day of rest with a telescopic rifle, but it was the perennial Uzi that always stole the day. It always blew my mind to get beyond the tangle of barbed wire, the remains of a Jordanian village, general debris, the grave-sized ditches, and a kind of moat that cut through the rock-strewn landscape, to stumble upon a page out of the Bible—now littered with broken bottles.

Southwest of the shattered glass of the shooting gallery, I followed the wadi up to some grazing sheep, their shepherd trying to steer them on a safer course. The sylvan setting encouraged me to say more than salem. Smiling at the wooly animals, their blue tagged ears the color of the Palestinian's license plate, I remarked, "You have many sheep."

"Money," he replied, "my money is home."

The young man spoke little English, but I thought it was strange that a poor shepherd could imagine I'd be asking him for money. The Israelis might mistake me for a Palestinian, but this sheepherder could only think I was an Israeli. That I was a bona fide American tourist whose visa was about to expire, nobody could imagine upon first glance.

The wadi reminded me of the Negev where I found a Dutch girl's passport that had been swept away in a flash flood, but that was more than a hundred miles away and there was no rain in sight. Some blossoms opened up in the Zin Canyon in mid-December, but these flower choked hills were the Holy Land in my book. The one enduring miracle for anybody to see was the annual winter/spring transfiguration in January right above Gilgal, when the manna from heaven impregnated Mother Earth with the promise of a million blossoms—an unbroken promise since time immemorial. Flowery words, until you know the barren hills of summer (the almost endless Godforsaken summer), razor sharp in places where the ascetic tested his mettle. And then you know why green is the Arab's favorite color.

Above one of the principal canyons are grassy knolls that give way to strata upon strata of partially carpeted limestone that was a giant stairway to the heavens for the prophets who came before me. For the semi-nomadic Semites who tramped these hills before Moses crossed the unseen Jordan below, these turd-littered steps two and three feet high were the walls of the First Temple. Early holy men knew the sky was the Dome on the Rock, and inspired wanderers from the east left Dead Sea Scrolls in many caves the length of the West Bank. Then as now the only valid sacrifice to God was the ego, and in return for coughing up his empty pride one New York hobo's cup runneth over. That is why this rock garden of Eden, every square yard painted with the colors of the rainbow, countless herbs and plants unknown to me beyond the sage in the sun and the sturdiest philodendron in the rocky crevices of the shaded north side of the mountains, were left to some Old Testament characters and their livestock and one curious stranger who never knew whether they were cursing a wayward goat or shouting an indecipherable salutation or warning across a canyon chasm that went unanswered. These Palestinians live in caves, some of them with their families, who cultivate the upper plateaus illegally but as they have perennially.

It is easy to lapse into poetry (or doggerel) in the land of the prophets, easy to see how things were connected in so tiny a land; and incredible coincidence and contradiction were part of the magic. The hills were alive with the sound of bees—and bombs. Below me were two tanks. The first time I saw the armored monsters I already knew there was trouble in the

Ramallah area, and I thought the tanks were guarding one of the mountain passes that afforded easy access to the valley; but upon closer inspection I could see the rusting relics merely bore mute testimony to the Six Days War, their silent cannons pointing towards Jordan. Smaller weaponry, rusted blades from much longer wars, littered the battleground and I even found a helmet that probably belonged to a British soldier before the War of Independence.

A white aircraft with red markings heralded the screaming approach of paired jets, numbering about 14, sweeping up the West Bank. My hands automatically cupped my ears (though I have spent four years in the airborne Navy), and no defender of Jericho could have been more unnerved by the piercing blast of the ram's horn, as noise remains the most debilitating weapon in Israel's arsenal of intimidation.

A little later I incredulously watched what appeared to be a dogfight north of Ramallah. As at least one of the plans went into a spin and I awaited explosions, a tiny white butterfly fluttered into my line of sight.

It was an air show, but the butterfly won the prize in my eyes. Three or four warplanes involved in the aerial acrobatics above me swept down out of the mountains zooming by Jericho and, with their cargo of death flashing over the Dead Sea, disappeared northwest of Massada. I had hiked up to the Israeli Mecca, circling around to the northwest as General Silva had before his Roman Legionnaires breached the more accessible defenses of the Hebrew citadel. Today, the children of chic American Jews make their Bar Mitzvah atop Massada, and Israeli officers are sworn into service with the Old Testament in one hand and a more serviceable weapon in the other. The Holy Land, this eternal battlefield.

Of course, the main event is supposed to take place in Armageddon about a hundred miles to the north, just south of Nazareth in what is now called Megiddo. It is a favorite tourist attraction of Fundamentalists and a Mecca to the Southern Baptists waiting to be raptured out, who, if anything, have been more inclined to travel in Israel since Reagan's bombing of Libya. With their local reverend on hand and a what me worry look on their face, they have a ringside seat if the world should end on their Holy Land tour. Their Israeli guides milk their obsession for what it's worth, but the tour buses to the land of milk and honey never make it up to Kibbutz Meggido, where Mona and I, refusing to work in the ubiquitous plastic factory, got the boot after an overnight stay. (We had to take or leave the 4 a.m. shift.) The Jezebel in charge of the volunteers was as driven as the mad charioteer who had lived down the road. For Tel Meggido was the home of the original Captain Ahab.

I looked down at Jericho. Rising up sharply from the ancient oasis were cleft-lined cliffs, not unlike my present perch, where Christ had his 40-day struggle with his soul. Directly below Quaranta (Qarantal) where Jesus, quoting Moses, replied to the Devil, "Man does not live by bread alone," is the Temptation Restaurant—on what may as well be the Jericho Turnpike. I had passed by the Oldest City in the World, (where the oldest profession also seems still to be flourishing,) several times before I made my little penitential climb up to the Mount of Temptation, which I really thought was just another Byzantine monastery. But amongst the hallowed hollows, which had housed hundreds of holy men in the third century and was a pilgrimage site for the unholy Crusaders, is a gilded cave of the Greek Orthodox. Here, that breakaway rabbi, the man from Nazareth, spurned the riches of the world.

So they say. I simply came as a caveman, arriving at the closed doors of Qarantal about two o'clock and waited in the blessed shade, too hot and tired to be bothered by the lost time until the reopening. Beyond the palms of the really charming town, with shades of the British Mandate, inns gone to seed in an indigenous village, is the no-man's land and the majestic mountains of Jordan that rose from that great salt sea. One almost forgets the tumbling walls that are joshed about so often. Heavy artillery reverberated the length and breadth of the grand canyon, and as if responding to a blast from Joshua's trumpet, the Qarantal doors opened prematurely and a young man stepped outside.

Apprehensively, the neatly dressed watchman looked me up and down. He looked above us, he looked below us. "Where is your group?"

There is little independent travel in Israel. The watchman seemed suspicious and, pointing to the unseen River Jordan to where John baptized Christ, he said that the Ein Hajla Monastery had been robbed at gunpoint.

"Where are you coming from?"

"Here in Israel," I replied.

"Israel!" he shot.

"Israel, Palestine, whatever you want to call it."

"What do you call this country?" His eyes were piercing.

Jesus Christ, I said to myself, what have I gotten myself into now. "The Holy Land?" Not good enough.

"Is this Israel or Palestine?" he demanded.

Looking the passionate fellow in the eye and feeling a hypocrite for it, I sheepishly said, Palestine. Though I'm really not sure what to call this unholy mess now. Incidentally, in the Golan Heights, high above Kibbutz Snir where we got a letter of recommendation, our Druse friends insisted we were in Syria.

Shaking my hand and opening the huge monastery doors before the scheduled hour, the young Palestinian said, "Welcome."

"Welcome," he repeated. "Welcome."

2

The Why and the Wherefore

This was not the most ambiguous welcome awaiting us, and of course, everybody wanted to know where we were coming from. But the Sixty-Four Thousand Dollar Question was, Why? Especially in late '86 and early '87 when traveling east of Istanbul seemed at best an invitation to a kidnapping—thanks to a sensationalist press—and if you happened to be in Greece also being bombarded with "Midnight Express" propaganda. The Greeks weren't about to lose the few tourists they were getting to the much cheaper and more interesting Turkey across the border.

It is true a synagogue was bombed in Istanbul after we sailed from Byzantium, by then literally rubbing shoulders with Iranians in a shared taxi in the very shadow of Mount Ararat. No Noah's Ark, but almost everybody's house was also our house. Nor was this trip out of character for a couple of over-the-hill hitchhikers. Peru's Andean interior was not very safe in 1965, nor Argentina in 1976, not a month or two after separating from Mona in Bogotá where an explosion in the CIA's Air Panama office shattered the windows in the adjoining hotel where we were sleeping. In 1967, the Huks were practically outside our back door in Northern Manila, and in northern Sudan in 1968 we were suspected of spying for the Israelis. In southern Sudan, I was thought to be a banned missionary (that beard does it all the time), stirring up the pagan Dinkas and Shillucks, who were then as now fighting a civil war against the oppressive Moslem government.

What the Israelis couldn't handle is why a couple of veteran travelers—one who happened to be Jewish—would see the whole world (including Taiwan, excluding communist China and Australia) before coming to Israel and then, as an afterthought after new passports were issued to us in Turkey. And didn't that stamp raise a few eyebrows at the Ben-Gurion Centennial Celebration when I took the day off from Kibbutz Sde Boker to mingle about the dignitaries like some displaced Bedouin—right there in the Wilderness of Zin. One reason why we first went to Africa as early as 1964 and in all those years of wandering in the wilderness we had never gotten around to visiting Israel was that I approached travel to the Holy Land as I had regarded the Bible itself—ho hum.

Somewhere on the road to Damascus or some such place, I realized the Bible was a fascinating book. However, never achieving any degree of familiarity with its contents or Palestine/Israel, I was always seeking the less traveled road. At least since I stopped going to Times Square on New Year's Eve. I knew the Holy Land was a tourist trap about the time Mona and I had abandoned the idea of working on a kibbutz—when we were the acceptable age. The Holy Land, like the Holy Book, had been bandied about by charlatans so much that I didn't know either from Charlton Heston and Hollywood. But until my first or second week here, I was as ignorant of the shameful exploitation of the holocaust as reporters pretended to be and knew little of the seamy side of Israeli life.

All I could be certain of was that Israel was such a small country, and it was a "big wide wonderful world we live in," and how much more romantic is the unknown quest beyond that little bit of the West. In my book every trip had to be a journey to the East, but in 1967 returning from India, I interrupted my land and sea voyage around the world to fly from Tehran to Lebanon, getting as far south as the Israeli border. The Six Day War cut short the intended side trip, and I contented myself with Baalbek Tyre and the pearl of the orient, as Beirut was called. It was unscathed by the war and still pretty much the drunken sailor, I was bowled over by the best bars in the world, virtual museums, where a libation could be served on a sacrificial altar and the barstool could be the capital from some acropolis. Such a beautiful city on a lovely sea.

The people appeared to be friendly enough, and in my foggy mind there was no intimation of the violence to come. I vaguely remember the refugee camps, but after India the dispossessed were commonplace, and there was no privation that wasn't anticlimactic. Nor did I connect the Palestinians to Israel, such is the miracle of communication or biased reporting and my own calloused ignorance. And I wasn't particularly interested in the fact that my ancestors (my parents being Sicilian) were probably Phoenician. I didn't give a fig for roots or refugees, as this branch of the family tree has been slow to grow.

I could have entered Israel via Cyprus, but at that stage of my journey

I couldn't see going out of my way for Israel. Almost twenty years later, I was still being told that Cyprus was the way to enter Israel. This time around it was on my way, but there really is no easy way to enter the Promised Land, if you'll forgive me a simile, and we had to return to Turkey since we could not go from Turkish Cyprus to Greek Cyprus, where a ship sails regularly from Limassol on the southern part of that divided island. With this ship in mind, we had made our way through Nicosia's no-man's land to the border—a sort of Mediterranean Berlin where the Turkish soldiers cheered us on, knowing full well the disgruntled Cypriots of the south would turn us back with an insult. "Don't you know the United Nations doesn't recognize the north?"

And I don't know if I recognize the United Nations, since it was okay for tourists to enter the Turkish Republic of Cyprus via the south. And it was all right if we entered the south via Syria, which we seriously considered doing. That entailed sailing from Turkish Cyprus to Syria, which had seduced me with its brochure about hosting the Mediterranean games, and then embarking for Limassol, the only port-of-call in scores of leagues that is served by the Greek line plying these troubled waters, before putting in at Haifa. But Mona was somewhat hysterical about this aborted plan and hotter heads prevailed. We never did find the Syrian Consul anyway.

A quarter of a century after kibitzing about living on an Israeli commune—really not such an appetizing idea after serving a four-year hitch in the Navy—the move seemed appealing. We had given up our New York apartment and I was virtually unemployable as far as civilized work went.

We knew a kibbutz wasn't exactly a picnic, but we held onto our image of a health farm, and we needed the mental and physical therapy that a return to the land promised. In other words, old salt that I was, I still didn't know the Left Bank from the West Bank, but being up the river we sailed from Marmaris, Turkey, for Rhodes as enraptured out as any holy roller at the gates of Armageddon.

Actually, Rhodes was the new Jerusalem and a stopover for crusaders of all persuasions down the ages. In one of the most charming walled cities in all the world, we walked down memory lane, as we had left Turkey the same way years ago. But the island is still Greece and the trap as well oiled as ever—even in the most unlikely places. We had repaired to a quaint tavern to wait for our ship to come in and called for the check when the embarkation hour was drawing near. I objected to being overcharged for tea. The proprietress reminded me I also drank water, fishing for a tip beyond my means. When I said there was no charge for the water, she complained that Mona had been sitting there for a long time while I was out walking.

Traveling in a Moslem country, I usually mistook the sensitive person for a Jew though the Moslems are the most hospitable people in the world. After months of traveling around South America, merengue'd and mambo'd out of my mind, Latin Beaten into submission, I thought I was hallucinating when I heard Bach emanating from a general store. I asked the owner of the shop if he was Jewish, astounded that such heavenly sounds could waft on the tepid air of that dark continent—in a 1976 rife with revolution and repression. In Argentina, journalist Jacobo Timerman spoke to the conscience of the world about the desaparecidos. And in the devalued currency of sensibility, wasn't generosity the other side of the coin? Devalued in Israel, he thought.

One reason we looked forward to visiting Israel was that Mona's well-off friend had invited us to stay with her, and never did the lap of luxury look more inviting. We couldn't take any more hotels or the hassles that come with shopping or eating out when you are nearly broke. This is why, (after leaving Mona's friend) despite or because of our age and lifestyle, we had become prime candidates for a kibbutz and were willing to work six days a week just to stay off the road—and know where our next meal is coming from, even if it is a wild assortment of raw vegetables and cream cheeses with nary a bagel. We dreaded leaving this "cushioned rut" as one inmate of a Golan gulag put it—but back to Rhodes. The reader must know from whence the traveler has journeyed if the journal will have any validity.

I did drink something stronger than tea or water that day. If ever there was a Flying Dutchman seeking a welcoming harbor, it was I; and if anybody milling about the docks that sultry night looked like a desperado of one Diaspora or another obeying some unspoken law of return, it was this over-the-hill, under-the-weather graybeard singing "California …"

If I'm stretching the Law, irreverent in my irrelevance, my wife's feelings dockside were a different kettle of fish. Except for Mona's first visit to Germany, she never stood apart anywhere in the world and meditated in monasteries and churches with the ease of a monk. She was transported by a muezzin's call to prayer, and it was her universality, finally, that made her special. Still, she was thrilled that at last she was going to Israel, embarking on an experience she could not fully share with me. I was the landlubber who watched his Women's Libber sail beyond the emotional confines of the humdrum. Although it wasn't exactly a Promised Land Mona was going to, she was at least returning to a childhood filled with talk of Israel, the synagogue's Kaddish and Hadassah. Mona was going home again, where the mezuzah hung over the door.

Israel means more to the working class Jew. This was what centuries of sacrifice at the Christian altar was all about. The rivers of blood that remained a blot on the mind but ultimately emptied into Israel and gave root to those seedlings little boys and girls bought with their pennies when they were growing up in New York. Such a marvelous symbol of a family's newfound roots in ancient soil. I could just as easily live in Israel as anywhere else, including Sicily. But I was glad that, as opposed to cosa nostra, which usually meant mine, this was Mona's thing and if it led to freedom, God bless her.

"Are we really going to Israel?" Boarding the ship, Mona was one of those gullible Americans Israelis like to joke about. Paloma, dove, the bird of peace, taking her to the Promised Land. Israel's praises could have been sung to the tune of "Somewhere over the Rainbow," and Mona could have been the young Judy Garland setting out on the yellow brick road. "California, here I come..." was more my cup of tea.

3

Sailing for Mare Syriacum

"...right back where I started from, so open up your Golden Gate, California here I come." A few laughs from fellow passengers. As the lowered stern of the ship was transformed into a gangplank, the Winnebago or whatever the hell it was with the California license plates that moved me to song drove up the portable ramp. Pedestrians mostly in pairs boarded the Paloma, but chaos reigned as motorcycles, backpackers, and a curious assortment of vehicles in no particular order flooded the ferry, and I foresaw yet another Greek tragedy, as the Hellenic captains will take on as many passengers as their tubs will carry. Standing room only.

This was one reason why I had tried to engage the driver of the camper in conversation, thinking of that night many moons ago when Mona was able to sleep in the front seat of a jeep somewhere on the not-so-high seas of the Mediterranean. What's new in California, I asked.

"I haven't been there in years." He was a middle-aged man with a much younger wife or daughter accompanying him, and he spoke with an English accent. Even his suit had a British flair about it, and I thought about the Reverend Pike driving into the Negev Desert in search of an authentic religious experience. He had with him a young blonde and a bottle of Pepsi. Their bodies were discovered some time later, the bottle long empty.

The attempted sea-jacking of the Achille Lauro and who-knows-whatever terrorist acts of which I was unaware was fresh in the minds of the security and immigration officers. Most of the baggage carried aboard was gone over with a fine-toothed comb. Everybody embarking on the Paloma was asked where they were going and, if they were not disembarking at Cyprus, who did they know in Israel. Certainly, the Don would have been suspect if Sancho wasn't with him, but I passed the quiz with flying colors. There was one character who even I had doubts about, as he apparently didn't know where he was going. But he didn't look like an Arab, and I guess that was good enough for his interrogators—as it should have been for an aimless wanderer like myself.

We were pretty much a mixed-bag, but most of the passengers were kids, the goyim of Europe going to a pre-booked kibbutz. Not to the Golan Heights for sure, these were street people, snowbirds heading south for the winter.

In a week's time, young Aryans would be sweeping the streets of Elat, earning a few shekels to get a Red Sea suntan or work in the plastic factories of any one of the dozens of kibbutzim south of Beer Sheba. And they were being transported to the Promised Land in a floating parking lot. Shallow youth without hope, a mockery of the actual Exodus.

I mourned the good old days when a ship was a ship and you could tell the bow from the stern and boarded her mid-ships. If a young man or woman was uncertain of his or her gender, there was at least romance in the air. It was a ship that moved me to poetry and didn't I write the classic Ship of Fools book, maybe the most romantic thing since Jack London rode the waves. Ah, the Visivicia, that Casablanca-bound passenger-freighter out of New York, flying under a Yugoslavian flag, as were the passengers dancing to "Aquarius." Gargantuan servings of not the best cuisine was included in the price of the $180 fare—25 cents for a bottle of potent pivo and the hashish gratis. Last but not least as we used to cliché, was the near luxury accommodations.

But as the Talmud says, and I have long demonstrated, no pursuit is more debilitating than travel, and when I dragged my ass up to the plastic second-class cafeteria, all I could think about was a place to sleep. I no sooner dumped my canvas sack in a booth to stake my claim, when a disheveled girl was telling me that her sleeping bag was there first. I was about to start a mutiny when Mona reminded me of my age. I was the spitting, foaming at the mouth image of Beyond Good and Evil Friedrich Nietzsche himself. Adrenalin pumping, I made for the Purser's Office waving my letters, the most prominent from the Turkish Consul in New York, which was like a declaration of war from Greece's most bitter enemy.

It was nearing midnight and I demanded a cabin before I turned into a pumpkin or worse. "But your ticket is marked Deck Class."

"But I paid for a cabin." We were entitled to a cabin for a night.

"There are no empty cabins."

"And there is no empty space on the deck. Besides," I added. "In this day and age do you really expect a couple of middle-aged people to roll around the deck the whole night? Do I look like a Goddamned hobo?" I glared at the First Class passengers pressing towards the counter for their keys. I'm not exactly a journalist, but I was sure as hell bad news. The Greeks have a habit of taking a half-full ship out of service and transporting two boatloads of passengers on a ship that falls far short of the advertising of the first ship. Ah, but the Paloma did have a gambling casino, one arm bandits, two arm bandits and was a bird of prey whose feathers I was ruffling. I am so tired of the Turks with their atrocious "toilets" getting the shitty end of the stick when the Greeks' lasting gift to civilization has been the Trojan Horse, a replica of which, incidentally, remains in Turkey. In a word for all that philosophy that may as well have been handed down to us by Martians, it is a deceit that is eternally perpetuated by pseudo equestrians.

Ship's policy dictates that Deck Passengers remain behind bars in a quasi-quarantine at the stern, but an open hatch allowed us access to the rest of the ferry and many escapees camped out on the carpeted floor of the First Class Lounge. By midnight it was wall-to-wall Deck Class passengers, but a steward nudged the prostrate passengers to move on. Only one girl screamed about the indignity of our situation, but this Jonah was saving his energy for a bigger fish and where there is a whale there is a way. With Mona and my bag in tow, I stormed up to the disco, collared the purser, indicated I was mentally ill and strongly urged I be placed in the Paloma's hospital, if indeed one existed. The disco would be closing in a couple of hours and, contrary to ship's regulations, the bedeviled officer would permit Mona and myself to sleep on the couches in the back. We sacked out while better heeled Israelis danced the night away.

Rosy fingered dawn saw a haggard figure stepping over pregnant sleeping bags, momentarily stopping at the ship's railing to peer out at the sea and contemplate the human condition. For all of the outward-bound paraphernalia, lacking ideals, these kids were stuck in an artificial world, going along for the ride and an even tan. Wearing my Liberty Ferry t-shirt for the occasion, gift of a Turkish Cyprus shipping line, I swore I would never go down to the sea in a ship again. I went to the stern, as I have done on countless voyages and meditated on the churning Mediterranean. It was the gentlest wake, the sea hardly disturbed as a surreal ripple merged with a becalmed Mediterranean, like our lives without a trace of our passing.

Little sign of ships and then the rugged shoreline of southern Cyprus, her mountainous cap veiled in mist. Limassol. Almost two months since we attempted to cross the border and board the ship here. Our journey to this side of the island is a metaphor for the gulf between Greece and Turkey and the Cypriot pawns, apparently doomed to another conflict. For the Liberty Ferry was really a harbinger of war, a barely disguised troop ship. Upon boarding her Cyprus-bound sister ship in Turkey, I wondered why 95 percent of the passengers were young Turks, males. Emigrating farmers? Then I realized most of the young men had short cropped hair and I remembered my boot camp days. For all of the romantic songs, these guys could have been a part of my military past. Except for the cigarettes. The "smoking lamp" never went out and the darkened ship was alive with a thousand fireflies. Fifty miles out to sea and the midnight local was thick with smoke and that endless Turkish chatter in this endless Middle East summer.

Memories, memories. One has to be an idiot to have spent as much time as I have, on, near and under the water, and not to be as reflective as the sea. More to the point, one has to be an idiot to have done all this, period. But true genius is the other side of counterfeit idiocy and it is only in instability that we know the calm and storm of the sea. And it is just this sort of hot air that makes waves and churns out the color of the rocking boat. Ah, but I must stay this course, mustn't be too literary, a diversionary reason for censorship.

In fact I simply wanted to stick to Israel and limit these sometimes unrelated flights of fancy, but not only is everything coming together as I retrace my steps, following that pre-laid thread out of the labyrinth, but Israel is so oppressive. Far beyond the Palestinian problem, and maybe it's because Israel is not real, and I can not dwell in it or on it and must escape. If Israel isn't small enough with all its abrupt divisions, the unreal patchwork of land and the unrelated inhabitants, Cyprus was a shell-shocked precursor of what was to follow; a microcosm of a microcosm, a splitting of the atom that explodes into war. Mile upon mile of barbed wire winding its way across a wasteland formerly farmed by the absconded

Greeks—still waiting to return to their usurped property, though it must be remembered the Turks were the persecuted minority for a change. Until Turkey stepped in.

Where the Turks allowed Greek owned farms to go to pot and homes not destroyed fall into disrepair, the Israelis disrupted the ecology far beyond the impact of the modern kibbutz (and the runoff of the toxins needed to sustain them), which replaced indigenous villages, also destroyed. There is a surreal lack of continuity here, an unnatural air like the Turkish cigarette smoke out at sea, hanging over the land that cancels out the otherwise almost pristine remoteness of a place like the Wilderness of Zin. Of course, testing secret weapons in that grand canyon doesn't help matters. Israel, Cyprus, how could I ever expect to get my land legs back on this terra infirma. I did go ashore just long enough to stretch them—and be hassled, as this was a Palestinian jumping off point for Lebanon. At least a few bodies had been left in their wake in the nearby yacht basin. That Palestinian wake unable to merge with the sea of humanity until the West Bank is Arab.

Editors worry about a category instead of accepting sui generis on its own merits, though even I must question my Brooklyn baroque. I will try to modify an almost involuntary vice that is my verse-curse. Compensatory poetry for my crudity. Such fluidity seems to speak lightly of the Middle East tragedy, but it is simply a matter of following my nose, and the truth will out. I can only assure I never aspired to being a Perlman or any other man for that matter and any pearls I may pluck from the oyster are providential.

A becalmed sea became my mate's Muse, but the voyage convinced her that some things are better left unsaid. Would that I too could resist to tell all. But then I would be guilty of the sin of omission, if this is to have any historical value. Anyway, I trust Sancho's interludes will give balance to this uneasy rider from La Mancha.

Mona's entry for October 26, 1986, our first day at sea aboard the Paloma, after that unforgettable first night, reads: finally, after Tony did much yelling we got a cabin.

My most memorable encounter with a passenger was with a New Zealander, a living and breathing Maori whose recent forebears feasted on boiled missionaries—although we did not discuss the culinary delights of his fantastic country. He said he was returning to Israel and expressed great admiration for a people who stuck to their guns.

I thought of the South Seas harpooner who sailed on the Pequod, but my friend had a friend in Jesus.

The ship was still in port, Mona was enjoying her two-by-four cabin, and I was watching the sun set from behind the bridge when the Maori joined me at the railing. After an exchange of pleasantries, he asked me if I was Hebrew. I said I had a tendency to skim through magazines from back to front, but . . .

"I'm hassled because of my color," he said, "but you know my ancestors did not originate in Africa. We are the most civilized of the Blacks." (He also said he'd spent some time on a kibbutz.)

I remarked that I could not comment on that, but I did have some familiarity with his lineage and I told the Maori about my experiences with the Dyaks of Borneo. I knew the kampong and I imagined it was similar to the kibbutz. But I could never dream to what extent the kibbutz or even Israel was an extended family and how dangerous to peace is any form of tribalism. But let me put this ship into port. Not any port in a storm, but a portent of things to come.

4

Terra Sancta or To Haifa and Have Not

A golden dawn, but no Golden Gate and yet for all the Mediterranean color, Carmel, the hilly backdrop of scattered houses, opened windows on my fading San Francisco. But that too was water under the bridge, and come hell or high water I would escape the cursed heat. The Dead sea, the Red Sea, the Sea of Galilee could wait. Jerusalem was supposed to be cool by the end of October, and so, euphoric, we made our way to Immigration. Wildly, I declared my genius at Customs, but was surprised at the lack of security. Only the chaos had the stamp of the Levant, until we were walking on the over pass that spans the railway tracks.

We had hardly set foot in Haifa and we were accosted by two over-the-hill Israelis who wanted to buy anything we might be selling. Our radio was their first choice, and I can see Barry Farber wince at so unsubtle an "anti-Semitic" swipe at Israel. If that wasn't enough, Mona's October 27 entry reads that one of these senior citizens is from San Francisco, which should indicate I'm as facile as I am fraudulent, except that these are the facts. I believe it was Somerset Maugham who said, if I may take the easy way out, we cannot write in fiction (non-fiction as well) those coincidences that befall us in real life. And our fate is all the more absurd, including Maoris, when we are unmoored. In fact, it is life's synchronicity that unnerves me and sends me down to the sea in scripts. And then in thrall to the muse, the facts take a backseat to what may only be a ruse, having fun, but then the spirit moves me and journal and journey be damned—I am in the Promised Land.

Both of these former Americans settled here after the War of Independence, at that time losing their citizenship, their American passports, and for some time had been crying over spilled milk. "The biggest mistake of my life was coming to Israel." But it took more than these characters to dampen Mona's spirit, and we checked out the railway station, our baggage none the lighter for the encounter. Regrettably, since it was only the milk train that serviced Jerusalem and it was already midmorning, and I was hot and tired from lugging around that ton of Turkish brochures that would launch my...Noah's Ark. The whitewashed railway station was so peaceful and the usually slower train is really the only way for civilized people to travel anywhere on land. Barring riding the rails, it's the thumb if you don't have a limousine at your beck and call. That's not to be flip, but we didn't want to take a bus to the bus station. Aside from the envisioned hassle that would entail, we were practically broke. Hitching abroad has become as much a means of transportation as it has a life style. It is almost the extent of my social life, and there is nobody more sociable than the intrepid Samaritan who heeds the thumb.

When I say we were almost broke, I'm making allowances for the approximate air fare to the states in case it came to that, as we've become a little bit more cautious. The old-timers, the unofficial welcoming committee, was still at it, and I thought if Lawrence Durrell's Cyprus was "Bitter Lemons," Israel wasn't exactly a bowl of cherries either. Colonialist Durrell seemed to be too enamored of the Greeks without a thought for the Turks, who became a scapegoat after the English pulled out. One could say that in Israel, America was the colonialist, the poor Israelis and the Palestinians a failed dream. Haifa had been servicing the 7th Fleet for years, and up close the main drag looked a little like Norfolk, Virginia. The Fleet wasn't in, though, and the honkytonks were deserted.

Having no luck, we made our way to the bus station, and here's where memorabilia does not stimulate the memory, because the bus drivers issue a handful of tiny 50 aragot slips, destination-less receipts, instead of tickets that add up to the fare. Which wasn't much, since Jerusalem was only about three hours away, though Haifa is in the north, and the capital is centrally located, if you don't count the southern Negev. We could have been taking a bus from the North Shore into Manhattan, except the bus had a somewhat decrepit English look about it and the aisle was piled high with duffle bags and less pliable luggage that you would expect to be stored in the baggage compartment. But this is forbidden by law, and the security reason given for this is that a terrorist could store away a bomb and walk off undetected, while anybody attempting to walk off the bus without his bag would be reminded of the oversight. An American Israeli girl wanting to take the greenhorns under her wing warned us about hitchhiking, though a literal army had their thumbs out. I said as much and our self-appointed guide replied that several soldiers had been murdered while hitching.

Where the road forks outside Tel Aviv, we began a long ascent to Jerusalem, passing the wreckage of the Six Day War as we neared the Holy City. Our friend pointed out the rusting hulks of vehicles lining the sides of the highway, a kind of war memorial to the fallen. I guess I retained the Hollywood version of Jerusalem, and it was not the kind of introduction to the Holy of Holies that I could envision, though I normally don't cross my bridges until I come to them. This was like being hit with Pearl Harbor when you arrived in Hawaii. The difference is that in Israel, especially Jerusalem, you cannot go very far without stumbling upon one war memorial or another. And that's discounting soldiers.

For all that, a good part of the ride was through a Queens and a Long Island in a sea of Arabs, a sprawling suburbia indistinguishable from a thousand other places—until the road climbs those limestone steppes, cutting into the artificial forest that encircles the Golden City. We were now in the Jerusalem Hills and that grayish white city reflecting limestone blocks that blend into the scenery. Arriving at the Central Bus Station on that unseasonably hot day, the Hilton Hotel dominated the skyline.

It was a short walk from a bus station that took me to South America and almost any town with its half-in, half-out—have-not—bus station that keeps the third world on the move. This Central Bus station, partially open to the elements, is not the larger Arab bus station on the other side of the tracks that does not have the benefit of soldiers. They were sitting on the concrete floor, backs against the wall like lessons in studied casualness (belied by Uzis)—a world away from the Hilton—as good a place as any to telephone Mona's friend. Actually, we had little choice, as the bus station was bereft of a waiting room.

We took in stride the transition from the carbon monoxide jungle of the bus station to the rarified air of the Hilton draped in Hebrew art and artifact. Truly one of the most tastefully decorated interiors of any hotel in the world and a virtual showcase for Israel. If Mona couldn't contact her friend, I wasn't about to waive any letter of recommendation fishing for some paltry discount. After trying desperately to phone on her own, Mona had the desk clerk put in the call for her.

In a few minutes Rebecca had arrived, impressed at so grand an entrance for a couple of parvenus. But she could not know this was not par for the course, as I beyond paradox (Turkey was already a dream) luxuriated in the air-conditioning and esthetically cheerful colors. Mona was delirious, as if delivered from a night out in the bus station.

But as the culture shock sank in, I felt lower than ambergris. Was this just a simple case of battle fatigue? And what kind of an arrival was this for a Quixote or any crusading knight who liked to journey back in time. Without a sense of place, I was at sea with myself.

Mona's symptoms were taking on a more severe form. Almost hysterical when she couldn't reach Rebecca, she was now ecstatic. My wife had a friend in the Promised Land. I had to be alone, and here is where I part company with Don Quixote, for only a complete fool always traveled with a partner, especially if she happened to be his wife.

What probably turned me off about Rebecca and her family was that they were like Americans, but only more so. In New York they all bought jogging outfits and on our second night in their home, in a nice condo above the Holyland Hotel, they were asking us if we wanted to go to a basketball game. The normal fare was the nightly horror movie, the video choice of the condo. I wish this were fiction, because we couldn't have found a more representative family of the upper middle class. When I expressed surprise that in tiny, and I thought austere, Israel each resident in her building was entitled to two parking spaces, she remarked that the people needed an inducement to get ahead. And how did the yuppie Israeli feel about religion? When an orthodox Jew was a little slow in crossing the street, she joked she would like to run him down. She ranked the quixotic Hassidic with the Arab and claimed that the Palestinian workmen had sabotaged the construction of her condo. Almost every time we went downtown, a place was distinguished by what atrocity the Arabs had committed there at one time or another. In the vegetable market is where they left their bombs, but now you see there is a grating under the counter, and the bombs can't be left here any longer.

We tried to overlook the hatred of our hostess, as we appreciated where she was coming from and were eating more than her vegetables.

In the old city I even went so far as to don a yarmulke and press my Roman nose against the Wailing Wall, looking for all the world as if I belonged there. With my checkered history I felt as if I belonged before those massive limestone blocks. More than Jewish faith rested on those walls. Christianity had its roots.

This was the sacred rock in the heart of Mecca. It was where a trail of tears should have ended.

So much history and emotion tied up with the experience of my fellow wanderers who I so often related to that I half expected to succumb to trance. But I rarely achieve a mystical state in the presence of others and the dovening of my black robed neighbors was distracting.

The Greek Tourist Office back in the States was pushing a go home again campaign to Americans of every nationality, the supposition being that we pampered barbarians (civilized?) had Hellenic roots. But any person who can get beyond his prejudices will find the lure of Israel more valid, for that Greek Golden Age for all its culture and antiquity is closer to the future.

It was a basically settled existence the Greeks enjoyed, while man's roots lie in the wandering search of the rootless nomad that left us with Abraham's biological imperative: walk. War followed wheels as exploitation succeeded exploration. The children of Israel exposed to the elements walked, and every day was a spiritual adventure. When they ceased to be God's yielding clay, a calcification called civilization set in. But if those limestone walls, what remained of Solomon's magnificent temple, were a result of a spiritual hardening of the arteries, all I saw was the spirituality of the Diaspora and the longest journey into night, the accessibility of the stars. Albert Einstein. And maybe it was just a case of waxing romantic over ruins.

In any case, I felt much more at home before this unadorned wall, an extension of the natural land, than I do before the polished pomp and circumstance of a church altar. I backed up from the wall as custom dictates, glimpsing a black man before turning around. An American, I thought, wail man, wail baby, this is the stuff of spirituals and all that jazz.

As the traveler, the eternal child footloose and fancy free, I see myself as a more likely descendent of Abraham than most Israelis. As for persecution, I should probably have an entry in the Guinness Book of World Records. And for all I know, maybe my father didn't go to church because he was a Jew. My father even had a Yiddish accent, but that was because of the English he heard spoken on the Lower East Side when he got off the boat, and later worked there.

At the opposite end of this wailing Western Wall that was reserved for women, Rebecca deposited a slip of paper between the huge blocks. Written on it was the prayer or wish of her daughter. She didn't remain there long.

Mona was awed before the ruins of the temple. She could only write "incredible" in her notebook. With all that emotional baggage the Jew carried to that wall, a Catholic's pilgrimage to Rome amounted to a picnic. As emotional an experience as the Hadj is, there is joy, completion, behind a pilgrimage to Mecca.

How ridiculous for any Christian to carry on about some statue moving or weeping. Such religiosity has only resulted in potentially spiritual people throwing the baby out with the bathwater and rejecting Christianity altogether.

It is much more credible and respectable to imagine the Western Wall to be weeping for the persecuted exile and to experience their sense of loss. If the wall didn't weep, it was living, the upper blocks heavy with weeds, flowers, a steppe removed from an introduction to my hills above Gilgal and the ultimate temple, Dome of the Heavens. To return to the old city, the wall, if approached from a different angle, was as divisive as Berlin's monument to persistence. And almost as well guarded, as this almost literal foundation of Judaism (actually the remains of the rebuilt second temple) gives some support to the Dome of the Rock above it. This Golden Mosque, the cupola originally being covered with gold, is not only the place from whence Mohammed departed this earth for heaven, leaving his imprint on an enshrined rock, but this second Mecca is also a symbol and a rallying point against Israeli occupation of Palestine.

Within a week's time, we would see prominently displayed in the

Druse's homes a picture of the Dome of the Rock and worshipping Moslems being gun downed by Israelis. The actual massacre occurred several years ago, but it's a continuous tit for tat, as the week before our arrival a soldier was killed on his way to the wall for one of the many ceremonies celebrated in its shadow. It doesn't take a prophet to foresee the day when an impromptu firing squad will fix its sights on the wall. Flames of rebellion are fanned by talk that the Israelis mean to destroy the Dome of the Rock, the actual site of Solomon's temple, where some Jews want to build the new one.

That Jewish orthodoxy proclaims the temple will be rebuilt with the return of the Messiah gives credence to the Armageddon school that sees the end of the world with His arrival. For the temple would have to be built on the summit of Mount Moriah, presently crowned with the Golden Mosque. The summit is also the site of the first and second temple altars, and any third temple built in the same place could trigger a third world war. There are Israelis who say there is room enough on Mount Moriah for the Mosque and another Temple, an eventuality as improbable as the arrival of the Messiah. There is room for a Temple in Saint Peter's Square also, for the Mosque is the Saint Peter's of Jerusalem, but the Pope would be as accommodating to the usurpation of his turf as the Moslem is to his.

When will we understand that religion has more to do with hoodlums than brotherhood. Gang wars. A division and a diversion devoid of vision. If the coming Messiah is to project the image reflected in the history of the church he'll resemble the Godfather. Will the Christian's Messiah be the Jew's Messiah? Will we recognize the true God by his white ass or horse? Or Cadillac? A Rolls Royce if He represents an Eastern religion. Will He or She go unrecognized by rejecting any symbol of status and the pursuit of power embodied in the speed and noise of a car? With a likely message as a return to nature, would not the Messiah walk and then as the ultimate act of humility hitchhike? Could I as king of the road be destined for a crown of thorns?

If any logical person would seriously consider the appearance of a messenger, could he or she envision a more likely scenario than the above?

Has the Messiah like the Jordan River been diverted in the desert of the twentieth century, leaving us with the mournful cry of his ass, who has made the journey back sans rider?

5

The Milky Way

But that's the view from Gilgal three months after the fact and maybe a little fantasy with too much water under the bridge. Sitting by the light of the electric—eclectic—heater, I'm unable to reread, much less rewrite, on this starry night. Quixotic? I'm at the foot of our mattress, which is spread out on the concrete floor of this cellblock as if I were Cervantes himself, the wounded survivor of the battle of Lepanto or some such place. My fighting or writing arm was injured in the vineyard, a not completely diagnosed ailment common to aging pruners of the unruly vine, which has to be pulled from the "trellis" after being cut down to size. And like Cervantes my aching arm is the impetus behind this chivalrous venture, as the pain wakes me in the middle of the night. When I crawl out from beneath the covers, I feel like one of those vines I have torn asunder where the grapes of wrath are stored.

This book could be the most honest thing to come out of Israel since Mark Twain set foot in the Holy Land. Read into this what you may, but Samuel I. Clemens entered Jerusalem astride a donkey, and it is said his ass was white. The Innocent Abroad also had his fill of Biblical baloney and like myself broke up his sojourn in Jerusalem with a side trip to nearby Bethlehem.

But let Messiah Twain give you his impressions of both towns. Little has changed in 120 years, except the begging and disease of nineteenth century Palestine replaced by genocidal occupation. Twain was spared Madison Avenue and the Byzantine politics of Israel.

"There was nothing more at Jerusalem to be seen, except the traditional houses of Dives and Lazarus of the parable, the Tombs of the Kings, and those of the Judges; the spot where they stoned one of the disciples to death, and beheaded another; the fig tree that Jesus withered; a number of historical places about Gethsemane and the Mount of Olives, and fifteen or twenty others in different portions of the city itself."

But for all that, quasi mythical Bethlehem beckoned.

A quarter of a mile away was Bethlehem of Judea, and the pilgrims took some of the stone wall and hurried on." And then describing an all too familiar scene, Mark Twain wrote "The Plain of Shepherds is a desert, paved with loose stones, void of vegetation, glaring in the fierce sun. Only the music of angels it once knew could charm its shrubs and flowers to life again.

In the huge Church of the Nativity built 1500 years ago by the inveterate St. Helena, they took us below ground, and into a grotto cut in the living rock. This was the 'manger' where Christ was born. A silver star set in the floor bears a Latin inscription to that effect. The grotto was tricked out in the usual tasteless style observable in all the holy places of Palestine. As in the Church of the Holy Sepulcher, envy and uncharitableness were apparent here. The priests and members of the Greek and Latin churches cannot come by the same corridor to kneel in the sacred birthplace of the Redeemer, but are compelled to approach and retire by different avenues, lest they quarrel and fight on this the holiest ground on earth."

Of course, Twain was anti-Catholic as well as anti-Semitic, but still this Protestant is pretty much on the mark: "I have no 'meditations' suggested by this spot. I touch with reverent finger...where the infant Jesus lay, but I think—nothing." Twain blames this on the "cripples and monks" badgering him, but I'm counting the angels on the head of a pin.

He, rather than the Bible, has accompanied Mona and me and might account for the acrimony. After the Mississippi, you can imagine how disappointed Twain was upon seeing the Jordan River or any other place in Palestine blown out of proportion by the biblical accounts that were about the only source of information for the passengers from the "Quaker City." At least they could see the Jordan. They even bathed in it and, of course, bottled the holy water.

From where I'm sitting, Twain's entry into Bethlehem astride a donkey is enviable.

The suburbs of Jerusalem practically merge with the suburbs of Bethlehem. If you're covering the few miles in a car and blink, you don't know you've left the outskirts of the former.

Rebecca drove as far as Manger Square, just outside the Church of the Nativity. Maybe she was in a hurry, but she had never been inside one of the most interesting edifices in Israel. Christ or no, Constantine's architectural curiosity was maybe the oldest existent church in the world. Mona, the perfect guest, remained in the car with her, and they drove to Hadassah hospital to see Chagall's windows.

Soldiers had their back against the fortress-like Basilica. Across the square was the police station. I felt well protected as, bending, I entered the church to follow in Mark Twain's footsteps, a bit more responsive to the spine tingling antiquity.

It wasn't exactly that front yard version of the manger. But after those faceless cubicles and the boxed in existence of modern Israel, how wonderful to look upon the furrowed face of antiquity and a durability that spoke of older gods. And how refreshing to lose yourself in the cooling chambers with one relic or another from every century. Enhancing my immersion in the past was the relative emptiness of the church. In between the infrequent arrival of groups, diminished by terrorist threats, I practically had the whole kit and caboodle to myself. As for importune monks, I barely got the evil eye, and that's because I hung around an inordinate amount of time and looked more the "terrorist" than the tourist.

I crossed the deserted square to pick up the Ministry of Tourism's map of Bethlehem with its list of attractions. The Milk Grotto—whatever that was—sounded like a must for the man child thirsting after adventure, so I walked the narrow lane lined with schlock shops, stopping at a likely hole in the wall. The only milk to be seen in this shrine was frozen on a canvas of Mary proffering a tit to the baby Jesus. Legend has it that a drop of Mary's milk fell to the floor and "changed the walls to its own snowy hue." In Mark Twain's day, the grotto had special significance to barren women so that "We took many little fragments of stone from here…because it is well known in all the East that a barren woman hath need only to touch her lips to one of these and her failing will depart from her."

Tongue in cheek or no, I had a literal thirst, and David's Well seemed like the real McCoy. Though I should have been a little leery about the official version of Bethlehem after reading that "the population consists mainly of Christians—a measure of the great faith inspired by this little town." The Christian population is in fact a measure of apartheid and nothing more, since Bethlehem is the West Bank, and many Palestinians are Christians. The rest of the population is Moslem.

On the way to the Well, I returned to the Church of the Nativity and tuned in to a guide, and then another. Conflicting reasons are given for the low entrance to the church. The Israeli explanation is that the low entrance made it necessary for the Bedouin horsemen, who regularly ransacked the church, to dismount before entering it. Closer to the truth is the air-conditioning effect of a small entrance. I would like to think the more charitable Christian version is more honest, the humbling effect of bowing down before entering a place of worship.

In the square, a tour group with a song in their heart was warming up for Christmas Eve.

The long-dry, weed-covered cisterns are actually a come on for the money-making attraction that is the David's Well movie house. For a number of years the now empty theatre has been showing "The Greatest Story Ever Told" for about five dollars. Few tourists got beyond the square at the opposite end of town, and the Palestinian projectionist was happy to fetch me a glass of water from a faucet. So all's well that ends well.

In nearby Beit Jala there is a Cremisan monastery. I didn't know if the place was worth considering, but I'd made the monastic rounds in Europe and had an idea the monastery was better suited for slaking my thirst. I started walking, but when a Palestinian school bus chanced by, I all but commandeered it—forgetting after all the brainwashing that maybe I had something to fear. But in the light of day I was acceptable, and the driver and children reacted to my performance in and out of the bus like I was a stand-up comic.

Culture shocks have a cumulative effect that results in hysteria, at least in my case. I had only to see the century old forest above the monastery, the vineyards below, and I was drunk before I sniffed out the bar after a tour of the bottling plant. The Italian bartender of this Silesian order was as generous with information as he was with the produce of the vineyards. Except for January's harvest of wildflowers, the place was as barren as Twain's Plain of Shepherds when the monks first set up shop before kibbutzim came on the scene.

Monasteries were the inspiration for all communes, including the kibbutz. How strange that so alien and ancient a culture could have so much in common with the kibbutz, but the early monks like the kibbutzniks had to be soldiers (in Europe), giving their all to their closed community. If the conventional kibbutz is without God, there is Maloch and the almighty dollar. Which is not to say the monastery is any different in that respect. Both kibbutzniks and monks have a penchant for gulping down their food. The monk must eat at a fixed time and usually cannot dally over his delicious meal and wine for more than twenty minutes before a bell sounds. In world famous Monte Casino, the monks have installed what sounds like a burglar alarm to summon the faithful to chow. The kibbutz is not quite so military, with more flexible meal times, but no worker worth his salt will linger over a meal for more than fifteen minutes. And certainly the cooking is no inducement to spend more than a few minutes with the unappetizing fare.

Four days into Israel and already I longed for Europe, at least the Europe the monastery projected. It was that battle fatigue, and monasteries provided me with sanctuary in past years. I wanted to return to Europe where history was above ground and the culture under.

Mona stayed at some monasteries with me. Yes, a curious romance with the road was my Monastic Merry-Go-Round, the European counterpart of Kibbutz Hopping.

My bartender was very talkative, almost confessional, and had I not preached to the monks of Italy. He had come here as a young man, and I think he was beginning to wonder what he had done with his life. I was asking myself the same question, though it wasn't as easy for me to keep a record. The wine only made me more depressed at this ungodly hour and heightened my desire for escape from my unromantic present. Just where the hell did I belong in this world? But I think I've always known I belong nowhere because I'm a part of everywhere, the rolling stone that has gathered moss—but not enough to grow too attached to any particular place. The nomad knows in his sauntering bones that this is the norm, but I wasn't about to walk out of there.

I asked a well-dressed man purchasing a couple of bottles of dago red if he might be heading for Jerusalem. He was, but wouldn't oblige me. The bartender told me he was the American Ambassador's chauffer, which only increased my chagrin. But the fellow had cause for caution.

A priest gave me a lift into Bethlehem, and there I shared a Jerusalem-bound taxi with a bunch of Palestinians, to the later horror of Rebecca. I hadn't been so uptight since we shared a taxi with a bunch of Iranians as far as Mount Ararat, within a few miles of the Turkey-Iran border. I don't know if the bottle I brought back with me absolved me of the sin of cavorting with the Arabs, or if my gift of Christian wine was taken as an even worse affront. But this gaucherie was balanced by a visit to the Holocaust Museum.

Rebecca practically insisted we go to Vad Vashem, as if to say within the walls of this house of horrors everything will become clear. But by now, we were even more exhausted and the last thing either one of us needed was the most graphic reminder of the holocaust—even if a tour of Vad Vashem should be obligatory, especially for the yuppie generation, who don't know Halloween from holocaust.

Long before I went into the museum, the horror of what had happened, the living skeletons, the dead ones, the ovens, the yawning insatiable ovens, were burned into my memory. But what has had the greatest effect on me was the photo I had just seen of three husky blond women relaxing outside a death camp, their grim smiles evil incarnate. A day at the picnic. And I asked myself, how do the Jews live with the idea of systematic extermination. The idea that all of them were marked for death by the Germans and that their annihilation was all in a day's work. Hardly anybody in the U.S. reacted half as vehemently as the animal humane societies do when animals are experimented on today. Is it any wonder then that the expendable pariah is seduced by the idea of conquest when the ashes have blown away. That the Israeli soldier becomes the perfect embodiment of the phoenix and only the truly strong can resist a prolongation of the macho image and the opportunity to be at the top of the pecking order. With justifiable anger and astonishment, the Palestinian asks, how could you of all people keep us down. But the pendulum swings from one extreme to the other, following a law of nature, and the martyr is destined to become macho just as surely as day fades into nacht. Without divine intervention.

Mona was so disturbed by the first part of the museum, she could not enter Part II. The perennial penitent, I saw the whole thing and came out of the museum extremely irritable. I chastised her for losing Rebecca's Hebrew book. I was overwhelmed by a sense of horror and oppression, and then shame for yelling.

Trees dedicated by the resisters to nazism had a calming effect on me. The sun was setting beyond the Judean hills and the horror was locked up for the night. We decided to walk back to the condominium, passing through a Hasidic neighborhood. The boys we saw could have been kibitzing on one of the better streets of Brownsville. No, only the dress spoke of Brooklyn. This was maybe Forest Hills, a million miles from the West Bank and the chamber of horrors down the street. But how well these transplanted youth took to Israel, without, it seemed, a thought for tomorrow, incongruous contrast to Rebecca's son preparing to enter the air force. I had asked him if there was any resistance to the draft, beyond the Orthodox non-compliance. He said no. These kids wouldn't be going into the service. On this warm summer night, cheerful in their white dress shirts they could have been waiting for their Messiah.

6

Kibbutz Hopping

The Dead Sea sparkled like a mirage through the eternal haze as we began our descent into the inferno of Israel's Death Valley. It was only a few short minutes ago that Rebecca had driven us to the bus station, with the advice that we make our way to the Golan Heights if we were looking for a cooler clime. She said she still might find my manuscript. But that isn't all we had entrusted to her care, and I was grateful with reservations that we could board the bus unencumbered. The Golan Heights. Counting on my posthumous fame, was she going to publish my book?

Israeli buses are much like Cyprus ships, those quasi troop ships we sailed on. Sitting behind us were several loud soldiers, unlike the better disciplined Turks, but like the inner city youth of America blasting their radio. Mona politely asked them to lower the volume, with no response.

Some moments later I made the same request to the soldiers. A curly blond, barely out of his teens and my age when I was in the navy, answered in English, "When I play my radio..." and here he switched to Hebrew in an angry tone that provoked laughter. In an instant's rage I was that sailor who got into a brawl on a bus with a marine larger than myself, pulverizing him. But more than a quarter of a century later my bark is louder than my bite and the extent of my regression was, "Fuck you, too." The soldier was up in arms and had to be restrained by his uniformed comrades. Had Curly been in uniform, maybe he would have been a little cooler. Still, I was amazed that so highly esteemed an army could produce characters not content with blasting their radios, ready to fight a man old enough to be their father. Did Curly think I was an Orthodox Jew, a condoned draft resister responsible for the Friday bus curfew in effect in a few hours' time?

The soldiers' hostility did not end here. One of them closed our window—which I reopened. At this point, several passengers rallied to our defense and we changed our seats, caught in the crossfire of Hebraic haranguing. An American emigrant in his thirties apologized for the behavior of the soldiers and almost got into a fight himself.

The last day in October was brutally hot. Looking out the window at the scraggly Jericho bus shelter baking in the heat, I was so glad we took the bus. We'd been so distracted by the soldiers that the three-hour ride to Tiberias was a tropical breeze.

The Sea of Galilee should have been inviting. This town, built by Herod's son and named for the Roman emperor, was a surviving pocket of history.

I wasn't about to look for a hotel and join the sunbathers in their little bit of the pampered Caribbean. I wanted to shake the hand that shook the hand of that man from Galilee or a reasonable facsimile, but to pursue a suntan on these hallowed shores was beyond the pale. The sight of the tropical tinsel only increased my appetite for true Golan Heights. Brooklyn Heights. It didn't matter where. I just hungered after the cool breath of autumn. Let the falling leaves, if they existed in this godforsaken land, be the magic carpets that would transport me to those transcendental heights that were the province of cool weather.

A bus transported us to Hagoshrim, after we'd been directed to the wrong platform. We could just as easily picked this destination out of a hat as it was written on a scrap of paper in my pocket. It was hot, but we would make a go of it. The man in charge of the volunteers left Izmir during the war and helped found the kibbutz in 1948. Small world, we could exchange some Turkish words with him, but there was no empty bed available.

The sun sinking almost as quickly as our feelings, we headed for the road. In disbelief, Mona watched my thumb go out. If the Golan Heights didn't sound scary enough, the barbed wire of the kibbutz was in the shadow of the watchtowers.

In fact, we were in the lower Golan Heights, changing buses at Rosh Pinna first. Failing to get a ride within the next hour, we boarded our fourth bus of the day, requesting we be left off at the highest situated kibbutz— where there would be no guesthouse to take the edge off our adventure and I would no longer curse the sun. A woman on the bus realized we didn't know where we were going and, happening to de-bus with us, struck up a conversation. She had been a dancer and had been to the States. Her husband was the kibbutz doctor. Kibbutz? It was nearly dark and cool, we could have been in another country. And we were, but this was kibbutz

Meron Golan, dutifully recorded in Mona's diary as being founded in 1970.

If we couldn't find work, our dancer friend would invite us to be her guest, as she and the doctor were not members of the kibbutz. We now entered the flat of a member, the friend of the American woman we would have to meet. Waiting for this liaison, we were offered cake and watched a toddler at play. And such was our introduction to occupied Syria. The Brooklyn Heights were more exotic than these garden apartments in limbo, and I was overcome with the emptiness that such an environment invokes. I have simply spent too much time in Queens, and it is for that reason that I can never get far enough away.

The American hailed from Philadelphia and was not very happy about our visit. Like any bourgeois American, she couldn't understand how we could just pick up and go and happen to chance upon flower rimmed Fort Apache, not a mile from bombed out Kinnetra in Syria. Even this early in the game, we may have been suspected of spying, but I think it was more a matter of people disliking those who embody that spirit that should be their own for a particular calling. When the kibbutzniks stopped being pioneers, the door was open to Philadelphians. Or as a German Wandervogel said of Kibbutz Degania in 1909, "Where lively people are together no one needs a program. Poor in soul are those persons who always have something laid out. Every day brings forth our wandering gratitude for a rich overflowing experience." Yes the word was wandering and the wandering Jews were unprepared for the promised but precarious land, sustained by the acquisition of an ever illegally expanding homeland.

But the Philadelphian was a therapist. "We don't need volunteers now. Besides, you have to go to Tel Aviv and be insured. You just can't go kibbutz hopping." Famous last words. But she neglected to say we were over the age limit and would never get insured. We were curious about Helen, I believe that was her name, and the pad she shared with another woman, but as far as she was concerned we were a couple of trespassers. I would have been angry had I known how many American tax dollars went into Kibbutzim, but we considered ourselves lucky that it was dark and we couldn't be turned away without the buses running. Helen found us an empty apartment and accompanied us to the chow hall. "After breakfast tomorrow, you'll have to take the bus to Tel Aviv."

The dining hall was on the second level of the kibbutz complex of offices and lounge, where we met the dancer and her doctor husband. The doctor had received his medical training in Italy and was a shot in a flagging arm. In an air thick with Hebrew, he serenaded me with Italy's humanizing vowels—pleasantly juxtaposed to the coughing, throat scraping of his lingua franca. And if that wasn't enough, he poured me a glass of wine. Blessed Sabbath. Friday was always my favorite night. Halfway through the bottle I said that Israel's adoption of Hebrew as their national language, but jettisoning those values that stemmed from the ancient tongue was throwing the baby out while keeping the bathwater. I'm not sure if the doctor understood me, but he and his wife were disappointed when they learned we had to leave in the morning. Not really surprised when he was informed he would not be allowed to have us as his guests, he acknowledged, "This kibbutz is a closed community, they are not an open people." As in Turkey, fledgling doctors are required to serve in the less desirable posts, and he was not here by choice.

The ashes of war had hardly cooled when settlers were brought into occupied Syria. But even the most zealous Zionist of the Hamenchaud movement needed a little extra inducement to live on the slopes of this Etna, and the Philadelphian had found a home away from home. The place was plush by Israeli standards, which is not to minimize anybody's commitment to Israel, but with familiar surroundings and a modicum of security—three squares a day—the omnipresent noise of war or its simulation becomes as acceptable as LaGuardia Airport to the residents of Flushing. And you knew Syria wasn't going to attack Queens.

Meron members were lulled into a sense of security that comes with familiarity and a measure of fatalism. Helen said there hadn't been a terrorist attack in years and if war broke out, they would die a little earlier in the conflict than the Israeli's in Jerusalem.

Just as our Jerusalem friends were entertained by horror movies, maybe reminding themselves that it was the peace they were enjoying that was the illusion, the members of Meron Golan took a hike up to the hilltop bunkers on their day off. From the fortifications atop a pyramidal hill they could look down on Syria and the ruins of the Six Day War. But today was a beautiful day, the bunkers were pretty much intact, and I don't think too many people were visualizing those six horrible days in 1967. I thought this group of hikers would lead me to a scenic site or some ancient ruins, but this told all in the exposed barbed wire and gun placements and did not require any archeological probing.

The doctor and his wife accompanied us beyond the kibbutz gate. We had stayed for lunch, so we'd gotten off to a late start. This was of no great concern to us, as we had no destination and only wanted a lift before it was dark. The doctor had told us about the "hospitable" Druse who lived nearby on the lower spur of Mount Hermon. This sounded great even if the nicest thing most dictionaries could say about this Arab tribe is that they are members of a fanatical Syrian sect. Warlike.

The doctor motioned a passing army jeep to stop, and we were on our way to the "Mountain Chieftain" (Mount Hermon in Arabic is Jabal al-Shaykh). Mona, who had been cultivating a nice friendship with the dancer and her children, now found herself in the back of the jeep with all the radio equipment, speeding along this high plateau that we only knew from screaming headlines. I hardly had time to introduce myself, riding shotgun as I was, before we were left off at a junction where a road ran right up to Syria, taking the soldier with it, and leaving us standing in the dust and desolation of the Six Day War.

Across the road was a battered tank, with a little fence around it. On the plaque were the names of the fallen on yet another memorial. The cotton puffs that had greeted us in the morning were gathering into storm clouds that would seem a permanent part of this picture, but it was so good wearing my jacket instead of dragging it that I was lifted above the dismal scene.

I was on the high road to adventure, but it was at times like this, when I could revel in my vulnerability that Mona would lose faith and throw me into a ditch to divert my flow. Yet, Don Quixote could not have a more loyal partner. Every inch a lady.

Often, a dragging anchor prevented us from being swept out to sea, but most currents carried us into safe waters, and I didn't think our copilot would desert us now—in this, of all places, the source of the River Jordan. We were heading for that biblical "Mountain of Snow" (the translation of the Aramaic Tur Talga).

My partner was so much a part of me, I could not see how unique she was until the editor of the Cape Argus at the end of our road expected an Amazon. Yet, God's fool raged against his wife for developing into a sensible middle-aged woman who would shelf that book of poetry that had seen us to Kilimanjaro and Africa's Arabah almost twenty years earlier. And didn't we have our Great Rifts then, at least since that day at the bottom of the Ngorogoro crater in Tanzania where I had to forego a feast that would be held in my honor the following morning because Mona was waiting for me that night and I was compelled to trudge up the slopes of the extinct volcano in the dark with a couple of grunting and growling (to scare away the lions) Maasai warriors.

So often had I wandered into situations not privy to anthropologists, so often surrounded by a surreal reality, that I did not have to go to Israel (but I take that back) to realize I was indeed chosen, and the criteria for that choice was that I had kept my covenant with God and stuck to something more durable than guns. More shooting from the hip. When you are this far down the road, it's time to pack it in.

We had little luggage, and I insisted it was a day for a walk. That is the attitude that has carried me around the world—never wait for Godot or any other Goddamned thing that interrupted the flow. If God helps those who help themselves (as the pilgrim's sign in Jerusalem read), it seemed people who drive are more likely to stop for hitchhikers who make an effort and have more faith in their feet than in their thumb. Maybe it's because you look helpless in the middle of nowhere. In France a man who had never stopped for anybody gave me a lift when he saw I was running. He wondered what the emergency was. I told him I was cold.

A bus passing in the opposite direction sped on to Tel Aviv, illegally. It was not yet sundown, but the Hasidim had little say up here, and the driver was acting with impunity until he reached the populated area, at which time the sun would have sank low enough for him to be within his legal rights.

Soon we were piling into a tiny tin pickup truck that sagged under the weight of our young benefactors. We were deposited outside of El Rom, I believe it was, a Druse village. A rushing stream was beneath us, behind us the hardscrabble so suitable for tanks. This was scenery you could get your teeth into. I raided the apple orchard watered by the brook and luxuriated in the uncommon lushness that cushioned its banks. Munching our way over a wooden bridge, I broke into song. "We ain't got a barrel of money, maybe we're ragged and funny, we'll travel along singin' a song side by side."

The woman at my side was not amused. There was little traffic, but there is a little known rule of thumb regarding hitchhiking. Your chances of a ride do not increase proportionately with the volume of traffic. It is on the less traveled road that you will encounter the more agreeable person. A large pickup truck came to a halt. I had no doubt about the status of the other drivers, but I couldn't make out this guy. I still didn't know the Druse from the Druids, but the fairly young fellow behind the wheel was obviously a man of means, and I thought he might be Israeli. Finally, I had to ask our newfound friend what his nationality was. He was a Druse, the proud owner of the apple orchard I had plundered, and we were invited to his home for tea.

We were in Hajdal Shams, the friendly town the doctor had told us about, but the first thing that caught my eye almost pulled it out of its socket. In the framed drawing near the doorway I recognized The Dome of the Rock where Israeli soldiers were machine-gunning Palestinians outside the Golden Mosque. Our friend explained, and I dimly recalled reading about the atrocity some years ago. What shocked me into a paranoid state was that this Syrian Arab would openly display this revolutionary picture with its arabesque call to revenge. Like any other brainwashed American, I half expected the unsmiling Arab to kidnap us or whatever it is the Druse does. Thinking that the provocative picture would have to be illegal or outlawed, I wondered what this brazen effrontery to the Israeli occupiers was all about. I would have been more suspicious of the man had I known that the assimilated Druse of Israel proper were loyal Israelis and an important part of the army. We were after all flush on the new Syrian border. Just up and then down the street was no-man's land.

Nazih's wife brought us a large tray filled with tea and cake and then in Arab fashion disappeared. I nodded in agreement as he continued his vilification of the Israelis, awakening me to the fact beyond the abstraction. "How would you feel if the Russians occupied New York?" Anything was better than Koch, I thought, but I saw his point. Israeli citizenship was being forced upon them. Nazih was waiting for Syria to liberate him and did not want an Israeli identity card. Someone had been injured in a protest the other day. As he vented his spleen, I stuffed myself with cookies and made ready to leave.

Would we like to stay and eat? I told Nazih we really had to find a place to sleep, half angling for an invitation, but he allowed us to be on our way, plying us with apples before we left.

It was good to get our cold feet back into our shoes, but it was beginning to drizzle, and there was no hotel in town. We headed for Newe Ativ, not sure what the place was that Nazih had recommended, and caring less. Just as it looked like we were in for a bath, a jeep rounded the Mount Hermon road and pulled up to what must have appeared to the occupants as an apparition. Where were we going? We said we were looking for work and before you could say tramping to Jerusalem, we were on our way to their Kibbutz. I looked at Mona as if to say, You of little faith, but wondered if the word was out on the over-the-hill hikers snooping around the Golan Heights.

7

The Killing Fields

We had been pressed into service for Snir by a seductive blonde. Shanghaied by an American Mata Hari. This wasn't just any port in a storm.

"What's a nice girl like you doing in a place like this?"

This most attractive of the young women squashed in the back of the dripping jeep was an American/Israeli soldier. Before going into the army, she had returned to the States.

"And you gave up the good life for this?"

"I have nothing in common with people my age. They're childish, they have no values. They bore me."

"Ditto for the people my age."

"Are your children grown?"

I thought about Turkey, where we finally felt compelled to lie about our "children" to be more acceptable to the Turk. Their raison d'etre, if not their identity, was in their offspring.

The girl continued, "How romantic to wait until your children have grown up to really see the world. We don't get many people your age volunteering to work on a kibbutz."

"Well," Mona said, falling into my lap as the jeep made a sharp right, "we always wanted to work on a kibbutz."

We headed up a sharp incline. Our friends wanted to show us the mountaintop fortress of Nimrod. Again, Turkey came to mind, as one of the most imposing sites in all of Anatolia is also named Nimrod and has statuary of near mythic proportions surrounded by people hostile to the government. The Kurds could be the Druse. But Turkey's Nimrod is almost inaccessible, like so much of Anatolia, and this less heroic version of an invincible castle had changed hands many times. In the twelfth century, the Crusaders made one of their bids for the Holy Land here in the shadow of Mount Hermon. Nothing overshadowed the Nimrod of Apollo.

Our driver was Joseph, a paratrooper in the Lebanon War. He got out of the jeep and stretched his legs in the slackening rain. I looked warily at the closed citadel, in no mood to play the tourist. Joseph pointed to the valley below. "Snir."

"That's our kibbutz" he went on.

What a great view, I thought It looked like an hour's hike to Snir.

He told me the area was mined. "Stay away from the red triangles."

I was angry at the soldier who had given us a lift a few hours earlier. He knew we'd be hiking about and yet made no mention of the mines. I looked at the hilly sagebrush country surrounding Nimrod. The Wild West, the Wild East, but in the failing light of the gray day Golan was ghostly. Below, the Banas River was shrouded in a vaporous forest, and fog eerily lifted from the mined miasma. A deathly silence fell over the land.

Snir. It sounded so sinister, but apparently the kibbutz was named for Mount Hermon now hidden in the mystical mists that bathed the Heights. The Bible refers to Hermon as Sirion, but the mountain was also known as Senir to the Amorites. Did the kibbutz leave out the 'e' for its namesake? This is a country of short cuts. From the inspirational Psalms we have "My soul is cast down… I remember thee from the land of Jordan and Mount Hermon." Fountains below, mountains above, something to look up to and worship. Snir. Smile when you say that.

The image conjured up from books was at some variance with our reality, but even on this darkest eve of our arrival, we dimly felt as if we had arrived. We had reached this watershed where we were no longer the uninvolved observer, but I knew I was as much the spy who came in out of the cold as a quasi-Zionist. But I kid myself. I simply came in out of the rain. Yet in all fairness to me and Sancho, the kibbutz was still that innocuous fun place of our youthful dream, and that Madison Avenue fantasy pre-dated the '67 war and its ramifications. In any case, the Israel of the Ministry of Tourism always resembled pre-Civil Rights Movement America. There were no blacks or Arabs in these pictures. Hollywood had come to the Holy Land.

We would be the "guests" of Joseph. The former paratrooper was a Moroccan Jew who shared his concrete cubicle with his Danish mistress. We would become volunteers just as she—though not quite as gung-ho. As is the kibbutz custom with paratroopers, Joe's parachute was transformed into a bedroom canopy. The billowing silk gave an airy ambience to the hole-in-the-wall that the young blonde found sexy. She looked on admiringly as Joe cut up a tomato and prepared a little snack. Confiding in Mona, the petite Dane said she would never marry an Israeli. Anna, I believe her name was, said she couldn't bear her son going into the army, and then she decried Israeli's invasion of Lebanon.

"How could the Israelis do such. a thing?" Then what was Anna doing in the midst of the Devil's Triangles. Paranoid because of my own duplicity, I wondered if she was playing the devil's advocate. Did they really want to know how we felt, coming from the Druse as we did with that Amnesty International look. Alone in '76 it was enough to elicit a nocturnal call from the Death Squad in Tucuman, Argentina. Remembering our icy reception at Kibbutz Meron, I made certain they knew I was a Navy veteran and could understand Israel had to protect her borders.

"But such brutality?" Anna questioned.

The pseudo warrior, I said, "That's war." Joseph was warming up to me.

I did believe what I was saying up to a point, but was still feeling schizophrenic from my turnaround. Hardly an hour had passed since we left Nazhi and his wife, and my dizziness was bringing on a dementia that placed me in another dimension. My idiocy paved the way to acceptance. In a gung ho moment, I was offering to go on guard duty if it came to that. First impressions, you know. We could not chance being put out to pasture in the morning. Not having a home, I was at home anywhere. At least for a while.

A life of extreme circumstances made it easier for Mona to adjust to outrageous situations. She had me. The traveler for all seasons, a chameleon, and the turtle who carried his home on his back. Uncomplaining, she moved to the adjoining apartment, bare but for a bed. A broken window let in air heavy with chicken shit, but within an hour we were eating chicken in the tastefully designed cafeteria and meditating upon the abstract woodcut of Mount Hermon placed above the doorway. The soldiers eating, their Uzis at their feet, may have been distracting, but Mona had survived the Sudanese civil war and the Mark Twain steamer that took us to Juba. My petite mate was a regular trooper. Without a hint of the truck driver about her and remaining the innocent abroad, she had no problem relating to Anna and Joseph, though he struck me as too much the playboy to stay put in Israel.

The war had not erased Joseph's lothario look nor had the kibbutz inculcated the kind of commitment that would keep him on the farm. It took a bigger Dane and an older dame to keep Joseph in check. What the heck, even Joe picked avocados when he wasn't scraping up the chicken shit from the "factory" floor. It was convenient that the volunteers were young and many of them brought up on a diet of "Exodus." You could easily see it was in the best interests of the kibbutz that the young women were seduced into staying on. Volunteers who did not form liaisons were less likely to remain on the kibbutz for more than a couple of months, many for a couple of weeks, though supposedly they were obligated to work for three months. A Dutchman who claimed he was actually in charge of the livestock had already been at Snir for five years.

Kibbutzniks say British subjects are much less likely to be hired because of their heavy drinking, but I sometimes wonder if it's because the young English people who would like to volunteer are less inclined to be in a reclined position. Some of the girls we had already seen had that "no sex, please, we're English" appearance about them.

It has been stormy weather for the Israelis. The avocados were ripe. On the eve of 1987, kibbutzim had a limited appeal and, insurance or no, the fruit would be picked by Quixote and Sancho. But at Snir on the front lines, most of the volunteers were girls.

We had just learned about the young Americans killed by a mine outside of Snir in 1982, when we saw the announcement for the Saturday night movie: "The Killing Fields." My experiences are fantastical enough without fabricating what could only be suspect, but at the risk of appearing fictitious, I'm compelled to stick to the facts; so you can appreciate why I feel God is trying to tell me something. Or were the kibbutzniks sending me a message. Such are the wages of synchronicity—and the resultant "paranoia." In "The Killing Fields," coincidence didn't end with the unsafe geography of contested territory. If I recall correctly, one of the reporters in the movie is imprisoned for spying. Of course, Mona and I barely qualified as bad news, bound to see similarities between our reality and the true movie and consider that we were dumped in those evergreen orchards, to tell it like it was. We had set out in search of Noah's Ark, but Mount Ararat in turkey was only a stepping stone to that equally elusive covenant of the ark.

We had Sunday off. Uri, a slight dark man in charge of the volunteers, arranged for Mona to pick up our foul weather gear, bedding and toiletries.

I headed for Banyas Falls, turning right at the now closed kiosk. A left turn could have spelled disaster. Not a hundred yards away is the still unmarked area where the Americans detonated the mine. Did the Israelis leave the area unmarked because it was the most likely terrorist approach to the kibbutz, or was it the kibbutzniks' apocalyptic approach to life, sneering at the danger. Or was it their propensity for only doing work that would reap monetary gain and an unwillingness to take on undesignated tasks. Was the installation of red triangles the military's responsibility? Whatever, you couldn't accuse the Snirites of sloth.

Hyrax, perhaps. These marmot-like creatures abound in the Banyas canyon below the kibbutz. Zoologists have determined that the hyrax is a relative of the elephant, but they are the "rock badgers" of Proverbs 30:26: "a feeble folk, yet they make their houses in the crags." Thinking these animals were marmots and associating them with the mountains of more temperate zones, I thought they had descended from Mount Hermon, which had already become an obsession with me. Actually, the hyrax is a tropical animal that exists throughout Israel. If it is related to the elephant, so am I.

The cascading Banyas. I reveled in the music of the white water and the sight of the unsuspected jungle contained by the gorgeous gorge. I was oblivious to the rain. A war could be raging above me and I would never know it. After the heavy rains, the Banyas didn't amount to more than a turbulent stream, but I stood on its rocky banks as if before the mighty Iguazu itself where I remained transfixed for hours. Falling water is not a rarity in South America, and all things are relative.

I was coming to think the whole kit and caboodle was mine. Balzac said the world was his because he understood it, but the natural world is mine because I love it and we can do no more than love, while it is doubtful that even France's greatest novelist understood anything beyond unnatural human nature. Touché.

Hyrax, Balzac. Balls. The Banyas, or Banias or Paneas as the Greeks knew it, was a veritable stream of consciousness that would ultimately fertilize Israel and Western thought for centuries to come.

But is this any way to write a book? I remember Norman Mailer's letter to me, after I sent him a manuscript I wanted him to deliver. I figured with his stamp of approval. But he borrowed what he needed and wrote that I was talented, advising me, however, that I should stop smelling my armpits. Get on with the show was the unspoken admonition, but the river of Pan is a pied piper that lures me to its source. The path is not straight.

One does not traipse through the tulips to get there. Crossing the small wooden bridge spanning this sliver of Styx, I sloshed up a muddy slope. I felt eyes upon me. From their craggy perches the hyrax watched me intently, all a furry innocence, until I was on a level with the equally curious cows looking bloated and unbiblical behind the red triangles. I thought, if one of these poor devils was to step on a mine I could be blown away with him (or her). Staying on the path, I hastened my pace, but the bovines smelled my panic and stampeded, stopping me in my tracks.

But the pipes were calling, and mined pastures gave way to glen and unattended grove, altars and moss-covered sanctuary. I could easily imagine Pan and his frolicking nymphs beside the bubbling brook and the ancient Greeks having one hell of a religious experience. "Give me that old-time religion, give me that old-time religion, it's good enough for me."

The succeeding Romans may have planted the sycamore trees that line the Banyas, but this was always a place of light and a more seductive shadow, as freckled as the bark on the sycamores.

The Greco Roman or Hellenistic legacy in this nymphomanical neck of the woods was almost a flesh and blood version of the Moslem's afterlife paradise. No doubt the Syrian officers had a crack at the good life here, heaven on earth, before the '67 War sped them on to their reward. Nearby were the remains of the Syrian Officer's Club and a pool they had built, where diverted water flowed through a cemented enclosure before it rejoined the Banyas. I hoped I wasn't playing Russian roulette by pussy footing about. Later, I learned the volunteers spent their summer Saturdays here.

Otherwise bucolic scenes were belied by unseen mines that would keep the Banyas area in a near pristine state for years to come. But mines seemed the only deterrent to destructive over-development, and maybe in some macabre way they were a mixed blessing. Snir would be safe when the cows came home, after they had detonated the mines. In the meantime archeologists must look covetously towards Golan. Some of the greatest finds are yet to be found in what could well be the "Baal-gad in the Valley of Lebanon" (Joshua 12:7). Many Israelis were amateur archeologists, a condition likened to people living near the sea being fishermen, and I wondered if Moise Dayan that incorrigible collector had a hand in placing these hunting grounds off limits. The lethal fouling of the nest is the saddest irony, and it was as if a ring of fire circled the Banias of the Bible:

"...upon this rock I will build my church and the gates of hell shall not prevail against it."

If I begin to take me or anything else too seriously, I have my antidote on hand. Here's what the inclement Twain has to say about Banias: "We followed the stream to where it gushes out of the mountainside, 300 yards from the tents, and took a bath that was so icy that if I did not know that this was the main source of the sacred river, I would expect harm to come of it."

Before following the Banias to its source, Twain camped near the site of the Syrian Officers' Club. He had clambered down the Golan Heights through the groves "of the Biblical oaks of Bashan" and then "entered this little execrable village of Banias and camped in a grove of olive trees." Then as now there are fig trees, pomegranates (Chinese apples) and oleanders.

At breakfast I put away a little food for the road and let Mona recuperate from her week's travails. Already she had been transferred to the toilet paper factory—after three months in Turkey an irony that had not escaped us. We still have the poster of the small child and his white fluffy dog up to his ears in yard upon yard of unraveled Blanche (250 sheets in every roll), the sophisticated man's toilet paper.

My plan, if I can use such a word, was to see about work at Newe Ativ, getting there in my own good time. Falling rain promised a spiritually uplifting day, a mystical drizzle perfect for this triangular Terra Sancta. I'd already gotten my feet wet, but in this part of Palestine, steeped in Pantheism, nothing but total immersion would result in proper baptism.

Pan seemed to thrive around mountain springs and lush surrounding, but for the later religions, hope sprang eternal in the desert. Maybe that's where the holy men went wrong. I knew something of the refiner's fire and fiery visions had to be tempered with mountain dew and the soothing sounds of a bubbling brook. I wanted to hike up along the Banias to the bombed out bridge and the road and then hitch. But the trouble with this walk, when I was not cowed, was that the cascading water was a Siren's Song that literally lured me on to the rocks and froze me into meditation. Only tying me to a mast or stuffing my Elysian ears would stay my course. But venturing forth without taking the requisite precautions, found myself rooted to a fountain dedicated to the Sylvan deity Pan, God of panic and ecstasy. Things hadn't changed. Most people couldn't get high unless they had a rush of adrenalin.

Supposedly, Christ came this way to discourage orgies and build a more spiritual church; and certainly the wandering Jew came here if he existed; but of the many pictures of him I've seen, I don't recall seeing Christ meditating by a stream. Rather, he is always associated with some grandiose gesture atop a mountain, walking on water, or at the Galilee shore, hands outstretched, but really never getting into the water. I could get closer to this Christ if I could picture him swimming—being a lifeguard. Instead, he is seen working miracles before some mob, a regular Charlton Heston who prefers showmanship to the transcendence of his humanity in the perfect peace of solitude. Rather than being an inspiration with his resurrection—real or imagined—Christians are given questionable comfort by his crucifixion, an image burned into the mind of anybody who loves churches as much as I do. Is this morbidity any better than an orgy? The Way was through meditation. Is through creation. Gandhi at his spinning wheel. In the end Christ was a man, a messenger, maybe a magician, a physician, a healer—and if he didn't exist, Hollywood would have created Him, which it did in part. The saddest thing about this long playing fable is that it has muddied the Ineffable.

I was in this ambulatory what-me-worry state, somewhere between the bombed out bridge and the Syrian Officers' Club, when a man swathed in Arab headdress materialized at a bend in the path. I had been coming up here and going below the falls in the opposite direction every day after work, and the only sign of human life away from the actual falls had been a Syrian tank at the bottom of the gorge. My first reaction was Jesus Christ, and he could have stood in that very spot, very much resembling the swarthy swathed intruder (discounting the blue-eyed blonde foisted upon us).

All that remained of the village that Mark Twain had slain was an oven and a Moslem shrine. The nearest Arabs or Druse were at least several miles away on the Syrian border and not about to be sauntering.

This encounter reminded me of my experience in the Canadian Rockies the previous summer, when I ran into a black bear. I stood my ground trying to read the eyes on this bear of a man whose disconcerting towel or quasi turban partially hid them. As his white headpiece fell from his mouth to reveal big brown eyes, a man with an automatic weapon appeared behind him. That was it. If they were Arabs, they were terrorists. I fingered my pocket knife, the absurdity of my situation taking the edge off my fear.

I strained to see the sensitive eyes of a Jew, Arab headdress not withstanding, or a likely terrorist. I looked to his eyes for the answer. They were capable of compassion, but would that exclude a resistance fighter.

Whoever he was, dark and unsmiling, he approached me and asked, "Who are you?"

It was at times like this that I had an identity crisis.

The last time somebody waved an automatic weapon under my nose was in Argentina in 1976, and my answer provoked a made in Connecticut gun butt to my stomach. Still looking the dark man in the eye, regressed to a primeval fear that erased my limited experience with an Israeli, I assumed that in this Holy Land any kind face behind a gun belonged to a Jew. Arabs, of course, were not permitted to own weapons. And in Arab countries I had assumed that the more gentle face behind a counter was Jewish. At odds with the Israeli saying that the Sabra is only hard on the outside, but the Sabra is born in Israel, and this tough-skinned fruit is something of a mutation.

If appearances were only skin deep, eyes but cloudy windows on the soul (clearly, my own apparently vulnerable orbs had proven to be Venus Fly Traps), and the Arab's humanity the equal of the Jew's, anyway, I had little doubt about the identity of these men when a woman came into view.

I hadn't heard of women terrorists. But who was I? Saint Francis preaching to the birds?

I answered the leader's question with a faltering one of my own. "You're not an Arab?"

"No," the broad-shouldered man answered.

"Then why do you have that thing covering your head and face?"

He replied, "I am from Yemen. It is the custom for Jews to dress this way also."

There was a young man accompanying the girl. All but the Yemeni were training to be guides. He was already a guide taking his group on an unofficial field trip, but contrary to what the guide said, I didn't believe that man with the Uzi was anything but a soldier. Our guide took us downstream to where the Banias merged with another brook fading in the distance under a canopy of rust colored leaves, drawing me in a mesmerizing descent to another time and place. Autumn in New York. In my disorienting flight on a falling leaf, I was anywhere but in the Middle East.

As the group prepared to leave this enchanted glen, I asked where they were going.

"You can come with us," the younger man responded.

"Where?" I asked.

Delighted by my interest, the aspiring guide replied, "It will be a surprise, come."

8

The Jewish Alps

Better an unpleasant surprise than the déjà vu that follows the ingestion of a guidebook. And if I wanted no guide and I had five, so what? They were unexpected, and it was all part of the serendipitous joy of being unprepared. I was already middle age when I finally got into the habit (when I remembered) of packing a Boy Scouts of America "Be Prepared" canteen. And then only after I came down with hepatitis after drinking from a mercury tinted (better than tequila) stream in Mexico's Copper Canyon. I'm afraid my motto remains, through little fault of my own, be open to God and let the devil take the hindmost. To have been in Marco Polo's boots before the advent of the travel book and let the devil take Mark Twain.

We ascended the Heights through Twain's oak forest and seemed destined for Kibbutz Meron, when I shouted, hold on. But we had just about reached our destination and were stopping in the driving rain after we turned off the road and entered a sparse and stunted limbo.

I was stuck to my seat and I wasn't budging, unless you made allowances for a little shivering. "What the hell...what are you doing?" I hadn't ruled out a kidnapping.

"We are picking mushrooms."

"Jesus Christ."

Perhaps, and out of the mouth of babes if the eminent but decidedly unorthodox scholar John Allegro is correct in his The Sacred Mushroom & The Cross. Also, the author of People of the Dead Sea Scrolls, happy-go-lucky Allegro, the first British representative to work on the scrolls, convincingly shows that "Christ" was actually the personification of a fertility cult, a kind of code word for that fun condition produced by the partaking of that sacred fungi, Amanita muscaria. So that your first Christians, the true fundamentalists, if you will, ate a fungus and called the experience Christian, "but every aspect of the mushroom's existence was fraught with sexual allusions, and in its phallic form the ancients saw a replica of the fertility god himself... "son of God" ...a purer form of the god's own spermatozoa... To the mystic it was the divinely given means of entering heaven." And so spake the noted philologist about the Fly-Agarics, the little known skeleton key to the heavenly kingdom, stored in the proverbial Judeo-Christian closet along with the other skeletons.

Be that as it may, I can't say muscaria grew in this ghoulish grove, and I wasn't about to find out. The soft rain that had so caressed me above the cascades was a windswept flood that would dampen the spirits of a muscatel aficionado.

"Aren't you coming?"

"You guys got to be kidding. I told you I've been picking avocados in the rain the whole week, and you're kidnapping me?"

"Nobody is kidnapping you. Picking mushrooms is easier than picking avocados."

I actually liked fondling the pear-shaped fruits, and there was an art to plucking the pulpy pears from the West Indian trees that bear them. You just don't yank the firm fruit from the stem, but gently separate her at the nipple, leaving at least a quarter of an inch of it to nourish the avocado on her voyage to Europe.

The Israelis planted the tropical laurel, a grove in which the horned Pan himself would have felt at home hoofing it with the European nymphs who sometimes worked a tree with me. I honestly can't say I minded being up a tree.

Harvesting the alligator pears in the older orchards was like making your way through a steaming jungle, and more than one time the damn aluminum ladder would give out from under me and leave me out on a limb.

I can't be sure I was ever insured, but the kibbutzniks appreciated my pluck and believed me when I took a day off because I was "sick," going up to Nimrod on the less crowded Sunday. I never could get used to working on my day of rest. But picking avocados was really the least exhausting of the cotton picking field jobs I'd had. The gathering of the avocados required a little deliberation, opposed to the all-arms approach of picking apples, say. Avocados so resembled their leaves in color and shape that you were forced to work slowly and, with me, it's easy to come to a meditative standstill.

So these guides really couldn't call me a poor sport. Indeed, if I'd been wearing that yellow rain coat issued to me, rubber bands applied securely at the wrists to stem the flow of water as I reached for an over-hanging avocado, I could have been persuaded to add a little color to this blackest forest. But enough was enough. It wasn't as if I were a stranger to muscaria or muscatel far that matter, having gone mushrooming in France. In the Florida cow fields not far from where I lived, the fungi are hallucinogenic. Farther south, you can go whacko in Oaxaca, where I believe Huxley found his doors of perception in some Mexican witch's hut; but my experience has been pretty much limited to the Campbell Soup variety.

All but one of the guides disappeared in the enveloping vapors as Beatrice remained behind with Dante. The chilled girl had stayed in the car with me.

"Are they really picking mushrooms?"

"If they can find them."

The magic of majun and not the mushroom or moonshine shattered my own windows, permitting pollution as well as aesthetic perceptions to enter my proud tower. Long before I read Allegro, even before the Beatles descended upon Marrakech, I ate majun in the fabled city itself. My religious experience almost duplicates Mohammad's flight from Jerusalem, heaven-bound on the back of his steed. Roxiante, less reliable transport, provided my own taste of heaven, but I was more like Icarus, and my own horse with wings of wax faltering in limbo also allowed for a hell of a time. An experiential roller coaster.

If the rider and not his transport makes the trip (and vice versa), an explorer's baggage partially accounts for the multi-dimensional limits of my encounter with the Divine—knocking an death's door. Not the fundamental Awakening of Buddha. My head-on collision with the Godhead wakeup was enough to "kill a horse," if not its quixotic rider. Strangely, eating this exotic delicacy was much like munching the ujidadas that my Sicilian mother still makes for the Xmas holidays. The only ingredients lacking in Mom's dish being the hashish, instead adding dough to bake her tasty fig cookies. Maybe that's why I thought majun would be a piece of cake. But this is not the place to sing the praises of oriental confectionary. That is done in the inimitable but unpublishable American Voyager. Yet this book of revelations, an explosive original also ahead of its time with the impact of Allegro, driven mad by his colleagues, could be rejected for the same politically incorrect reasons: An "experimental" genre bender ahead of its time—in spades when it comes to "Palestina" (as my Israel Ministry of Tourism map indicates). Perhaps the Second or Third Intifada will be more timely.

Somehow the energy that ignited my soul, loosened my screws, scrambled my egg-lift-off, was channeled into more familiar territory, as buttermilk, birds chirping and the flowing song of the desert brought me down to earth. Terra Sancta was characterized by a terrific intensity that was comprehension without compulsion. Without hallucinations, kaleidoscopic circus, crystals, and that whole grab-bag of tricks that marks the voyage of your LSD trip. Other synthetic stuff. Nor were there miracles, water changing into wine. Instead, snatches of internal crystallization alone were intoxicating. The brightest sun had burned away my fog, unveiling ineffable sensations, images borne of intensity, intention, innocence, an innocence, that was there in the first place.

Years later I met a rich Moroccan who spoke about his own magical mystery tour, his first trip, and how all others were anticlimactic. The major difference in our reactions to majun was that, while he found himself above the tallest trees looking down, I was looking up. I was the tree, the chirping birds in it. When I attempted to fly, I was free of a fixed orbit, a comet hurtling—literally—through the galaxy. Let Carlos Castaneda put that in his pipe and smoke it. And this was before Don Juan's own controlled flights of fancy, power trips borne of discipline—finite—unlike my own unhinged launching into space. But ultimately, Eros was in the saddle, the phallic fungi of the Fertile Crescent overshadowing desert cactus. Flooded with the feeling and innermost knowledge or intuition that, if there was a Christ, who I rarely thought about, he had also drunk from the Big Dipper. And if a son of a gun like me could have such a shattering religious experience (opening a Pandora's Box, when I thought my hand was going into Mom's cookie jar), then maybe Jesus was just another son of God, like Buddha, Mohammed. And all the miracles alluded to in the word play Allegro alluded to, symbolism.

None of this diminishes the Sermon on the Mount, because the message has always been the same, when inspired, at least since the Vedas showed the way. Coming from a mere mortal (son of God notwithstanding) it should be all the more inspirational, as everlasting life is the eternal moment and only our ego and a not-so high priest stands between us and that experience the pure would preach to the uncomprehending. And didn't Thomas Aquinas say that everything he wrote was like hay compared to that kernel of wisdom that came with his moment of truth. Which begs the question, What was he eating?

About ten or fifteen minutes passed. It was an eternity. The guides returned empty handed—except for the Uzi. They hadn't seen any mushrooms. We drove to El Rom, a lake that is barely visible at the bottom of a black pit. I peered through the mesh-wire fence and tried to imagine what this inkwell would look like on a nice day.

I believe the guides drove me to Newe Ativ. This moshav is one of those oddities that is rendered nondescript by its incongruity. Location cancelled out whatever appeal it could have for me. Newe Ativ is among other things a ski resort that is situated between a hostile Druse village that sits on the Syrian border above, with orchards below. Junked cars are a kind of connecting link between the two communities. The rusting autos on the side of the road mark the gateway to Majdal Shams, while Newe Ativ extends a more rustic welcome with a bar, a kind of last chance café in the high desert that is tended by a Druse teenager who speaks little English.

About to be cast adrift again, seeking any port, I asked for the man in charge of hiring. Getting nowhere with the unlikely bartender, I sat down before a cold and vacant fireplace. There wasn't a ghost of a chance it would be lit, and I didn't have the price of a cup of coffee. When three Englishmen sat down at an adjoining table, I checked out the pool hall and was directed to a suburban street.

The moshav is something of a private enterprise, and from the little I've seen of them, seem to be more habitable than your run-of-the mill kibbutz. Halfway to the recruiter's house, I met the man on his way to his jewelry shop, which faced a kind of courtyard. The inroads of capitalism could not erase that unfinished look so common to places east (and north) of Suez. That fly-by-night (flies by day) look. But Snir was getting in a long

69

awaited crop of Europeans any day now, and there would be no room for us at the kibbutz.

I can't say we were dreaming of a white Xmas, but the road did not beckon and I wasn't going anywhere until I had climbed Mount Hermon. Earlier in the year I had climbed a good part of the way up Mount Olympus, failing to sit in the Throne of Zeus. It is a beautiful hike to the cozy refuge and I was looking forward to a similar experience. Mount Hermon was, after all, the Mount Olympus of the mid-orient, home of the more durable gods. I may be your least prepared climber, but there is a Mount Cammarata in central Sicily, and I am a chip off the old block. Dante says, "Nature is the art of God" (art is the nature of God?) and I believed that certain mountains (Atlas) were altars to God(s?).

Newe Ativ attempted to be borscht, but came out smelling like bunkers. Few things bug me as much as wet concrete, but the recruiter was a charming Frenchman; so if this wasn't the Jewish Alps, maybe I was in Chamonix. In his shop was everything from Tiffany to schlock, which he made and sold. A Jew from Paris, he appreciated my eccentricity and plugged in an electric heater for me when I removed my shoes and socks. The craftsman also plugged in a kettle and set about soldering while our water boiled. We spoke a mélange of French and English.

"Can you tend bar?" he asked.

"I can learn." If I don't get drunk in the process.

"We will need waiters and waitresses, cooks. Can your wife cook? We have two restaurants." They had everything but Jackie Mason, but New Ativ needed the old Mort Sahl.

"Do you need entertainers? My wife and I do a song and dance act at Snir. Actually, I thought I might be able to operate the chair lift." The next best thing to sitting in the Throne of Zeus. That could be arranged. But where was the chair lift?

"It's on the top of Mount Hermon."

By Jove, I'd really be siting on top of the world!

My new friend told me to call him in about a week. I hitched a ride with a Druse heading for Banias. In a couple of minutes we were below the imposing Nimrod, the "Banias" of Mark Twain's declaiming. It is curious how he goes on and on about "Nimrod, the Mighty Hunter of Scriptural

Notoriety" and then calls the fortress of that name Banias Castle "the stateliest ruin of that kind on earth...thousand feet long... We wandered for three hours among the chambers, crypts and dungeons...trod where the mailed heels of many a knightly Crusader had rung..." Before they were defeated by the Arabs, he might have added.

"We wondered how such a solid mass of masonry could be affected by even an earthquake, and could not understand what agency had made Banias (actually Nimrod) a ruin; but we found the destroyer... our wonder was increased tenfold. Seeds had fallen in crevices in the vast walls; the seeds had taken root, tender insignificant sprouts hardened..." and "...forced the greatest stones apart... Gnarled and twisted trees spring from the old walls everywhere, and beautify and overshadow the gray battlements with a wild luxuriance of foliage."

It turned out that this middle-aged Druse had to test the Banias River for toxicity. He parked his car at the side of the road and filled up a test tube. There were various reasons for the increased levels of impurity. The protective fence had been breached. I walked to the Banias parking area, announced my volunteer status to the man in the ticket booth and headed for the purifying pool, where Twain and countless pilgrims before and since sought to wash away their sins. I thought the word banias stemmed from the Latin banos or bathe, when I first heard mention of it. Nor was this Peter's Pan. Paneas became Baneas with the arrival of the Arabs in the seventh century, because these invading Semites pronounced a P as B.

I retired to a great ochre colored cave that put a smile in the gray day. This must have been the original tunnel of love, but I contented myself with finishing my lunch at the very source of the Jordan. The rain with its rivulets flowing down the unabsorbing hills diminishes this miracle in the desert, but most visitors to Banias arrive here after a very hot dry day and they can only babble about this Banias springing forth from the fecund foundation of Mount Hermon, which beckons from miles away. Some of the more poetic witnesses to the birth of the Jordan liken the Hermon to a womb. Paneion, pandemonium, pantheon of sexuality and a good place for this pagan to quietly enjoy his avocado. And what, really, is a pagan, as the word stems from paganus or country folk. Rural. Whatever, old man river himself, Nelson Glueck wrote, "The scent of pagan sanctity hovered long over Paneas—even after Christianity became the official religion of the Eastern Roman Empire..."

Glueck goes on to say that victims were thrown in the pool, reminding me of the Mayan sacrifices. The universality of sacrifice. There is something to it, but if man wants to appease his God, he must sacrifice something of greater value than his son or daughter. Let him cast his ego into the water. You can't move a mile in Israel without bumping into some universal symbol or a reminder or even the birthplace of a great historic figure who has his mysterious origin here. Turkey was an even greater historical cornucopia, full of surprises. For all I know, Saint George the patron saint of England was born there, but right above me was the Moslem shrine of Sheikh Khudr, the saint who slew the dragon, by George. Was the serpent he lanced really Pan? Outside my cave out of reach was the sort of niche that housed Mary in many a church, but it had sheltered Pan. If Christians knew the true origins of their religion, they would panic. I for one (well, I was baptized) remained a fan of that old time religion.

Celibacy, the self-effacing castrating, the seemingly insane behavior of the desert fathers, begins to make sense when you can appreciate the high of those happy hermits materializing in the third century Holy Land like mushrooms after the rain. It does seem their Christianity was really without Christ, or more accurately, like myself those mad monks above Jericho, where the "fly" most certainly flourished, felt like Christ. Sitting in their caves they knew in their nakedness the power and glory that transcends sexuality. The emperor did indeed have no clothes.

One of the tragic ironies of misreading the scriptures and the Christians' emphasis on Jesus Christ as God, rather than simply referring to God, is the isolating of the Jew, reinforcing a justifiable (when one considers what was done in his name) Christophobia that accentuates the them-us syndrome. Christophobia is, of course, the other side of the anti-Semitic coin. Beholden to a questionable bible to which the Falwells have the answer, "Christ" becomes a ploy for keeping the flock in the fold. These chosen ones await the rapture, though politics of Israel complicates things, as Jewish acceptance of Jesus is required for the End Times tickets to paradise for both. In the end, the average Christian and Jew remains an infidel.

So for a more biased appraisal of Paneas, I refer you to the pious Twain. I think that he of tongue-in-cheek fame had his lingua franca in the right place when he says, "It seems curious enough to us to be standing on ground that was once actually pressed by the feet of the Savior. The situation is suggestive of a reality and tangibility that seems at variance with the vagueness and mystery and ghostliness that one naturally attaches to the character of a god. I cannot comprehend yet that I am sitting where a god has stood...surrounded by dusky men and women whose ancestors talked with him, face to face, and carelessly, just as they would have done with any other stranger... the gods of my understanding have been always hidden in clouds and very far away."

Was this the distance that separates Twain from God...and never the Twain shall meet. The American way?

For an un-American reading of God, as seen within the Judeo Christian framework, I must quote from a postcard I picked up in Mexico, along with my hepatitis. The quotation appears under a photo of a snowcapped mountain towering over a sparkling lake:

> Busque a Dios y no lo encontre,
> busque mi alma y no la halle,
> busque a mi hermano
> y encontre a los tres.
> or
> I searched for God and didn't encounter him,
> looked for my soul and didn't find it,
> I sought my brother
> and found all three.
>   —Fedor Dostoyevsky

A quotable thought, even if John Bartlett doesn't think so. Maybe that's because the author of the above is actually Mexican. In Israel, where half the population is Arab and the other half at war with itself and needs an enemy for unity, such a sentiment is seditious.

9

Snir

Singing in the Rain.

"Without a song the day would never end, without a song the road would never bend, without a song the Jordan wouldn't roll..." With all the rain we were getting the river didn't need any help from us. But as we had to be in the orchards at six, a song was called for. Long day, short diary (Mona's):

Nov. 3rd, Monday. Starting picking avocado—(much easier than grapes) not too organized. Go back to cafeteria for breakfast and lunch. Coffee break in shack. Finish about 2:30. Met Tovla (living with English volunteer), been to states. Says every member adopts a volunteer—surprised to see people our age working as volunteers—picking avocados in rain. Talked about not believing in God—Jews now have Israel and no longer have the need for God or religion to keep them together—but observe holidays. Large dining hall, food large variety—use leftovers. Uncomfortable eating all meals with so many people.

I won't soon forget Tovla, our foster father. About 35, he was a balding ball of energy. He and Joseph astride their high hydraulic lifts would plunge into the older and more accessible trees. With machine speed and precision, rescue the stunned fruits from the splintered orchard. I groaned more than the trees at a desecration that wasn't even cost effective, but the equipment satisfied the Israelis' penchant for "progress" and was pleasing to veterans without a war. Tovla was a jovial coil, the happy warrior always ready to spring into action—and one day in his army uniform he marched away from us (along with Joseph and a few other reservists). Our foster father met his wife in the States and took her back to the old country to live on Snir; but how do you keep them...and within a couple of years she had left the kibbutz with her child, leaving the loquacious lothario to his own devices—which turned out to be the most attractive English volunteer at Snir.

Ellie was from the slums of London, but she was pretty and patrician, older than the other girls; and there was nothing cockney or cockeyed about her. Rather, blonde and blue eyed (what else?), pert and petite. I can say I wouldn't mind meeting her in a dark alley. I enjoyed sharing an avocado with Ellie. If the truth be known and I'd been on my own, I would have stolen that pixie away from that fast talking salesman. Tovla sold lamps or some such thing in the States, when he didn't drive a truck, and he really wasn't this woman's speed. He was more of an American than I was, while his prized volunteer was something of an idealist. But Exodus must have been on the bestseller lists of Europe; and Ellie made her own exodus, finding herself broke when reality caught up to her.

She was disappointed when Tovla said the Israelis didn't need God. To this Declaration of Independence I had responded that maybe Israel's triumph, was its tragedy. I asked him about the article I had just read in the Jerusalem Post, something about the president of the United Kibbutz Movement embezzling twenty-nine million dollars. Tovla's eyes widened, like he was surprised I could read, but then said how terrible it was, all of us busting our balls in the orchards for peanuts and some fat cat making off with the milk and honey. But Mona and I found ourselves up for adoption.

Nov. 4th, Tuesday. Difficult getting up at 5:30—English girls wake us in morning-picking avocado again, finished about 1:00—rained most of the day. Members lounge closed—volunteers only have their bomb shelter for socializing on many nights. English girls going to Elat—warmer. Working to make enough money for Egypt.

Nov. 5th, Wednesday. Worked today in toilet factory. Tedious. Danish girl manager. Six Swedish girls very aloof. Danish flirting with Israeli men. Tony left at 12:30. Couldn't breathe—air musty. Tried to get TV. Room opened. Bomb shelter closed.

Slim pickings here. Mona's background in shorthand is showing. And yes, I did spend a very long morning with nary a chirp out of me in the toilet paper factory. All you can eat, though. Really, they had the icebox stocked with Popsicles (out of ice cream) that the girls, homesick for their near arctic patria, scoffed up. It excited one odd kibbutznik to see these Lolitas lap up their ice pops. Plenty of cookies available, also, but the quantity of food never a problem at a kibbutz.

I starred in one of those old Jackie Gleason skits, where the hapless fat man is overwhelmed by a speeded up conveyer belt that leaves him waste high in pie. Except that I had to transfer cartons of toilet paper from the conveyer belt to a dolly and the boxes simply fell to the floor when the belt was accelerated or when my own dolly, stuffing the boxes with Blanche experienced a burst of energy. But there were slack periods, and I could stand by watching the belt roll along like some truncated Jordan. It was the best job in the dust filled factory, and when the Danish girl wanted to rotate me to another position, I developed my breathing problem. Bad as the air was, stacking this crap on the rack was the least hazardous job at Blanche's. After I left, Mona was cutting the cardboard rollers that the toilet paper is rapped around. Placing the long spool before an unprotected blade, sawing the cardboard down to size. One careless move and you could lose a finger or nose. Mona fed the serrated cutter for about an hour and then said, Shove it. Initially, her Swedish partner tried to brow beat an apparently spoiled American into completing an unpleasant task, but then seeing just how dangerous the job was, abandoned the operation herself. The big Swede punctuated her refusal declaring, "In Sweden such unsafe conditions would never be permitted." In Turkey, such a factory didn't exist and Mona thought of all the times she was caught short.

Nov. 6th, Thursday. Worked in laundry today—Tony picking avocados. Sewing buttons and elastic bands—boring but relaxing. Worked with two Swedish girls, more friendly than yesterday. Dining room can get noisy. Dogs always waiting outside. Hundreds of socks. Borrowed heater from member. Said Arabs cut barbed wire on border many nights. Met Canadian woman, invited us—many non Israelis making home in kibbutz.

Mona appears to be going around the bend. At least, she'll be able to darn my socks properly. The Canadian never set a date and we never did visit her.

Nov. 7th, Friday. Back to picking avocados—5:30, more organized this time. Finished about 12:00 for day, being Friday and beginning of Sabbath—evening meal everyone sitting together, prayer before starting, dinner—all volunteers sat together—chicken again. Strange dog bothering Tony.

When Mona says "more organized," she is referring to the harvest.

How could she forget all the mud, the tractor that towed the workers bogging down. Joel, of Philadelphia, is worthy of mention, really a good natured guy. Last Christmas the volunteers sang his praises thusly, "Joel, Joel, the angels did say..."

Joel came here via the Negev. He said the kibbutz was getting too large and he wanted a change of scenery. Married and in his early thirties, Joel has been here about ten years. In Israel that is.

As for that strange dog, I think he had been eating too much insecticide. He wouldn't allow me into the First Aid office. I did manage to pick up my ration of prophylactics, entering the dispensary when the dog had been shooed away by a familiar face.

Nov. 8th, Saturday. No work today—rain on and off as previous days—Tony hiking. Spoke with Schmeul—has taken dog from Lebanon—named after terrorist. Uri told me again yesterday about leaving Wed. Communal eating is very difficult. We visited with Schmeul—parents from Syria.

When I dared to look in Mona's black book, I wondered how I was going to stretch these lines into a book?

We spent a good three hours with Schmeul, the closest thing to an Israel hippy. So out of the Sabra character that I had my suspicions. I'm pretty sure he worked in the chicken factory, while I couldn't walk within a hundred feet of this carnal house. I believe that Schmeul, with the unfortunate volunteers, swept up the mess. I think every member had a crack at ringing the necks of the chickens, or however it was they executed the birds. But there was nothing chicken shit about Schmeul. He had tropical fish, the tank providing most of the light for the pad where we were invited to crash when we got our walking papers. A comfortable mattress filled up a good portion of his living room, and it wasn't long after the spirits materialized that I found myself inclining more and more towards the horizontal. It was a pad better suited for pot, and I got that old feeling. Which is not to say I was feeling my age.

Schmeul showed us his garden, no marijuana growing there. There was a big drug problem a few years back, and the authorities blamed it on the volunteers and got tough. This Syrian Jew was trying to make a go of kibbutz life, telling us the problems he had his first year here. I'm not sure if it was his lifestyle that bothered the members or what, but he said people were beginning to see things his way. His garden appeared to be a victory of sorts. With a war every few years, many returning veterans seemed to constitute a transient class. I remembered the Israeli I met on the Bolivia-bound train in 1976. He was just a little coy, smug or dopey, about his visit to purchase drugs. Schmeul spoke about his Syrian background, but I don't have any recollection of persecution of his parents.

Nov. 9th, Sunday. Strange working on Sunday—back in toilet paper factory—sweeping, dust all over. Tony, library.

Can't say I blame Mona for being brief. If she says a little less, she will have said it all. I feel guilty about my cushiony job, but I wasn't needed in the orchard and I refused to do what I was there for—the work the members found least desirable. As I said to Uri, I thought the kibbutz was supposed to be democratic, to each his needs, from each whatever his capacity, never pleading guilty but paraphrasing some communist manifesto borrowed by the kibbutzim.

"What kind of work do you do?"

I told Uri I was a writer, and he arranged for the feather bed. Writer, library, they seemed to go together, even if the books were in Hebrew. Over the years, volunteers had left enough books behind, most of them in English, to keep me labeling them for a day or two, provided I caught up with my reading in the process.

It was about this time we met a tall young American Jew from California. His father was the kibbutz doctor, but he preferred to work in the kitchen, a kind of permanent KP, rather than work in the rain. Mona said his father was spending his summers here in Snir, but that this was the young man's first or second visit to the Golan Heights. Although the father was a volunteer, who I should have seen as a patient. His duties were limited to the dental chair, while his son playing his Hollywood card for what it was worth, did more than slice the tomatoes.

A very attractive Swedish girl who couldn't have been more than eighteen actually believed the dentist's son would be able to star her in a movie. They would go to Hollywood together, and she would leave the toilet paper factory behind. There was no chance of this Valentino making his aliya, literally his "ascension," in Israel. He told Mona that to become an Israeli was a step down for him. From what, he was never very clear about. What the aspiring yuppie meant was that Israel would cramp his style—financially. He said he had more girls than he could handle, Christians. In Israeli society such mixing wasn't kosher. Obviously, Snir smiled on such goings on and is considered one of the more radical kibbutzim, being the first kibbutz to permit children to sleep with their parents—after the terrorist attack on the children's house in nearby Dafne.

I don't think the California dreamer was spending much time with his dad.

Nov. 10th, Monday. Visited Ariel again, from Holland. Patrols area—tells us how dangerous it is to take short cuts. Cow stepped on mine. Some places not marked. Told us how difficult to become an Israeli citizen. Had to be circumcised and learn Hebrew. Likes hunting. Wife spent small fortune to get him a gun. Said he would have invited Tony to go hunting with him, but thought Tony would decline. Israelis too complacent about security. Says Arabs cut border fences at night. Tony says when returns to kibbutz after dark gate sometimes open. Ariel, tall, thin, seems to be living on edge. Wife and children pleasant, but something strange about him. Party in bomb shelter/disco. Schmeul, DJ.

Circumcise yourselves to the Lord. Remove the foreskin of your heart. Jeremiah. Whatever, Ariel let it all hang out, at the same time speaking a universal, if rarely practiced language that sat well with the Snirites.

A party that couldn't bomb. A bomb shelter is an inspiration for the disco of the future. Profiting most from a darkened enclosure is a gambling casino.

In Stuttgart, a centrally located hotel, On The Platz, is actually under the Platz. A holdover from World War II that was my home for a bad part of the week during my down and out days in Paris and the rest of Europe.

So there was no view in Snir's disco, but déjà vu, and that down-home feeling fortified with Maccabee beer, and Mary Jane. As they used to say in Palm Beach, a good time was had by all, but there was this inescapable reminder of war that was so easy to bring me down.

The best laugh I had was provided by the Dutch cowboy, also a volunteer and no relation to Ariel, more down to earth. Maybe his lofty name is why I could have confused him with his countryman, the Flying Dutchman. Jumping up and down pogo stick fashion, with his Israeli partner, a male member, he was the incarnation of Pan himself. He seemed straight enough in the stockyard where we had met. A little peculiar, as he had a charming way with hogs, which you might not expect on a kibbutz; but they were like the coveted forbidden fruit. The veterinarian was literally tickling the fancy of a huge far-from-kosher pig. Then another porker, scratching behind the sow's ears, demonstrating his way with animals, underscoring his importance on the kibbutz. He was a horse breeder in Holland and, tiring of the horsey set, made his way to Israel where he thought he could be useful. As a hillbilly from all too flat Holland, he felt at home in Golan. Most of the Snirites were from the city, he said, and it was necessary to grow up on a farm to understand animals.

"I'm indispensable. I practically run things." Like most of the Dutch, he spoke English well. His hair was like hay. Another tall Aryan, he enjoyed his role as a kind of Snir overseer. "I am here five years. It is difficult to teach the Israelis anything. They will only do something if they think it is their idea. You must not tell them directly."

His dancing was less subtle, going bunkers, bouncing off the twisting Swedes and English girls. Now, Israelis from every land got into the act, but there was no upstaging the Dutchman, the horseman of the apocalypse, cowboy of the kibbutz.

The dislocating absurdity of a swinging bomb shelter so out of synch with its surroundings flashed me back to that Casablanca-bound freighter, where all manner of castaways turned up. Turned on. Except that the Age of Aquarius is already that disappearing wake that follows every ship, gone with the wind. Curiously enough, it was in the middle of the ocean that our theme song was "Jesus Christ, Super Star." And now, I wonder where you are.

The bomb shelter was our introduction to volunteer social life. The English girls who awakened us cleaned up the bunker our first night on the town. It was their responsibility, really, their going-away party. The girls would have liked to spend more time in the TV room or members' lounge, but when it was open the Israelis never let them watch anything in the English language. It irked the members when the volunteers would watch a program broadcast from Lebanon, one in particular, proclaiming salvation through, Christ, but no matter what the volunteers listened to, they could count on some kibbutznik switching the channel. Without so much as an excuse me (I really don't think the expression exists in Hebrew) or a glance, a young man would idle up to the tellie and turn the dial, as if the girls weren't in the room. This "arrogance" drove all the volunteers up the wall, but at least I had an opportunity to see just how American Israeli TV was. Game shows to compliment Rebecca's horror shows.

The lounge also showed films that brought you back to where you were with a start. I was chilled as one film demonstrated preparedness for chemical warfare—the proper way for children to wear a mask that was too large for them. Excluding my experiences in the nearby groves, the one time I really transcended the scent of the factory and the lingering smell of war was that Sunday morning that I awoke to a snow-crowned Mount Hermon—the Kilimanjaro in miniature glistening in the cool, clear air beyond flowering vines and tennis courts. Until the Wednesday when we left, it was our lodestone.

Mona interrupted her packing to put aside an avocado for a sunny day. I have a title for your book, "Up for Adoption."

10

The Forgotten Ones:

The Druse of Majdal Shams.

"A Syrian village is the sorriest sight in the world, and its surroundings are eminently in keeping with it." From "Innocents Abroad."

On the next page, Mark Twain and his group are very thirsty, their goatskin is dry. They halt before a wretched Arab town "perched on the side of the mountain, but the dragoman said if we applied there for water we would be attacked by the whole tribe, for they did not love Christians." They must journey on. As the innocents were two hours donkey ride from Nimrod castle, we must assume they had just skirted Majdal Shams, on their road from Damascus.

Our entry into Majdal Shams recalled our approach to Jerusalem, but nature wasn't as accommodating to the Druse town. Trees and overhanging cliffs almost camouflaged the Capital's war relics, but there was nothing to overshadow these rusting chassis that sat on the side of the road as prominent as the Palm trees on a Syrian boulevard. Some of the machines partially blocked the road. Israeli authorities could claim that outside Jerusalem war's debris was a kind of memorial, but inside and outside Majdal Shams, the junk was a monument to neglect. Shams' shame advertised to passing tour buses the Israeli sentiment: See how dirty the Arabs are?

Without a dragoman, we dragged our own asses up the steep road, passing high above Nazhi's house. I longed to see some of those mud-plastered homes that Twain grew to detest and to catch a glimpse of the past. When Clemens came this way, he really didn't know a Druse from a Druid, and we remain pretty much in the dark. At least I do. Some say their Diaspora was out of Egypt and they even have their own Moses, but they see me coming and this may be apocryphal. One thing for certain is that the fair-haired inhabitants of Majdal Shams came here from Lebanon and that the town remains a link between the Levant and Syria proper.

We hiked up to the little traffic circle that served as the town square.

Where you might expect a traffic cop (if there was traffic), Majdal Shams awaited the installation of the statue of a Druse hero. A small restaurant looked out on the unadorned circle and although the place could bear no resemblance to the town Twain knew, or rather thirsted after, I could go nowhere but up. All that can be said for Majdal Shams is its altitude or location. And a curse of the Third World, a concrete jungle that climbs up the imposing Mount Hermon, long past the point you would think it possible or practical. A magnificent frame or backdrop for this desolation that softened in the distance, as I could imagine the homes were made of a natural substance.

Mona was a little leery about remaining in the restaurant alone, but she was too tired to go on or up, and I wanted to get as close to the Syrian border as possible. I'm not one for cheap thrills, but it was there, and my Everest was out of reach this late in the day. I wanted to be able to say that something happened to me on the road to Damascus, even if it was the back road. But all was quiet on the Western Front. Above me was a U.N. observation post. A little further on, driven on, an Israeli tower and a Syrian tower, twin towers. I prayed both sides scratched their heads rather than pulled their triggers. Apparently, I was U.N.

So forbidding a terrain lent itself to the terror of this no-man's land. A truckload of Israeli soldiers took off up the mountain. I don't think they were going skiing.

I walked as far as I dared and then, ever your dutiful tourist, snapped a picture of the warning sign. Several ragamuffins sent to fetch me put me on the road back to the restaurant, but a couple of blocks short of the eatery, I spotted Mona and a young lady coming in my direction. Yes, we had been adopted. This time by a college student whose father owned the restaurant. Handa wanted us to meet her brother, recently returned from Spain with his wife. The young couple couldn't speak English; but her brother Ayman spoke Spanish fluently, our lingua franca. They had been studying in Spain the past year.

But the Ayoubs were as if to the hacienda born, and I simply did not know where I was until the perfunctory tea was brought and I was stretched out on the carpet. And if that did not bring me home, hanging from the wall was the apparently mandatory Dome of the Rock Massacre.

It was difficult for me to believe that this warm young man in his twenties was a radical poet and something of a Druse celebrity, but soon he was translating his book into Spanish for me. There was no mistaking that the Majdal Shams Druse were the soul brothers of the Palestinians, and this poetry a cri de coeur against oppression.

If Israel doesn't have its own Melville, it is because myth rather than truth drives the narrative. And if an open mind develops in a closed society, it abandons ship. Maxim Ghilan, a respected international journalist and politician in Israel, wrote "How Israel lost Its Soul," when it became obvious that the '67 War was started by Israel and not Egypt. Another trumped up justification for a quasi-genocidal occupation. A few years later, Israel's modern prophet would write what is clearly evident many years later: "Either the present state of affairs will continue to exist, dragging the country to its bitter end; or a movement for peace and renewal will replace it." And yet this is not written in stone. In this land of shifting sand, smoke and mirrors, a miracle is long past due. More realistically, as I've written to prospective publishers: "Israel's past and future is written in the pages of the present—between the lines. Bottom line."

We had thought of the Golan Heights as largely uninhabited. Was this what the American press wanted to convey? The Israeli authorities were, after the war, thinking that these Syrians would fall into line with their Israeli brothers. The Druse soldiers are to Israeli armed forces what the Sikhs are to the Indian army, but the Druse are also indispensable to the Syrian defense forces and as far as Ayman was concerned, a Druse loyal to Israel was a traitor.

On our journey to the south, in Ein Gedi we saw a dedication to Druse soldiers slain in the battle for this strategic oasis. Joseph had told us that in Lebanon the Israeli Druse had committed the worst atrocities against the Palestinians. I had a problem reconciling this brutality with the photo of the bearded patriarchs that hung from the wall of Ayman's home. Their almost Zoroastrian hats heightened their bearing and seemed to imbue them with a dignity beyond violence. Benevolent wizards, but then I thought of others in conical hats and long robes. Their religion appeared to be a composite of Persian, Christian and Moslem, but is still shrouded in mystery, even as it dies out and nationalism becomes the opium of the young. Doctrine and practice is the province of quasi-priests so that the only Druse, privy to its mysteries, are the deeply religious who apparently take vows. But from what I gathered theirs was a brotherhood without ritual and hierarchy. Ayman later pointed a finger to the upper reaches of Majdal Shams and said that an unadorned building little different from the others clustered around it was their meeting place. I don't know if this lodge could be rightly called a house of worship. The Druse temple, if it could be called that, was more like an ancient synagogue than a church or a mosque, but I do not think they are likely to draw that analogy. Looking out over a good part of Israel, the Druse spiritual center serves a community of about ten thousand.

Tea and cookies was followed by hummus and falafel, fresh vegetables and a cold dark night on the town. We had pastry in one of those mid-Eastern eateries that is the bane of the esthete. More concrete and those same unadorned tiles we tread (dread) the length of Anatolia and in every kibbutz and many an Israeli home. At least this hole in the wall could boast of a mural of a mountain scene and the temperature to go with it. The Druse social club was no warmer and the ambience designed to chill to the bone. The art closest to the heart of the young Druse is the Israeli occupation with a real or imagined portrayal in barbed wire and concentration camps. Even if the goulash portraiture was a metaphor for the imprisoned spirit, it had to have the ring of bitter irony for the Israelis—who I could not imagine condoning this kind of thing. But they must have. Harmless outlet, since so little could elude the tentacles of the Israeli spy network. The Druse knew how far they could go with their provocation and vice versa. Israel considered the unpredictability of a Syrian fanatical sect founded by Ismail.

An older man flipped me an apple. Above the desk was a set of Encyclopedia Americana sitting on a shelf. I had to hand it to those door-to-door diehards. Two or three young men spoke English, so I asked this group if they wanted to know how Americans saw them. The Druse were summed up in a paragraph or two which, I read aloud.

I draw a blank but for the pooh poohing of my quote, a lingering shadow about the Druse being a persecuted minority in Syria. Easier to remember is Webster's (1937) less political definition: a warlike tribe. But the Druse saw themselves as the new Jews in a Nazi regime, where instead of the Star of David an Israeli identity card was being forced upon them.

In the back of the club lay the unfinished statue, awaiting resurrection in the traffic circle. And some traffic to go with it. Guests were far and few between. Some young Germans came this way early in the summer. Ayman's friend didn't arrive too soon with a nearly full car. The fair-haired young man would take us to his house, and for a moment on that incredibly cold night, Rebecca's indoctrination impacted upon me. Were we nuts? I looked at my wife with that what, me worry, expression, only too happy to be going where there was a promise of oil heat, and little chance of a kidnapping.

Our new friend's house seemed to be newer than Ayman's, but its rough edges were softened by a bottle, a heater soon to be plugged in, and a urbanely witty character who already was. The John Belushi look-alike (the similarity ended there) was a pipe-smoking laborer who did not belabor the irony of constructing homes for the rich Israelis below in the St. Moritz of the Holy Land—where we were also awaiting employment. The whiskey, wine and raki flowed freely. After the Turkish delirium and Israeli deviousness, this motley gathering was a breath of crystallizing air. These Druse were simply bent on having a good time and not at the expense of the Israelis, except for maybe one dig that could have gotten under Mona's skin, had she not considered their circumstances—which really didn't seem that dire. The young Turks were too well adjusted and confident in a waiting game that seemed without rules. I'll never forget Belushi spread out on the floor like a pasha bullshitting about his court appearance in the morning for resistance against one Israeli edict or another.

Mona was convinced that the Syrian government was somehow supporting Ayman and his friends. We could not imagine how he could afford to study in Spain, ready to resume his studies the following month. Handa had asked Mona about kibbutz life, but if anybody resented their existence, they did not begrudge us our flirtation with the other side, never dreaming that Mona is Jewish—maybe never caring. There was no holding back.

To what extent liquor played in this emotional outpouring, I can't say, but an old wino like me would like to think that in vino es veritas.

Insincerity in sobriety and absolutely no honesty in arrogance. As I slipped into a stupor, I actually pitied the occupiers and their compulsion to live up to the superman image. Always on an apocalyptic one-upmanship, the guardedness of the guard. As opposed to the openness of the Godly.

Not to say these drunken Druse were men of God (though that may well be), but in my eyes they were more Sicilian than Syrian, if more sophisticated than my simpler cousins. There was something else about these unassuming people that took me back to Sicily. As loud and generous as the Sicilians are, they also have a secret society, though granted it is a less spiritual brotherhood than the Druse. In their mountain fastness, high above their orchards, the Golan Druse enjoyed a more independent history than most—at least when Mark Twain was here. Unlike the Sicilian crushed between the Mafia and the church, or the Arabs below, the Druse took on the wings of the eagle, apparently above it all. After the forced joviality of so much of the Middle East—and the Middle West—it was refreshing to meet a happy warrior.

When we returned to Ayman's home, he still wanted to talk, but I'd been floored by the one-two punch of booze and the un-tropical breeze, and I wanted to remain there—under a half dozen blankets. My gallant effort at conversation was ridiculous.

It was too cold to sit and I was too tired to stand. Ayman, finally tiring of my agitated movements, got the message and kindly gave up his matrimonial mattress, which was indeed on the floor but lacking the required number of blankets. Our host also furnished his honored guests with his heater. In their bedroom was a touching wedding picture of Ayman and his wife. They hadn't changed in the year or two of their marriage. Had I found my brother or, at my age, my son who turned up at Majdal Shams?

We wanted a taste of autumn and got a mouthful of winter instead. In Golan's Promethean perch, there was little coal or wood to be burned. In the morning the spilt water on the patio was a sheet of ice, but last week's melting snow, its sunlit crags above, became a siren's song. Unfortunately, after a sleepless night, we could go nowhere but down, looking forward to a defrosting. Mona interrupted our descent to photograph an old Druse armored in a ferocious handlebar moustache chopping some precious wood. But not before Ayman got the ancient's permission.

The young poet and his wife were reluctant to let us go on. A real friendship was developing, but we explained we'd most likely return in a few days. There was also Mount Hermon. No Matterhorn, but good enough for a guy who made mountains out of mole hills and couldn't pass up a pun, or a pub.

Until a job turned up, this seemed like a good time to get the requisite Nazareth out of the way, to speak to the man who spoke to the man from Galilee, actually, or the sacred mushroom. Either way, it was getting to feel a lot like Christmas, as the song goes. But, as always, we would play it by ear—making allowances for my tinnitus.

Ayman's mother had insisted that we take along with us yesterday's pita bread and some hard boiled eggs. And, of course apples, taking us down memory lane and those humbling staples and generosity that got us through the sixties, when we rarely knew where the next meal was coming from, or if it would ever arrive. On the road in much of Africa, depending on the climate, it was bananas or peanuts, until we reached South Africa, and we relied on the dark brown bread relegated to the blacks.

It was easy for us to identify with the underdog, which was Israel until we saw how much it had in common with South Africa, its best friend. Now we related to the people of Ishmael (Ismail). I could see them, like his namesake, the lone survivors on their mountain, to mix my metaphors, of a Moby Dick, the wrath of God, Armageddon provoked by those on both sides of the mountain who would play God.

Israel could become another Pequod and the driven Ahab the composite captain of the ship (of state) like that other Ahab, Israel's seventh king, at the site of that perpetual battleground, the Armageddon of John's Revelation.

11

Kibbutzing

Going Our Way.

A glorious sun drenching day, with apple orchards sloping below us. But there were no rides from any quarter, including a passing bus. Did we look like Druse? A carload of crowned patriarchs passed us going in the opposite direction. Majdal Shams was now out of sight; so, tired of walking, we stood our ground. This was a good time for Mona to take notes, but she was too disheartened to write and concentrated on her plight.

I chastised her, "I told you to wear a dress. You could have crossed your legs, showed a little thigh."

She stood up. "All right, Clark." A little banter for morale.

I would write myself, but my thumb is occupied and I am really too busy enjoying the weather and Druse rusticity.

I only wished there were less traffic and less rubbish in my bag, so I could simply enjoy our walk. Nazareth, or wherever my nose taketh me could wait. But even without a definite destination, Mona carried on as if we had to be there at a particular time. She reasoned we were hitchhiking. It was the business at hand, so we should be getting a lift, rather than just soaking up the scenery. What the hell, Mark Twain didn't travel much faster than us, with arrival came other problems. My only regret was that in middle-age my bag was never light enough. Yet, my pack was the shell on the back of a turtle, all the home I needed.

We continued our hike, stopping about every half mile, until a Druse family gave us a lift to Brechat-Ram, the volcanic lake down the road that I had seen in the rain. The lake looked no better on a clear day and there was an admission fee. Not our cup of tea.

Again, I asked Mona to begin writing some notes, but she was of my mind. If you are enjoying a place, why write about it; and if you aren't, why rub it in. So I am suspicious of those neatly packaged travel journals that purport to capture the spirit of the road. And anybody who brought their typewriter along was looking for a home away from home and is beneath contempt. Even a camera altered the picture and it is a fact that observation alone changed an atom. Jungle Jim aside, you cannot bring them back alive. For all the charm of many travel stories, they are but the stuffed animals of the taxidermist, devoid of reality's reek.

Mona drew another blank in her black book, except for the mention of Kibbutz Mahanayim, which is where we spent the night. But getting there was such a mania-go-round that my rage has provided me with perfect recall. My memory really has improved with spurts of adrenalin since going to Israel. Rested, we hitched a ride to El Rom. But how could I forget this noteworthy occurrence? We had walked down to the same stream, where we got a lift in the opposite direction two weeks ago.

But now, we had competition. An unsmiling old-timer not fifty feet up the road was regarding us with some suspicion. We had violated the first rule of the road (at least in the West) by jumping to the head of the line, and yet, ladies first. He was not concerning himself with such niceties. Turning my back on this Druse, I faced Mount Hermon and, just living in the moment, took out our pita bread. In an instant, the old man was offering me an apple.

In El Rom I suddenly became quite repelled and then depressed by all the iron doors of the shops that were like so many jail cells on our road to Armageddon or wherever it was we were going. An almost endless numbing drabness of the modern Middle East in such disappointing counterpoint to the remaining pockets of Arabesque that inspired other cultures with its intricate invitation to meditation. I could not believe I came this way three times, with its mystical, biblical connotation; and that now we were trudging to the end of town, once again being passed up by the same bus driver.

Outside of El Rom we stopped across the way from the police station, where a young soldier wearing a skull cap was speaking to an elderly Druse. I could imagine them talking about the finer points of their respective religions, what they had in common. Imagination made this a moving sight.

A pregnant dog sniffed us out, careless about the passing cars to Mona's horror. She finally struggled up the steps of the police station and probably had her litter. One gets a little superstitious when twice in a three-month period, a very pregnant dog seeks you out at the side of the road. Everything was pregnant with meaning. And the biting irony of absurdity, no pun intended. I soothed myself with the knowledge that you only see a country from the side of the road. For it is surprising how even in remote areas you become a fixture in a matter of minutes, no more obtrusive than a grazing cow looking up to gaze at the inhabitants of some village. Villagers become as unconcerned as the cow, and you may as well be some old crow that has alighted on a nearby fencepost to gawk. But you aren't gawking, you are an inconsequential hitchhiker, unthreatening and about to fly away.

In Turkey, the gypsies did take notice. We didn't give them a chance to take anything else. As startling a sight as you are momentarily, in minutes you are woven into the fabric of life.

The picture changes dramatically when you pull out a camera. And this wasn't just any country. But the most telling view from the side of the road concerns the passing motorists who could be candidates on "Candid Camera" in their undisguised reactions to hitchhikers. For nowhere can you better catch people in the act of being themselves than when they are behind the wheel, out of harm's way, on the power trip that driving is. The driver who stops for you is usually another kettle of fish, and you can't go very far on a good day without encountering that very special person who bothers to give you a lift and is likely, in most countries, to take you home or go out of his or her way for you, simply because the driver is a Good Samaritan.

They were in short supply, and we considered ourselves lucky when a bus stopped for us and we were on our way to Or Tal. This kibbutz was a spur of the moment consideration, as the weather had turned warm and this was the last stop before the dreaded valley. Actually, Or Tal was a ranch of sorts, apparently run by soldiers. A black Englishman drove us back to the road, suggesting we try Ein Zivan if we were seeking work. Within minutes, a senior citizen was taking us back to Ein Zivan, telling us that this kibbutz had a plastic factory and what a very nice place this was to work. Above the ranch, it had a splendid view. As I made to get out of his car, I told our benefactor I was allergic to plastic. He mentioned several kibbutzim in the valley, saying he was actually going to Safed, an "artists' colony" high above the Sea of Galilee. But first, the man had to continue on up the Heights to take care of some business. He would be returning this way in an hour's time and would take us to Safed if we were waiting outside the kibbutz.

While waiting for the volunteer overseer to turn up, I took out my tourist map of Tiberias to see what it had to say about nearby Safed or Zefat, as the Hebrews called this "ancient city of Jewish mysticism, now a favorite summer resort." It was just east of Mount Mermon (not Hermon) and an ancient synagogue. For innocents abroad a must. Playing it safe, we posted ourselves on the side of the road without so much as a grain of salt. Lebanon was not an issue with the Ministry of Tourism, and like everybody else, we tend to believe what we read, though we live the reality. One hopes the bombs had not yet fallen or were in the works as this was written: "The road continues northward as far as Metulla, whose 'good fence' on the Lebanese border..."

And how do you straddle the fence when so much of it is barbed wire twisted into an innocuous form? I walked over to the bus shelter as an ancient might approach an oracle, but the handwriting on the wall was run-of-the-mill graffiti. One yuppie was cured of his "fetish for plastic." Another malcontent said something about slave labor. As they had waited for their bus, nobody seemed very sorry about leaving Ein Zivan. A Good Samaritan was going our way loaded with apples. What else? As doggerel would have it, the man's son had just returned from the Big Apple, prompting a rise out of Mona, but the old fellow didn't bite.

We told Sam we'd spent some time at Snir, which only lessened our chances of getting an invitation. "Snir!" and he grumbled about communists, drugs...the old anti-left litany.

Down we went, and a gurgling stream (it could have been the mighty Jordan) rushed on to the Sea of Galilee. In the failing light, the valley took on a richer color, easing me into encounter with the ancient mystery. The road to Ha-Galil was level for only a few miles before we were climbing the opposite heights on the road to Lebanon and a spectacular view of the inland sea to the south. Heart shaped, harp shaped (the Hebrew name for it), the great lake was a lapis lazuli under a crimson sky, a wonderful water color that was fast becoming an ink drawing as we drew near Zefat, with not an artist in sight. I was the only mystic within centuries. Outside of

Jerusalem, Israel was as mystical as a Quonset hut. You would look long and hard for any trace of the Kabala. Sam let us out across the street from his house, but there was no sign of Sam's son. He suggested we try the "Youth Hostel" about a quarter of a mile away.

I'd never known a youth hostel to go for more than five dollars, but this place was asking thirty shekels for the both of us, off season. We reasoned that at that rate we would be broke in a week. We hopped on the bus to Rosh Pinna where we had changed buses two weeks earlier. On this cool evening with the night people so common to the Western world it seemed like a year ago, if ever, that we passed this way.

A shady lady asked us if we wanted to rent a room, which only increased Mona's yearning to return to the bosom of the kibbutz and get the hell out of Rosh Pinna. One of the earliest modern Jewish villages, this 'cementville' was old enough for a bus station with all the flavor of an airy port authority. It was lacking a waiting room, but we went to the adjoining cafeteria where we learned about Kibbutz Mahanayim. I was told the bus left later than it did, but we managed to jump aboard before it pulled out of the station, arriving at the kibbutz in no time, and in time to commandeer a station wagon carrying a few members back to Mahanayim proper—that is, the heart and soul, the dining hall. This is one of the largest communes in Israel, just outside the airport of the same name.

In fact, I think Mahanayim is named for Miami and is the Hebrew translation. There was nothing about these much older, more conservative kibbutzniks biding their time near a tropical sea (Galilee) that will easily dispel me of that notion. We were just under the wire for chow.

In the dining hall we met Eric who had already strayed from the fold, but had recently returned, determined to have another shot at freedom. Jonathan, temporarily in charge of volunteers, had tried to help prepare the retiring Eric for the outside world, but errant Eric could not cope with the unexpected.

From England, Eric was already in his thirties and tortured by his inability to leave his "padded rut," as Jonathan put it. I wonder if Jonathan, who would also like to break the unrelenting routine in this inhibiting habitation, introduced us to Eric to show him what price freedom. I thought about being confined to the base one or two duty days a week when I was in the Navy and wondered how anyone could prefer even a gilded cage to starvation. Going hungry, of course, was the only way I could travel and why I could go bananas over humble pie, freedom being everything.

Nestled in the valley away from the border, it is misleading to bring the military into this, for many, idyllic picture. My overriding memory of Mahanayim is of a golden-ager gliding down a walkway on his tricycle. Fortunately, there was no work for us and we never did see the heaters factory. Unfortunately, we didn't see a heater either as the windows of our room were broken, but numbing fatigue and enough blankets saw us through a sound sleep. Miami it wasn't.

We woke up to a beautiful day and a déjà vu out our jagged window. Fresh air and a little ragged around the edges, but the way I like it. A midwinter day in Florida, no ashes at this altitude.

Over a large breakfast we met Jonathan. He really seemed like a regular guy, to whom we'll always be grateful, but I kind of question his motives for driving us to the main gate. People in our position have been known to camp out on many a kibbutz where you can get lost in the crowd and get your three squares a day.

Bum's rush, or no, it beat walking and in minutes a creaking van was halting up ahead. There was only room for one in the front, so Mona opted for the back. We had decided that, as cool as the nights were, this was still no time to see Nazareth. With the Lebanon War forgotten, I thought we'd get up to Metulla and do a little fence sitting.

The van's driver, in his thirties, was going to Qiryat Shemona, just below Metulla and on the opposite road to Mount Hermon, if it came to that. We had just heard on his radio that the chairlift on Mount Hermon would be in operation tomorrow on Sabbath day. This may have been the earliest opening yet, and I thought that my French friend in Newe Ativ wouldn't mind our early arrival. The news over, my new friend, who I call Van, lashed out at the government, saying that because it was so corrupt it had created a dog-eat-dog atmosphere or, as he put it, "Everybody is eating each other—they follow the example of the government. Before, nobody stole anything. Now, you can't trust anyone. Only a war will bring us together." But the Lebanese War had helped divide the people, and what the country really needed was a genuine revolution.

Van went on about the working conditions, the long workweek. He would not starve, but he could not live on his salary. This was especially painful for him because he'd already been to the States and had a taste of the Big Apple. A kind of repairman, he was content in New York, but his father had fallen ill, and when he went home to visit him he got caught in the economic crunch. I was beginning to see the similarities between the young Australians and the young Israelis, who had gone to pre-Reagan America. Just as the Aussies went to Great Britain to be civilized, the Israelis went to the U.S. to be humanized. At least, if they stayed long enough, the Israelis returned a little less arrogant. But when we got to talking about the Golan Druse, Van called them traitors.

Whatever the charms of Metullah, it was not in the cards. My thumb for a mast, it did not catch a breeze. A girl soldier who was also heading towards Metullah, remained hitching in her spot an hour after we abandoned our idea of skirting the Lebanese border. Not a hundred feet away, I resumed my cigar store Indian routine, hopeful to see Dan before continuing up to Mount Hermon. That is, the River Dan, and the tel of the same name, which I had already seen. The more diligent Mona had little opportunity to play the tourist. Van, who'd gone out of his way to put us on this junction, had suggested we try the nearby Dafna if we were in a pinch for work.

Van had driven us up the Huleh valley. Not the Hudson, yet it was close enough to the Jewish Alps to evoke the spirit of the Catskills the first day of the deer season. Some of the "strongholds" in the upper valley had much in common with the Borscht Belt. On the other hand, Huleh valley was boxed in by the Lebanon mountains to the north and the opposing plateaus. But Golan an Bashan gives way to wetlands—what is left of it—and greenery that would not bless the rest of Israel till January. The acquisition of the Huleh Drainage concession in 1934 led to the "redemption" of much of the land in this "lake district," shrinking this pristine paradise to little more than the Beit Ussishkin Institute, its stuffed specimens against a large diorama of the teaming Huleh—before the Zionist reclamation from God.

The proliferation of fish and waterfowl, botanical treasures, had been replaced by farms and plastic factories. It was a grandiose scheme that could have met with less disastrous results in Uganda, but in so tiny and fragile a landscape the ecology was radically altered, a unique oasis in the desert that is Israel gone forever. Even the Dead Sea was being drained dry in the name of progress. Without the River Jordan and the Mare Mortuum, what was this land the Israelis had inherited. The Sea of Galilee was near toxic.

12

The Snows of Killer Mount Hermon

Writing about the remaining Huleh, a still existent swamp to the south, Nelson Glueck could write in 1967, "There are papyrus plants, reeds, bulrushes, high grasses, ferns, water lilies and exotic flowers of many kinds. Jackals, hyenas, some wild boar." Remaining was little water under the "Bridge of the Daughters of Jacob" and little sign of animal life. Like Abraham pursuing the kidnapped Lot, to paraphrase Glueck, we went as far as the River Dan and spent the night at Dafna.

Dafna has to be the Queen of the Kibbutzim, but her largesse does not filter down to the volunteers, now holed up in the bomb shelter bar complaining about the unsafe work conditions. They were too young to bitch about the accommodations, which were shacks devoid of plumbing. The prison-like cells housed the "child labor" imported from Europe. Above our cots hung a heater that emitted a pleasant glow and sufficient heat, but interfered with our sleep—which served us right, as we were really engaging in a scam. Not that we wouldn't have labored here for several days before going to the resort, if there was work to be done in the orchards or if Dafna was short of shepherds. But we were to be assigned to the perennial plastic factory first thing Sunday morning. The very first thing, as we were expected to report to duty at 4:00 AM. Nor did we expect to inhabit hovels.

"Did you expect the Hilton?" volunteer leader Judith, who somehow got around the insurance, chided when we demurred about living in a rabbit warren. Actually, the Hilton was a reasonable expectation if the members' quarters and the Memorial extravaganza was any reflection of the volunteer's digs. A small stream, tall trees, flowering plants and waterfalls (artificial) encompassed a tastefully designed memorial park and benches in view of quasi-deluxe housing. The around-the-clock plastics operation had made this opulence possible, and it, in turn, depended upon the invaluable volunteer—to the kibbutz what Pharaoh's slaves were to the pyramids. Or what the blacks were to the South African gold mines. It was a strange brand of socialism that excluded the lesser folk.

Transfixed by the falls, soothed by the pools, in the embryonic embrace of sun-drenched water, I was content to sit out this Saturday morning on the bench recharging my batteries. Judith was giving us another night to sleep on our decision, but Mona, acquiring my worst faults, was all for rushing into the Israeli "Sunday" stream of traffic—anything to avoid waking up in that concrete cellblock again.

Walking along the banks of the tree-lined brook that winds its way through Dafna, we met the man who had planted the seedlings. Incredulous, we looked at the towering eucalyptus, but the smiling Lithuanian who came here before the war was indeed one of Israel's first Johnny Appleseeds, a beneficent fellow who stood in such remarkable contrast to the Johnny-come-latelys who were creating the very conditions from which he fled. It was the cruelest irony, for if there was a lesson to be learned from persecution, it was compassion for the disenfranchised. The broad, still energetic old man was a prototype for the best joke to come out of Israel, the one about the venerated pioneer showing his grandson around the kibbutz he had helped found. The old Zionist says to the young boy, "See that road—I built it. I plowed those fields. I planted these trees. I built that house." His grandson replies, "Gee, Grandpa, were you an Arab?"

That's not to debunk or deflate the accomplishments of the pioneers. The joke really speaks to the industriousness of the Arabs—who really don't work on any of the esteemed kibbutzim in the Golan area. But there is no hiding how vital the Arab is to the Israeli economy. The boy should be asking his grandfather if he used to be a volunteer, but we have become Israel's best secret, or at least largely invisible of late and nothing to joke about.

There are many retired couples at Dafna from eastern Europe, Rumania and Poland mostly. But on that crisp morning looking to a pine and a chalet-like house framing the snow-capped mountains beyond, I was peering at a picture out of Austria. The squalid volunteer area, the Cannery Row down the road could have been a thousand miles away.

For a while it was truly pleasant strolling the grounds that Sabbath morning, until I came in sight of the tangle of barbed wire that ringed the kibbutz and would hopefully keep out the hostile have-nots. The slashing perimeter had been breached in the past and next door at Dan was the site of the horrible massacre at the children's house. This is the reason Israelis give for always having at least one armed adult accompanying a group of children. Increasingly this was the way of the world, barbed wire and broken bottles atop the protective wall of a mansion, a return to the castle's protective moat, the walls that still stand in Jerusalem (that Ben Gurion, tired of walls and with no sense of esthetics, wanted to knock down). As always, there were the seductive inner gardens, the sweet smell of success and security to neutralize the unsightly and, in other places, the incursions of the unwashed.

The Dan River is in depth and width smaller than a moat and flows below the rubble of the Tell.

At its source it is almost a pastoral scene with little of Banias' drama and mostly visited by soldiers. The first time I walked up this boulder strewn stream, a little disoriented by the huge eucalyptus, I forgot all about the closing time and in the approaching dusk found my exit barred. I couldn't believe that the guards would lock the gates without checking to see that everybody was out. I mean, I was practically in Lebanon and considered the interesting encounters that could ensue. But the same thing had happened to me at Nimrod, again an Arab guard locking me in a stone's throw from a not always impenetrable border fence. Luckily, the fences that locked me in were inadequate to the task and at Nimrod I went under, while at Dan I went over the fence— just as a jeepload of soldiers was pulling up to the gate to have their dinner on the bench opposite the entrance booth. Though they had their little joke, they knew I was from Snir and I was invited to dig into Snir's chicken and partake of some wine and beer. When it comes to soldiering these guys and gals have class—as long as you're not a Palestinian.

Mona never did make it to the Dan River. We soaked up some sun thinking we were on our way to Newe Ativ. But a couple of army officers and their dates were driving up to Mount Hermon all the way up to the chairlift, and that seemed better yet. If I had thought of climbing the mountain, the road was the only way up—and for a price. Highway robbers—the military—posted themselves at the side of the road and were asking ten shekels a head. I told the driver he could let us off there. However, sitting in the back of the jeep we went unnoticed and resumed our mobile pilgrimage to Baal-Hermon—what awaited us is yet another desecration in the name of defense.

Israel can probably boast of the highest parking lot of any size in all the Middle East, twice the altitude of Hunter Mountain. With very little effort you can make the transfer from car seat to chairlift. If you arrive early you don't have to walk more than fifty feet.

If you were going to climb a mountain sitting, you did not want to do any walking. It's the American way—which Israel seemed to be incorporating like a Star of David Spangled Banner, inseparable till a bitter end.

The parking lot was a beehive of activity, people picnicking in and out of their cars in a swarm of military—where there was once an altar to the protector of the mountain. If there had once been a throne, it was now portable, and for a few shekels, any man could be king. Surrounded by the snows of Mount Hermon, families from Tel Aviv couldn't get enough of it. They frolicked in the white stuff like this was the first and last time. A happening like a beached whale, Baal.

This holiday mood spilled into the coffee shop or snack bar.

A handful of people were skiing and sledding, and Mona had gone for a cup of coffee.

Leaving the hollow of this once sacred saddle, now a parking lot, I took the road opposite the chairlift and climbed the opposing peak. The road was closed to non-military vehicular traffic, but poverty goes unseen, and I came upon a bit of Antarctica, with even a base camp at the pole. Not two hundred feet off the road, partially covered tanks and trucks were parked outside a Quonset hut. Over the hump I went, expecting to be apprehended at any moment and wondering how the hell I managed to get this far into a restricted area. Was everybody out to lunch, a Shabbath brunch. Descending the road to Baalbek, I took a photo of a lone bush and then about faced. I was becoming so Messianic, I half expected to be taking dictation from some deity. How do I become privy to the incredible without being a messenger? Was it altitude or attitude?

My God, what a vision of the Holy Land was afforded the ancients who climbed out of their valley to pay homage to pre-Olympian deities. In a land of few soft edges, where much was monotonously hard and harsh and below the level of the sea, you could see forever, with distance a mellowing and commingling of the land and sky, a merging of the elements provided by a sea voyage. In such an impressionist masterpiece, where Baal painted the scenery, black and white gave way to a light gray that was ethereal. And as the narrow mind broadened, the vastness of this barely contained panorama swallowed up the claustrophobia of the valley below.

There was sanctity in its snowy inaccessibility, but today the Word was strategic. Hermon was more a military base than a resort—the end of the road for "Sunday drivers."

I joined Mona at the almost squalid snack bar, a strange combination of kindergarten and canteen. Soldiers warming up, kids raising hell. Resting on a table, pointing at Mona was a rifle. I moved my wife out of the line of fire and went up to the counter and there, as busy as a bee, was the Parisian Jew, my prospective employer. He was in no position to talk, but told me to call him in a couple of days and, with that, gave me a cup of coffee on the house. He sounded encouraging, but I'd seen enough snow to see me through the desert of an Israeli winter. And the desert was preferable to this Ballistic missile site. This had to be the dreariest après ski lodge—overground bunker—in the world, including Turkey, where they had discovered fireplaces...and something to burn in them.

As blank as the landscape before us was Mona' s page for Saturday, but then, the day had just begun as we trekked down the mountain. We got a lift to the scene of a battle, a memorial and more wreckage of war exposed by melting snow. This endless mourning, the inescapable reminders of the intrepid but tenuous hold on the land. Each memorial was beginning to resemble a station of the cross on Israel's interminable Via Dolorosa. As we resumed our descent, a Haifa-bound young officer and his girlfriend came rolling down the mountain, still several miles above Hajdal Shams.

But the mountain and its people had lost its grip on me, and unwilling to return to the valley, I settled on Qazrin or at least the nearby Field School that Meron's Italian-speaking doctor had told us about. It was a long enough ride, but as we entered El Rom, I got this sickening feeling as I feared the young officer would take one of the lesser traveled roads into the valley and leave us stranded near the police station and its pregnant dog. Luck was with us, though, and the chipper officer went a mile or two out of his way to drop us off at the Field School. Yehudiyya, I believe. The character who ran the place wouldn't give us the right time, much less information about the tourist attraction.

Later, his assistant chided us for calling on him at siesta time.

From the outside, this quasi-museum with its exhibitions looked nice enough, but in the two hours I spent waiting for the curator, I'd seen enough of the dismal surroundings to cool my heels and hit the road.

13

The Road to Armageddon

This proved to be an impetuous move. Nothing in sight moving. In the ominous light descending upon us, Qazrin's uptown was a ghost town.

Unable to attract residents to this gardenless spot, it remained bleak and incomplete. Too near a potential apocalypse to be appealing to your average Israeli, this fair sized city went without basic amenities, including a resident doctor. Our friend from Meron Golan called on Qazrin about twice a week.

Only a hint of blue colored the western sky. As the evening chill magnified our black mood, we looked longingly at the concrete coffee shop across the road. It gave off a dingy light, but like a couple of moths hungering after security, we looked to the hole in the wall as if it were a midnight sun. Having been on this carousel before, familiarity took the edge off fear, but who would stop in the dark, and did we dare allow ourselves to be picked up? Guiltily, I tried to calm Mona and asked her for just five more minutes before we would succumb to the lights on the other side of the road, and then I went into my song and dance routine, "Give me five minutes more, only five minutes more..."

It worked. A guy living in Qazrin was visiting his girl friend in the valley. Lady Luck was still smiling on us. His girl was a member of Kibbutz Gadot. But we may as well have been waiting for Godot if we thought anybody would come up with a bed, even though the volunteer leader had been a construction worker in Brooklyn. The young Israeli bragged about all the money he made under the table, but now that the tables were turned, maybe patting me out of one of my odd jobs, he wasn't returning the favor but pushing my face in it. The U.S. also brings out the worst in us.

Anyway, the chances were that the braggart was either an Italian Israeli or, most likely, working for Moishe's Movers, apparently, Israeli owned, easy entry for spies. Construction worker sounded more macho. We made our bed and would sleep in it—hopefully. And not in Gadot.

Leaving Gadot was a problem, but after the usual song and dance under a convenient street lamp, fearing but hungry for a lift, we were finally riding in the back of a pickup truck. Mona preferred freezing to taking her chances with the driver, but she needn't have worried. He reeks of perfume, but I tell him we're looking for work. Where are we going? Where is he going? A moshav. We'll work for nothing. No go. But in a few minutes time, we have found ourselves another lamp post. It is on the wrong side of the road, but our only concern is getting off it. The road that is. And now we are truly waiting for Godot.

My antennae are bristling. We can't get into any old car. Mona is saying to watch out for the blue license plates. Be careful, make sure the driver is kosher, but the road is almost deserted. And who do you trust, anyway. Only once in Turkey did I turn down a ride and that was because of Mona's infectious paranoia. So they were three men, but I could see by their hurt look we had nothing to fear. And doesn't Godot play such tricks on us? How many times does the wimp turn out to be Jack the Ripper? "Normalcy" was no yardstick for security.

We needn't have worried. Psyching myself up to throw caution to the winds and take the first ride that came along, I looked disbelievingly as a wreck of a car lumbered to a halt and a man knee deep in refuse opened the door of his jalopy. This had to be a joke. How could anybody in Israel be so obviously psychotic and on the loose. A stereotypic-schizoid tripping over the most insane assertions from the word go.

"See those sneakers on the floor? I won the marathon in those. I run a health food store. I'm rich…" Howard Hughes in Israel.

My head was reeling. I looked at the clutter and looked at Mona. She asked him about his store. He had some tidbits he wanted to give us, but where were we going, anyway.

I couldn't say I didn't know, or he would think I was crazy. "The kibbutz up the road," I said.

"Which, one? You mean Ayelet Hashahar?"

"Yeah, that's it."

I couldn't be sure if this health food nut was a fruitcake or what (most likely the latter), but Mona's curiosity wasn't that strong, and when we arrived at the kibbutz, she wanted to make a beeline for the cafeteria.

But our friend insisted we try some of his wheat germ and sea weed and made no bones about his desire to accompany us in to the chow hall. When I mumbled something about being too tired, he insisted we get together in a few days. With that, he took my Tiberias brochure and did a little skywriting above the Sea of Galilee: Yaron Scheyer, Ramot-hasvim.

Except the dollar sign that he wrote in the place of the first letter of his last name was as large as the lone cloud it covered. A kind of silver lining, a never to be fulfilled dream.

"See how rich I am," the caricature laughed. He then said, putting away his organic food, "There is no room for the entrepreneurial spirit in Israel."

I told Mona I felt somewhat guilty about running out on Yaron, reminding her that what he was to us, we probably were to "normal" people.

"Oh come on, Tony, he was doing a Jackie Mason number on us. A stereotype."

"You don't think he's crazy? You weren't afraid?"

"He just made me feel so uncomfortable."

I found it hard to believe that in this closed society the walking wounded could expose Israel's inequity, but maybe Mona was right and Mr. $cheyer was rehearsing for the Newe Ativ ski-resort. Still, I had to wonder if we were being baited with this anti-Semitic routine, for I was now pretty much convinced that we were under surveillance. And if we weren't we should have been. In any case, once again, adrenal exhaustion had left me in that twilight zone where reality is stranger than any dream.

It was past chow time, but a couple of kibbutzing old-timers would see what they could dredge up for us. We'd already told them that we couldn't afford the Ayelet Hashahar guesthouse, and that we were prepared to camp out where we were, if they wouldn't take us on as volunteers. To the rescue was an American cowboy, a Jew from Mormon country. I'm not certain of his status, but he'd been on the kibbutz for several years and was left the most habitable digs I'd seen yet. Carved furniture helped give the apartment a rustic ambience. A cabin in a bucolic setting. A strange young man in a cowboy hat (or was that an hallucination) who slept on the floor beside us, as we uneasily lay atop his mattress. Such a charitable act, an encouraging manner to bring down the curtain on the day.

In the morning we traded paperbacks, and I felt so much the richer for being poor. If we had the money we would have paid the sixty-two American dollars to stay in the guesthouse, which would have been a classic case of taking your coals to Newcastle. I mean, paying hard cash to sleep on a kibbutz was like paying your boss (for sleeping on the job?).

Of course, there are kibbutzim and there are kibbutzim and Avelet Hashahar, with its tiny museum, could have been a college campus in any backwater.

In the morning, a busload of black women were embarking for the Sea of Galilee. From their chartered bus, these American tourists will see everything they expect to see, even what's not there.

Across the road, we boarded a crowded Egged, wanting to get off at the Nazareth turnoff, but it didn't turn out that way. When things go wrong, I wonder if it's because something better is in store for us.

As we walked along a stream coursing towards the Sea below, a hippy couple from another time and place, but very much here and now, gave us a lift. It was only a few minutes' ride to the road that led to their kibbutz, but their warmth neutralized the effect of what followed. A late middle-aged couple, she was a clothing designer, while he was a retired businessman. They told us how wonderful Israel is and how happy everybody is. I assumed he was an advertising director, as he went on about the left-wing agitators making a lot of noise. Did he assume I was Christian? Did he think that if I was going to Nazareth, I would believe anything?

I stood in disbelief as the Jewish Ronald Reagan speeded on his way to Beersheba, about to make one of his "many" trips to the U.S.

Stepping lively in front of us were some left-wing agitators. Palestinians. Women and children with an engaging smile under their jugs. Whatever they thought about a middle-aged couple tramping to Nazareth, it made them happy.

An Israeli heading for the strategically located upper Nazareth gave us a ride and left us at the foot of the lower Arab city. Hungry and thirsty, we trudged through this limbo until we came upon a Public Works grounds and a pleasant shaded area with a picnic bench and a water faucet. We thought we had stumbled upon a park, until a curious foreman looked us over and, satisfied with what he saw, shook our hands. Just as I used to be able to distinguish a Japanese from a Chinese by the camera hanging from the neck of the former, I differentiated the Jew from the Arab by the latter's outstretched hand. Welcome, welcome.

The old town was directly below us. But there was still some high ground to cover for a better view. As we neared a church above Nazareth, we ran into the Rudolf Steiner advocate I'd met on the ship. My Swiss shipmate had been staying at a kibbutz that followed the teachings of the mystic philosopher so popular in German speaking countries. Steiner had taken a holistic approach to life, and the cultivation of food was an aspect of his philosophy.

The area abounded in experimental communes, and my friend had been working on a Christian kibbutz that had gone organic, following in Steiner's homegrown footsteps. I was surprised, even a little envious, when my shipmate told me that they did not work in the rain. All he could do, he said, was read. He looked content. He had not seen Israel yet. I was sorry when we went our ways and felt old. Rudy had the ebullience of the believer and was heading south with enthusiasm.

We went higher still, until we could see the Horns of Hattin, a twin hill of volcanic origin that is the site of Nabi Shueib, the traditional tomb of Jethro, Moses' father-in-law and prophet of the Druze. Was it the prophet who would be resurrected in the traffic circle in Majdal Shams? We had driven by, or at least under the Horns, unmindful that this was where the Crusader army was slaughtered by Saladin's Saracens. This is what one historian made of that fateful scene at the close of the twelfth century: "A militant and truculent Christianity, as false as the relics of the 'True Cross' round which it was rallied, met its judicial end within view of the scenes where Christ proclaimed the Gospel of peace, and went about doing good."

Immediately below us was an abandoned church now being restored by a Mrs. White from Wappinger Falls, New York. I believe the reconstructed building would house the homeless Palestinian boys in the area. Mrs. White, a volunteer, thought we would have no problem volunteering also. The decrepit church afforded a good view of the town and was directly above the Basilica of the Annunciation, which is built above the grotto where Jesus is said to have lived. The Basilica is a new structure with an almost conical tower that makes it the AT&T building of cathedrals. Dominating

Nazareth, this odd dome telegraphs to the pilgrims and to the world that this is the place.

Winding lanes lead to the Basilica, which is near the home of Reverend El-Assad, who I had to see about us working on the church. Mona waited for me at the Religieuses De Nazareth, a hostel run by French Nuns and an English nanny. The Arab priest thought it possible that we could be of assistance in some way—Mrs. White had suggested teaching—but should we become volunteers, we would have to buy our own food. I wasn't clear on accommodations, but in any case I didn't think it fair that, after putting in a full day's work, we were expected to provide for our meals. Actually, we would have been doing penance for assisting the oppressors of the Palestinians going without.

The hostel had a certain charm to it, palm trees shading the courtyard, but someone had applied enough insect spray to the room to kill a human. At least there were no surviving ants from the heavy rain the week before and the place was quiet. Secure enough, judging by the bars across the convent window. It was the cheapest place in town, and the only demand upon you is that you be in your room by eleven.

I had checked out the Hospice Casanova down the street across from the Basilica. But I saw a dandy leave this apparently ill house of repute, now truly regretting passing up the opportunity to be of help at the church, passing up what could have been a mutual learning experience—though Casanova was instructive. What would Christ Jesus think about that Tower of Babble opposite the Casanova—built more in the spirit of Herod than in Christ? And what would Larry King ask Jesus Christ?

There was little to hold me in Nazareth, especially money. Contrary to what the Ministry of Tourism writes, the town retains little of its original integrity or character of the preceding centuries. Saint Gabriel's Church, built in the seventeenth century, is an interesting intersection of past and present. It was constructed over a spring that is the source of Mary's Well down the road, where Gabriel announced the coming of Christ. I don't know if this is the same Archangel who blew his horn. Like many Greek Orthodox churches in Israel, St. Gabriel's is a crypt-like place abounding in bric-a-brac.

As I buried myself in the past that Sunday evening, my meditation was interrupted by an organized tour. Following on their heels a private party approached the spring, also a well, and the guide dropped the bucket, pulling himself up a drink. As the larger group was about to get into the act, their guide warned them about drinking the water. The private guide, an Israeli like the leader of the tour group, said this was nonsense, the water was pure.

To this, the other guide responded, "My group is American. They aren't accustomed to such bacteria."

But the Americans were permitted to lower the bucket and raise it—for a price.

"Anybody who has used the well is expected to make a donation."

When it comes to scams, you can't beat the Greek-Israeli team. But alls well that ends well.

I got my drink across the street at the Palestinian tavern.

Mona had a question about the Annunciation. "How is it the Basilica supposed to be the site of the Annunciation?" She read from her pictorial map of Nazareth. "It says here, 'built over the ruins of Crusader and Byzantine churches,' blah, blah, 'the lower floor enshrines the grotto...' but then at Mary's Well, according to tradition..."

"Are you going to nit-pick?"

With its outdoor tables, the tavern was a suitable bistro to get bombed. But I was cold and getting put off by the derelict appearance of the square outside the church. Anywhere else in the world such a site would feature a fountain and be maintained in manner such a historical or apocryphal spot deserved. In a land of concrete and rubble and nothing to define it, this was a priceless piazza, but it was also Arab, off the beaten path (just a little), and allowed to go to pot.

But then, you are lucky if you find the Synagogue Church, a holy hole-in-the-wall where Jesus is believed to have preached as a young rabbi. Here he read the prophecy of Isaiah that foretold the coming of the Messiah. Was he talking about himself, or that other guy?

In the morning, I paid nanny in dollars and got short changed, but this was the way in Nazareth and it led to Megiddo or Armageddon, a must on any tour of the Holy Land. Our brochure read, "Canaanite town habitated since 3000 BCE." People were still living there? We were on our way to the kibbutz of the same name.

Expecting to see a town, we drove by the mound with the smattering of palm trees. Pointing over his shoulder, our Palestinian benefactor said, "That's Megiddo, Megiddo, welcome, welcome." To Armageddon.

Two women driving to the kibbutz left us off at the jewelry shop just inside the main gate. Within minutes, we were talking to Hanna, the head of the volunteers, but she wanted us to go to Tel Aviv to sign the proper papers. I assured her there was no way—certainly not on the three o'clock bus—that we would go to Tel Aviv. Convinced I meant business, she said she would take the necessary step to put us to work in the morning. It appeared as if kibbutzim like Snir, in a danger zone, were less strict about who and how they recruited volunteers. And then they were a more liberal ("communist") kibbutz movement. But Hanna's overriding concern was to come up with some workers for the four a.m. shift in the plastic factory, and she rammed the red tape that stood in her way I pleaded with this overseer, anything but the plastic factory.

No customary day of grace? When we'd be working the wee hours of the morning? Plastic was a cruel master. Here in this pseudo bucolic backwater was the black heart of the kibbutz. In this mountain greenery, where man painted the scenery, a substantial pine forest had been planted. Switzerland, one member called the once barren hill opposite the kibbutz, the area that, according to Christian tradition, will be the scene of the war of the End of the Days. Armageddon. Below us was the chariot city itself, a tree topped hill or tel of rubble. A hell of trouble. Dust to dust. Plastic wasn't biodegradable.

But the kibbutz held its charm, and if Megiddo hadn't been occupied for five thousand years, less than fifty years of occupation or habitation had endowed the grounds with a sense of community and continuity, thanks to the remaining wooden dwellings. A cottage atmosphere, as Mona put it in a less lucid moment. But tall trees did heighten the hominess of our new home. Actually, a sharecropper's shack would be a more accurate description of the older quarters occupied by white trash and "niggers."

Moving out of the cabin we were about to move into was Iris from Long Island. As poetic as it is true. Her parents had just taken the taxi from the Ben-Gurion Airport outside Tel Aviv and were waiting for their daughter to finish packing before they would whisk her back to the airport and home.

"They don't even want to have lunch here." The volunteer daughter, maybe 20, was a little miffed about her impetuous parents. "Israel is my second home. No place like it in the world. I always try to visit when I have an opportunity."

The father is a little older than me and not quite knowing what to make of his daughter's successors, continues, "Iris just loves the kibbutz. On Long Island, she wouldn't get out of bed before ten, but here she is raring to go at five."

"It must be the plastic," I said.

Iris has also worked in the jewelry shop, maybe because of her connections, but concedes it has not been easy. "Hanna has been a marine sergeant at times, but she's really okay."

The departing volunteer has gotten her leader a gift, reminding me of my last day in Navy Boot Camp and how all the graduates had been encouraged to chip in for a present for the C.O. I could see how a Jewish Princess from Long Island would take great pride in toughing it out with Israel's paramilitary and come hell or high water—war—bite the bullet. Mona said that Iris could have been her before she met me.

"Just getting away from home and out of a rut made it easy to gloss over your present circumstances."

But even the goy boys became gung ho about going the distance, taking up the gauntlet. The challenge in all this, played for what it was worth, had even—had especially—served the Krishna cult well. You are also getting that from the horse's mouth. I don't know how long she signed on for, but Iris only worked at Megiddo for a couple of months, under par for a volunteer operation that could be called successful.

As Mona moved us into Uncle Tom's cabin, I hitched a ride with the Long Island family to the tel, to the consternation of the mother who wasn't sure she knew the difference between a Palestinian terrorist and a Sicilian tourist, if I may speak loosely.

"You're getting off at the entrance, the entrance is here."

"No mother," Iris said. "It's the entrance to the archeological site where he wants to get out. You'll love it here."

"Give my regards to Broadway." I said the magic word and walked into Megiddo gratis.

Layer upon layer of history had been unveiled, the remaining mounds capped with lonely palm trees. I thought of some desert outpost. But below the rolling farmland belied Biblical prophecy. A serene scene more lush than Sicily, thanks to irrigation, but always a coveted corner of the globe. Somewhere in this fertile verdant picture is Kibbutz Mizma. I had forgotten that we checked it out. In and out, in a half hour, but Mona had mananged to make a notation in her diary. Just the name, mind you, neatly written in red.

But these ruins were the lasting reality in this landscape. Agriculture and plastic was sustained by water still not easy to come by, and the Sea of Galilee and environs retained their strategic importance. A position that would make Megiddo a perpetual battleground, as long as there was maniacal competition. It was as if wars had been fought here so long that the collective consciousness of the races that inhabited the region or sprang from it would perpetuate what had become the inevitable. The mark of Canaan. Since before Necho of Egypt in 608 B.C. defeated Josiah, king of Judah. The occupation perpetuates this propensity.

The same values that drove Ahab lived on in Arab and Jew. But today's charioteers are cheered on by Christians waiting in the wings. I looked over the stables trying to picture horses in this land of asses. At the bottom of a pit is a Canaanite altar. Had Solomon himself worshipped there? At the top of the tel there is a stairwell that leads to Solomon's water tunnel, but my way was blocked by bars. Below me a cavern like a grand vault for Solomon's most precious jewels. Now long dry, the buried treasure water was worth a king's ransom. Much more. The secret tunnel tapping an unseen spring was the object of the invading armies' continuing search down the centuries. Ahab's chariots were nothing in the face of discovery and the poisoning of the life source. The tunnel snakes several hundred feet beneath the earth before opening upon the fenced in kibbutz and the frontier of "Switzerland." To emerge from this tunnel, time warp, with its eons of water under the bridge is to be Alice in Wonderland.

Tracey vaguely fit that description. She was an English volunteer who was either insane or instructed to tell us how great Kibbutz Megiddo is. Would she get a bonus? Was she a bounty hunter holding onto a live one? Maybe she liked us. Tracey earned thirty shekels a month and was running out of money, but intended to return to England, work and save enough money to come back to the kibbutz. I don't know what this young charmer did in Great Britain, but here was another dubious idealist who'd read "Exodus," and the kibbutz "mystique". Like Vietnam, see it for what it was and hate it or, having made that great emotional investment, want to hold onto the illusion.

We told Hanna we would work in the factory on the condition that, if we couldn't hack it, we would be transferred. I seem to recall Hanna (somebody did somewhere) showing us photos of what they manufactured. Whatever the horror, however, I was determined to have a shot at it, if only for the experience of discovering the magic of plastic. Besides, rain was in the air and if that was the price of keeping dry we'd give it a try. Hardhearted Hanna flew off the handle. I don't know how long she expected us to stay on, but she said we could get our walking papers in the morning. Rain or shine.

In the morning at the Tel, we were a couple of snails attaching ourselves to Reverend Maizie's group, the snitches who came in out of the rain, soaking wet. To the members of Leslie Tours—House of the Lord—with their Holiday Inn name tags reading, Oral Roberts, Jerry Falwell, Ronald Reagan and other unreasonable facsimiles, we must have looked like we just walked out of Revelation 11: "I will send my two witnesses dressed in sack-cloth and they will proclaim God's message..."

In fact, the fundamentalists from Broken Zipper, Arkansas, were having a lot of fun, engrossed in the room-sized Megiddo model around which they had gathered like moths before the "seven gold lamp stands." I could see the coming apocalypse coming to life in their eyes: "And the sound made by their wings was like the noise of many horse-drawn chariots rushing into battle..." (Revelation 9). The Israeli guide was a medieval theologian explaining why Megiddo, not a hundred miles from the capital, was the center of the universe and Apocalypse now, the Lord's tenants seemed to be demanding of the enraptured Israeli, their eye's shining—or we want our money back.

"Then the spirits brought the kings together in the place that in Hebrew is Armageddon." (Revelation 16)

Leaving the Reverend and his flock to the devices of their guide, Mona went into the coffee shop while I returned to the rain.

There were flashes of lightening, peals of thunder and a terrible earthquake...since the creation of man there'd never been such an earthquake...the great city was split into three parts and the cities of all countries were destroyed. God remembered New York and made her drink the wine from his cup—the wine of his furious wrath. All the islands disappeared, including Manhattan... Great stones of hail, each weighing as much as a hundred pounds, fell from the sky on men. And men cursed Ronald (whose last name means raining in German) Reagan. (Revelation 16—with a slight alteration)

14

After the Deluge
or
Drifting About the Sea of Galilee

With a weather forecast like that, it is not surprising that the devout Swiss have built bomb shelters under their condominiums. And I mean the other Switzerland, that enterprising place where the trees came with the country and money grows on them. I cursed the weather. Poetic license aside, the Israeli weather bureau could confirm that November 18 was one hell and high water of a day.

Tramping through Afula is such a miserable memory that only a masochist could give a play-by-play report, so suffice it to say that the rush hour found me on the hospital grounds above the town urinating behind some bushes before hopping onto a bus to get out of the flow of traffic. We covered so little ground—all of it wet—that I was convinced that it was in the spirit of Armageddon. We wanted to spend some time on the lake, but since we left the driving to Him, we could just as well wind up in the Negev that night if our ride was going there. As this pre-destined book would be incomplete without Megiddo or the Sea of Galilee, drivers were passing us up so that we would be standing at the right place at the right time when a driver would be going to Ein Gev—as opposed to the Negev, or even Tiberias, which would have left us in the dark.

In the failing light, we de-bused at the foot of Mount Tabor, just as the House of the Lord tour descended the fabled mountain.

Legend has it that Christ jumped or flew, perhaps in Don Juan fashion, from the Mount of the Precipice (Mount of the Leap of the Lord), fleeing Nazareth's doubting Thomases before alighting on the hill that towered above us, to be transfigured. In the Gospel according to Matthew 17, the Transfiguration is described as a change coming over the face of Jesus. He becomes as bright as the sun, his clothes as white as light, and if that isn't enough, Moses and Elijah get into the act. All well and good, but there is no mention of the Messiah being airborne. How anybody figured that Mount Tabor is the site of the Transfiguration is the real mystery, as Matthew is clear about Banias or Caesarea Philippi being the site of "on this rock I will build my church," and seems specific enough about other matters.

But I'm counting the number of angels on the head of a pin, and in any case, I haven't read all the gospels. An Israeli hit the nail on the head when he said religious sites were determined by strategic value. At an altitude of two thousand feet, with its monastery and church overlooking Jezebel and the Jezreel Valley, it was an ideal place to have a national monument. And then maybe Jesus did fly there.

That's not as farfetched as the Italian claim that Mary's house flew from Turkey to Loreto, Italy. We visited Mary's house high above Ephesus, where the mother of Jesus was said to have died. Had the real house flown the coop? It was simply too much for the land of the Popes that Mary's house could remain on infidel soil. But then the church is a house of cards built on the bones and tattered cloaks of phantoms. The real miracle is that the spirit of Jesus—man or idea—has survived the pomp and most incredible circumstance. Never did that old saying ring more true, "the closer one lives to a church the further he is from God." We never did see the monastery and church commemorating the Transfiguration, but it wasn't from a lack of trying.

By this time the rain had stopped, and in a brightening sky the Esdraelon was absolutely beautiful. I wondered if the change attributed to Christ wasn't a result of the charged atmosphere that also expanded your perceptions. As I clutched at straws, I looked for the answer in the field but saw neither hide or hair of a mushroom. In my own trance, I was convinced that a Jesus had to be a bit of a space case and that the beatific expression that would come over him was, in Stevie Wonder's words, "the sunshine of my life." Sure, his face took on a glow and what was a trance was transfigured into miraculous. It remains impossible to convey to John Doe the power and glory in silent meditation—just as the church and now all governments would give us a Roman Circus and empty prayers to stifle the liberating magic of meditation. I didn't have a soap box with me, but my own feet were off the ground.

After Tabor the road winds through the most interesting kibbutz country in Israel. Communes of every stripe and flag are tucked away in mini valleys and rifts of the rolling plateau or, like crosses, occupy a knoll not always seen from the road. How much of the land has been shaped by the hand of man I don't know, but the effect is natural and European, as much of the Palestinian squalor is veiled.

Commanding the most glorious view of the lake is a kibbutz operated by Argentine and Brazilian Jews. What an ideal place to work, we thought. But no help was needed. I thought of Lake Constance in Germany. We had such a view of that lake when we picked strawberries, but above the opposite shore was the Golan Heights and not Switzerland. Though the difference was erased by a sky that I could not deny. Catching the dying light, the hills of Jordan were hallowed, a Kingdom of Heaven reflected in the "Sacred Sea" below.

What you see is what you get and, just as Jesus made his momentous leap of faith, we had kibbutz hopped to En Gev on the opposite shore in the twinkling of an eye. Getting that ride was nothing short of a miracle, and we couldn't have picked a better place to spend the night or give some balance to our view of Israel.

Our benefactor continued on to the Golan Heights, as we entered a side gate that was being locked. We had arrived in Acapulco. Not fifty miles as the crow flies from that apocalyptic Appalachia and the patchwork quilt and guilt of farmland off the road from Armageddon. But how many light years was it from Megiddo to this nuevo Mexico, much farther from the Biblical Sea of Galilee or even that lake that washed away the sins, and dirt of Mark Twain. A matador's cape was drawn from the western sky (with a flourish), and under the darkened Ha-Galil, the lights of Tiberias twinkled.

I sat on a creaking bench under the palm trees, tall trees, and watched the fishing boats bobbing in the tiny harbor. I could almost hear a Mariachi band playing in the seedy restaurant at the water's edge.

"Shalom," brought us home. We had found Uri, a likeable guy temporarily in charge of the volunteers. His wife Malka also seemed very friendly and interested in the down-at-the heels Americans who had just walked into her apartment. As poetry and doggerel would always have it or me, their older daughter was engaged to a rich Mexican. The youthful couple didn't know if they could put us to work, but we were welcome to their younger daughter's room. Their generosity appeared genuine, and we ate in their kitchen instead of going to the dining hall. I believe it was a Peter's fish (named for you know who) that Uri had prepared himself.

How pleasant to have stumbled upon this Tropicana on the Kinneret. Uri doubted if we would be able to work in the banana grove where stalks that weighed 40 kilos were being loaded onto trucks. There really was something so laid back and Latin American about En Gev that, after my can of beer (North American), I went to sleep as if transported to Acapulco Bay—walking on water all the way.

The seaside kibbutz supplied a couple of restaurants, but this was a very slack off season and Uri, who repaired the fishing boats, told us there was no work to be had in or out of the water. We would simply be their guests for a couple of days.

Grateful and with more guilt than gelt I set out for the north shore in the morning, intending to see the historical or apocalyptic sights. But I had trouble hitching and teamed up with a man from the Department of Natural Resources or the Nature Reserve who was checking out the water pumps that were located every couple of miles along the lake. You couldn't have a better guide if it was the truth you were after.

The Sea of Galilee was dangerously low, and if it gets any lower, the toxic runoff of fertilizer, herbicides and pesticides would amount to patricide. Something was killing the birds and was endangering the lives of Israelis. This was the second person I'd met who was testing water for toxicity. The chemicals that had helped the desert bloom were more concentrated in the lower levels of the lake, the major supply of drinking water also, and a dry winter would precipitate a crisis. The balm abused had become a poison and, like much in Israel, had turned upon it. Magnified excesses had made Israel a microcosm for self-consumption. Water—one reason for war.

In the days of Josephus, we read, "the waters are sweet and very agreeable for drinking..." the soil surrounding the lake "so fruitful that all sorts of trees can grow upon it... One may well call this place the ambition of nature..." But the ambition of man had resulted in the fouling of his nest and created the risk of unintentional poisoning. Where water was so rare you realized it was everything and as coveted as Solomon's secret cistern.

Two-thirds the size of Lake Tahoe, Mark Twain put it as he tiraded against the Galilee. Innocently. Now, intentional contamination was a threat. As with any site of importance, the pumping stations were protected by barbed wire. It proved to be inadequate, as my monitoring friend didn't have all the keys to the pumping sites and was able to climb the fence to take the necessary measurements.

We shared some of the bananas I'd picked up on the side of the road before he picked me up. He gave me the address of a reserve on the Dead Sea where I might be able to work. Not far from the mouth of the upper Jordan, where the fisherman apostles had lived. I was the Florida beach bum who'd come home to roost (two years as a lifeguard). It seemed so natural to stoop for the spiraled shells and polished pebbles. Surely, the Guru of Galilee and his penniless apostles were the original beach bums—mushrooms inspiring their oceanic experience on a lake like no other. Banana groves were a bizarre addition. As I looked beyond the patches of reeds to the mountains and stepped over a rivulet, I knew I was part of a scene that had captured the imagination of an endless stream of pilgrims.

Every rivulet that gurgles out of the rocks and sands of this part of the world is dubbed with the title of 'fountain' and people familiar with the Hudson, and Great Lakes...fall into transports of admiration over them... If all the poetry and nonsense that have been discharged upon the bland scenery of this region were collected in a book it would be a most valuable volume to burn. (Mark Twain, near Capernaum)

I didn't make it as far as Capernaum. I got no further than the pumping station at the Jordan River. At the mouth of the river, the banana groves lend themselves to the marshes and there is almost the tepid air of the jungle about this mini miasma, but this is still the desert, as disorienting as ever, and the grove is an exorbitant drain on the water supply. Bananas have an enormous thirst, and the crop ready to be phased out had not proved to be cost effective.

Next stop was Capernaum, but it was getting late and I wanted to be back at En Gev by evening. I don't recall if this man was an Arab or a Jew (I have his name and address buried somewhere), but he turned around his pickup truck, which was maneuvering the most incredible tracks, and took me back to the Qazrin junction.

In Yellow Pages fashion, I let my thumb do the walking, but not coming up with the right number, I went into my Charlie Chaplin routine. I hadn't tramped a half mile before the thorny landscape yielded a lift to Kursi, near Georgesenes, where Jesus drove the devil out of a possessed man into a herd of swine—perhaps explaining why pigs resemble men so much. Here my benefactor continued on past the monastery and headed up to ruined Hippos, an important page out of Greek history. For me, another ride to the kibbutz.

An Israeli Acapulco is an unfortunate misnomer, as I can see a real estate mogul turning this tranquil fishing village into a flashy resort and the multiplication of tourists. Skinny dipping will be referred to as religious fervor.

We were on our way to "spectacular" Gamla when the soldiers we were riding with dropped us off outside their base high above the lake. This was a frontline military post, and many soldiers were oriental Jews who let out the kind of yelp or war whoop common to Arab countries. It was a sometimes eerie sound we had heard at celebrations and funerals, and I wondered what the present occasion was. If this delirious dirge wasn't ominous enough, a red fox crossed the road. The poor devil had probably been routed out of his den, but this conquering Caesar was nearing the point where he would be reading chickens' entrails and looked for the significance of this omen. I don't know what I would have done had a black cat crossed my path.

Observing all the oriental Jews in their encampment, I wondered if this wasn't a kind of Vietnam where the American Blacks had been disproportionate to their numbers. They looked tougher than your average Israeli, and they sure as hell made intimidating sounds behind their barbed wire.

But it was time to put our own show on the road and we walked up to a main road. We were within couple of miles of Gamla, when getting there became such a problem that I hitched in the opposite direction when an amiable driver of a jeep came by. Almost coming full circle, we wound up in an onion patch above the lake just in time for lunch. Then, having heard Ramat, a moshav, needed help, we were on our way, turning off at the Orthodox resort known for its segregated bathing north of En Gev.

Unable to find the volunteer overseer, we drove back towards the lake with a Moroccan motorist who, hearing our predicament, assured us he had an empty cottage and the only work required of us was to clean it up. Short of the lake, he turned around and showed us his cottage. And lest you think there are free lunches in Israel, we rarely slept anywhere without cleaning up a mess.

It seemed the North African was separated from his wife, who lived in a bona fide house across from his crash pad. We wouldn't be putting him out, nor did he have any hanky panky in mind, but would find another place to sleep where I'm sure his motives were less pure. Food? Maybe his wife would invite us in to eat. Turkeys in the huge coop opposite cheered us on, white clowns sounding like the fans in Ebbets Field bleachers when the Bums were still in Brooklyn and Jackie Robinson had just hit a home run. For an appetizer, I had enjoyed a marvelous sunset from a dizzying perch above the Sea, watched the sky take on the crimson of the turkeys' sideburns, but we were on a roll and passed up some couscous and all that goes with it, much needed R&R.

Morning saw us heading south via the north road. Soapbox or no, I was not going to pass up the Mount of Beatitudes.

A couple of rides put us on a side road level with the mount that bisected an avocado grove. Finding nothing edible there, we walked the remaining distance in the exhaust of passing pilgrim buses. An interminable caravan of uncomprehending Christians who could not hear the Sermon for the carnival or the chapel, as pleasant as it is. Beyond the parking lot, an open heart became the gateway to the Kingdom of Heaven, but preachers from the four corners had their crack at being Jesus. The simplest message in the world was interpreted for the touristy flock scattered over the grass, and if the pilgrims were spared a theme park, the manicured site did not evoke the spirit of the Man (or idea) and the ground He walked on.

As a matter of fact, most places associated with Jesus are under the ground. I was beginning to think ancient Israel was a nation of troglodytes until Mark Twain set me straight.

It seems curious that personages intimately connected with the Holy Family always lived in grottoes—Nazareth, Bethlehem...and yet nobody else in their day and generation thought of doing anything of the kind...

It is exceedingly strange that these tremendous events all happened in grottoes—and exceedingly fortunate, likewise because the strongest houses must crumble to ruin in time, but a grotto in the living rock will last forever. It is an imposture—this grotto stuff—but is one that all men ought to thank the Catholics for…it is infinitely more satisfactory to look at a grotto than to have to imagine a dwelling place… The memory of the Pilgrims cannot perish while Plymouth Rock remains to us.

In Mark Twain's day, the Mount of Beatitudes was located on the Horns of Hittin, conveniently near—at that time—Nazareth, a must for pilgrims. The Holy places on the lyre-shaped lake played second fiddle to enterprising Nazareth on the crossroads of the east. Below Nazareth and the then beatific mountain was "the battlefield of nations…Tamerlane, Tancred, Coeur de Leon or Richard the Lion Hearted, Saladin; the warrior kings of Persia, Egypt…Napoleon—for they all fought here," on the road to Armageddon, while the shores of Galilee were steeped in squalor. Capernaum had not been resurrected (though Christ preached here) out of the mire.

But in time, the lakeshore property became prime real estate, and that picturesque hill overlooking Tabigha, site of the Multiplication of the Loaves and Fishes (and the addition of myth) seemed like an ideal place for a Sermon on the Mount. Besides you couldn't have all your pilgrims going up to Hittin, especially when you had Jethro's tomb up there also, attracting the dangerous Druse who paid homage to their prophet.

That Hittin was the traditional site of the Sermon put the custodians of such happenings on the Horns of a dilemma. But faith moves mountains. Of course, Twain could have gotten his mountains confused, but bigger things have been maneuvered in the name of milking the pilgrim for what he was worth. The turn-of-the-century guesthouse on the Mount was not open to guests. At least not to pilgrims of our ilk. Papal visits were more common, apparently, but a terrified nun let me have a drink of water. What is more likely is that the Mount of Beatitudes was the site of an altar to Baal and in a large sense remains so, but I pictured the hilltop at a time when a pilgrimage required more than a boost up the steps of a bus. Beyond the parking lot was a tombstone in memoriam to Mrs. R. H. Hager who had come here to die.

Japanese were snapping away; Spanish speaking picnickers had strayed from their priest; but there was an unbiblical cord that connected this crowd with the Holy Land. The Mount had all the spirituality of a shopping mall with a view, indication in these end times it is not the esthete nor the meek who has inherited the earth—what's left of it that is worth looking at or listening to. A panorama that pleased the worshippers of Pan was panned by Twain and mostly ignored by preachers who couldn't see the papyrus for the paper, that it is through transcendence, truth (among other things) that one can comprehend and live the ideas of the Masters. There is beauty without morality, but there is no morality without beauty; and if it remains an immoral world, it's because people are blind to it—and it must have taken a magic mushroom to open the eyes of the Israelites. And potluck, peyote…a mind-blowing head blow, for everyone else since. With intent.

I expected Stations of the Cross marking the way up to the Mount, but the site of the Beatitudes hadn't been moved for a freebee. Besides, Jerusalem had the original Via Dolorosa, with many convenient gift shops situated between stations, where, along with reliquaries, you can buy a t-shirt that reminds you "Israel is Real." And if you don't buy that, "Don't Worry America, Israel Will Protect You." No, Israel didn't need another Trail of Tears. Let the bus transport the pilgrims to the Mount, and if an enterprising TV evangelist had his way, a waterslide could be constructed— it would have to be interdenominational—from the chapel to the Sea of Galilee. Not only would it make a big splash with all faiths, including atheists, but you would get the pilgrims coming and going. This rapturous ride ending in baptism or heavenly demise would be for fundamentalists teetering between Apocalypse Now and paradise on earth. A more believable alternative to Rapturing Out, this long ride would be known as the Slide to Salvation.

An appealing idea because we really didn't know how we were going to get off this mountain, as we weren't about to run the gauntlet of pilgrim buses. The chapel with its pruned and groomed grounds was really an island in a sea of avocados and grapefruits. I actually thought the road pointing in the direction of Tabigha was the Via Dolarosa you might expect in another country, but this was kibbutz property, and I couldn't be sure where the rutted track led. Taking our chances and all the grapefruits and avocados left to rot that we could carry, we marched in the direction of the main road.

We couldn't be certain this track connected with the lake road, as there were no workers about on this Friday afternoon.

So I left Mona to her munching and, without the bags, went ahead to reconnoiter. There was access to the road, but the gate was locked. With some snooping, I found a breach in the fence and fetched Mona. We climbed over the bent wire and tossed our bags to the side of the road. That's why the lady is a tramp, and the most marvelous mate any hobo could hope to have.

We no sooner had picked ourselves up and brushed ourselves off—half fearing arrest—when the UN Peace Keeping Force pulled up to us. The Observers were Canadians from Newfoundland. And you can't find more amiable Canadians than Newfies. They were stationed up by the Syrian border and were simply taking in the sites on their day off. These black and white fellows later made our day, when they took us to Tabigha. Now they were going to Capernaum. This may have been their day off, but Israel had cultivated this extraordinary grapevine accompanied by paranoia, and who can fault them for questioning our quest. Our caper in Capernaum and environs. We were living in a goldfish bowl—and feeling a bit claustrophobic. Who was the UN observing?

There is something very eerie about the Galilee. If you ignore the anomaly of bananas, you are left with an almost empty geography (and sky) and a history peopled with ghosts. Further along the shore, there was a multiplication of loaves for the multitudes, there were renegade rabbis and unruly rabble, but the fishermen salt of the earth have been sanitized out of existence. Kefar Nahum is Hebrew, but the white temple is Greek to me. Even if the columns of Capernaum are Corinthian. Jesus, or someone like him, taught in the partially restored synagogue, a fisherman of souls, maybe even fish. A beautiful lake, but I strained to see sails or ships, signs of a living seaside.

Yet another ghost has been dredged from the depths of antiquity to breathe life into the nihilistic now. It may turn out to be more popular than a waterslide if somebody comes up with the money to launch the "Jesus Boat." "The 2000 year old boat found last February on the shores of Lake

Kinneret (Galilee), dubbed by the Holy Relics lobby the Jesus Boat, is in need of a Good Samaritan if it is not to revert to dust." "Holy Relics" lobby. That's a good one, courtesy of the Jerusalem Post (*The New York Times* of Israel, mostly a hollow echo on occupation). Not so funny is the article opposite that. Above a photo showing three students to a desk in a crowded Arab classroom is the headline, "Israel's neglected Arab school: an affront to the conscience of our country." An occupation with 'conscience'?

It was so easy to drift away from the Palestinian presence—when they are not protesting "no water supply, no toilets, no telephone...." Especially when you were on a magical mystery tour. We finished our lunch at the multiplication table. Curiously enough, there is a Mensa Christi there— the Table of Christ. Tabigha is really quite nice in its Byzantine simplicity, the history of the shore embedded in the floor. But for all the marvelous mosaic, it was time to get off the beatific path.

"Just like Lake Tahoe." In a moment we were driving to Tiberias with an Israeli who was unfamiliar with "Innocents Abroad." Or he thought he picked up some innocents abroad, of the mind that if we believed (as presumed gentiles) the miracles associated with the Sacred Sea, why then it was also an alpine lake.

The minute we were dropped off in Tiberias, I was commandeering a car bound for the south shore.

15

Journey to the Dead Sea

Though we did manage to see Kibbutz Deganya and make some people paranoid, we didn't see much of Tiberias, named for the Roman Emperor Tiberius, but associated with the creation of the Talmud and once recognized as the country's fourth Holiest City. Of course, there are only three cities in Israel, nevertheless, much of the town remains a sacred site for the Orthodox Jews, who are up in arms over the Miamification of ancient burial grounds. Actually, Tiberias, with sections of the walls standing and some decent old homes overlooking the sea, is one of the most habitable places away from the Mediterranean—but then most of Jewish Israel is a spartan encampment.

A strong wind portending winter whipped up the waves and sped us on our way in a shower of spray. A likable pair of veteran kibbutzniks were returning to their former home, Kibbutz Asdot Ya'acov, for a visit—and we just so happened to be going there. We had left behind yet another war memorial, marking the spot where I expected to see the exiting Jordan. After human life, one of the great casualties of statehood has been the Biblical river. I'm not sure I ever saw it, but call me Old Man River, as drained and diverted as any sacred stream emptying into a Dead Sea.

Fortunately, our big-hearted friends knew the head of the volunteers, and no fiction writer would dare fabricate such a day—and night—as darkness saw us seeking out Paula, "mother of the volunteers." We were luckier still that there was no work for us and we were able to join Paula's real son Aaron and his wife in the Shabbath supper. Paula sat with us later. She was a broad woman of that Slavic salt of the earth type and had come to Israel in 1932. She may have been at Asdot Ya'acov the whole while, if indeed the kibbutz existed then.

Her daughter-in-law was desperate to leave the communal life, and I had all I could do to get through the family meal without a breakdown. Friday seemed to be children's night, and my nerves were by now jingling like Santa's sleigh bells. If I'll be forgiven the analogy.

Getting to Bet She'an was no piece of cake, and again I had to seize the moment when a couple stopped for an armed soldier who was also hitchhiking. They wanted to boot us out of their van, but looked to the soldier for his feelings. He was for letting us be—though he never uncradled his Uzi.

We were left off at a road block before a junction that read like Bawanna. Here, the white man's burden included stopping vehicles with blue license plates. A young English born soldier allowed us to stay in the soldiers' shack while they attempted to flag down a ride for us. Clearing away some garbage, he fetched some water for us and told us to be at home. It was Saturday and the buses weren't running. Even American tourists could be caught short. The slight soldier said the other night they had to fire upon some Arabs who were drunk and didn't stop to be checked. Our friend really seemed like a nice guy, hip, almost apologetic about the situation. Theirs, not ours.

The Jewish Englishman returned to his post. An hour or so passed before he came up with our ride, a hotshot aviator bound for Jerusalem. He joked uproariously with the soldiers before speeding off into the wild blue yonder with his newly acquired cargo. When I pressed this cool looking blond about all the laughter, which any self-respecting paranoid would think at his expense, the flyboy confessed that he warned the soldiers he would bear no responsibility if we got heart attacks—and proceeded to do his best to provoke cardiac arrest.

It was a narrow winding road and often you could only see a hundred feet ahead of you before the road dropped out of sight, but our aviator was above the clouds, deaf to our chastisement. I cautioned him about hitting an Arab or something harder, but "Israel has the best Air Force in the world." Our pilot barely slowed down for a wide-eyed Arab traffic policemen as he sped through Jericho before depositing us near a bus stop off the Jerusalem turnoff. Not too far from where the Disneyland Bedouin seduce the camera-toting tourists with their camels and tour buses make a refreshment stop.

An interesting hour or so passed before two men let their curiosity get the best of them for the middle-aged couple as they trudged on to the Dead Sea and gave us a lift. They pointed out the former deluxe Jordan hotel at the water's edge and how vulnerable the Israelis were to invasion here to justify all the barbed wire that stood between us and the sea. Within minutes, we passed under the Qumran caves and were dropped off at the oasis of Enot Zuqum. This nature reserve didn't require our services, but it seemed like a place worth exploring.

Fresh water springs fringed with reeds are home to a species of fish that are found the length of the Rift Valley. Supposedly, the planet's earthshaking contortions eons back enabled these fish to make their way from Lake Victoria in Uganda to the Sea of Galilee. But the Great Rift is no longer the African connection, as a few feet away from where I stood was a lifeless lake of salt and sulphur. A kind of asphalt jungle that has been all but steamrolled. It remains a beautiful sight, but at the rate the Dead Sea is being drained for its mineral wealth it will one day be the lowest highway in the world. An exaggeration, but there has to be a limit to the extent of the extraction from this Biblical curiosity. A desecration of nature.

Wherever Noah got his asphalt it was used to coat his ark. But no sails livened a lake that the Talmud stated was the "most remarkable" of the "Seven Seas and Four Rivers" that surround the land of Israel. It wasn't until 1835 that an Irishman and Maltese sailor actually attempted to sail on the asphalt strewn lake. Maybe there was something foreboding about Aristotle's warning that anybody cast into the Dead Sea would float forever—as the salinity level of the landlocked sea is six times that of the Mediterranean.

I thought it incredible that anything so surrealistic could be so close to the nation's capital, but then Jerusalem was not of this world. With dusk approaching, the sun already behind the towering cliffs, we pointed our thumbs in the direction of Kibbutz Qalya above the Qumran caves. Given short shrift, we headed in the direction of the caves, as camouflaged by geography as its sacred scrolls were obscured by history and hysteria. In clay jars stored away for centuries, until they were chanced upon by a Bedouin goat herder in 1947, were the most revealing revelations concerning Christianity's origins. The Essenes, the authors of the Dead Sea Scrolls who lived in the clefts above the rift, were, if not the first "Christians," the followers of their own Jesus or "Teacher of Righteousness." A hundred years before the birth of Christ these holy cavemen awaited the return of their own Messiah. And who is to say that Jesus wasn't he, though changed outwardly.

The Essenes' scriptures discovered by a Moslem seemed like a wonderful bridge between Christian and Jew to any spiritual person, since the Essenes' scrolls were the essence of spirituality, exuding the universality of the Way, unencumbered by the rites of Passage—but as such, a threat to some religions, the scrolls have been spirited to an air-conditioned cave in Jerusalem, its message essentially buried by the politics of church and synagogue, on view for about five dollars in the museum. Jesus was to Judaism what Luther was to Catholicism.

We were back on the main road before dark. Again, we said we would exercise caution, but impartial, we ignored the soldier's warning about blue license plates and climbed into a jalopy driven by a barefoot Palestinian. Mona was scared, and I was a little uncomfortable myself, even though in the failing light I felt in the presence of a good soul; but again, brainwashing was holding sway as Palestinian is synonymous with terrorist. But if I couldn't trust my vibes, I could believe my eyes. I couldn't believe that this simple fellow who went unshod could have anything but the most noble intentions. It was he who feared the hitchhiker. As he passed a pair of young Israeli males who were perhaps European, the Good Samaritan slowed for a look. Then glanced at me and ran his finger across his throat to show why he wasn't stopping.

Mare Mortum Salsum. In the most ghostly light, cakes of salt were glaciers in an aquamarine fjord—and then there was only barbed wire and blackness, as we were swallowed up by the night. My paranoia returned. What if this guy couldn't afford a pair of shoes? But soon, we were at the bottom of the road for Kibbutz En Gedi, a beacon directly above us. Our benefactor let us out of his junk heap. I felt the fool before this barefoot wretch who beamed good will. There is little cause for suspicion unless your benefactor anywhere speaks English. Anyway, it never ceases to amaze me that there still remains in this world so many gentle souls—and most of them apparently going our way.

I was surprised why so obliging a soul did not drive us up to the kibbutz gate. Generally, barefoot people are not in too much of a hurry, but I was too tired to consider what kind of a reaction our pal would have drawn from the Israeli at the gate. Feeling a little vulnerable, we climbed this west bank until a bus came along and dropped us off at the security post. I hoped that in the cover of darkness we could steal into the chow hall and stand our ground, but the guard wasn't having any of this. Whereupon, I waved my Snir letter of recommendation, all but demanding sanctuary for the front-line volunteer and his wife. The long and short of it is that, within a few minutes another bus, this time bound for Jerusalem, deposited us at the En Gedi Reserve.

Such a Quixote the Nature Reserve had never seen. What to do with him and his partner? We found ourselves sitting at a patio table outside somebody's pad listening to a lot of jive talk from a jazz musician who lived at the kibbutz. This questionable cat was doing his damndest to impress an attractive volunteer from Holland, but he returned to his Dead Sea settlement without a Dutch Treat. Indeed, I would have thought (and I shouldn't rule that out, gray beard or no) that this chick was making a play for me if I already didn't know the score. She was trying to sell me on how swell it was working here for three dollars a day. The girl had her own kitchen, conceding, however, that she ate a lot of spaghetti, since food was not included in remuneration. She only worked a few hours a day, cleaning up after the guests who stayed at En Gedi. Israelis couldn't be expected to do house cleaning or be maids.

Neither could Mona. She wasn't having any of that. Men were permitted to do the more desirable work, like maintenance, out of doors, and maybe as a guide. I had been a guide in Mexico and was really excited by that prospect, but the man in charge of volunteers was doing his army reserve duty, which meant we had Sunday off, and that was okay too. We scrounged up some leftover food and had a mini-dorm all to ourselves.

In the morning it sank in that below us was the Dead Sea of school day fantasy. It was one of those childhood fascinations that become the most lasting obsessions—like big tits, if I would indulge an Achilles heel, a cure-all for the disturbed youth. Geography was my favorite subject before I ever dreamt of floating, and the whole class knew that you could not sink in the Dead Sea—without benefit of Aristotle. It must have been in National Geographic that I saw a photo of a non-swimmer floating and thought that was the cat's meow. Though I went on to do more dramatic things, bathing in the lake and being unsinkable was for some time in the category of walking on water.

So, as dream came to the fore, incredible Ein (the i is optional) Gedi, inspiration for the Song of Songs, played second fiddle, as a Quixote and his mate made it posthaste for the rock strewn shore. Mona got no further than the restaurant, but I went on to the water's edge to gaze upon the most beautiful barbed wire in the world. Dali-isque, salted stalactites encrusted the barbarous coil. But it was still barbed wire, and I recoiled at the desecration. The Dead Sea was my Jordan River and a bath nothing less than a baptism. Rising above this sculpted Arabesque, I made the plunge. Ick! Oily, greasy, kid stuff. This foaming phosphate was the abomination of the prophets, a liquid Hell (baptism of fire?), and I absconded this scourge of Sodom and Gomorrah.

Curiously, I had no compulsion to float, but then I really have developed into a swimmer and had been a Florida lifeguard so full of hot air that the Atlantic was my Dead Sea. I had become unsinkable. If every man has an unconscious pilgrimage to make, the realization of a forgotten goal, this was mine. Or was my fascination with staying afloat an unconscious metaphor for keeping my head above water.

After grabbing a bite with Mona, we walked a mile or so to the Ein Gedi Reserve, explained our circumstances to the warden and entered the oasis free of charge. The sign above the entrance warned about leopards and stated only groups were admitted, but the warning was waived, and we were on our way. A short distance from the gate a shelter for viewing the wildlife took on a special significance, for the small building was dedicated to the Druse soldiers who had died here in the War for Independence. This is as good a place as any to record the additional information about the Druse I have garnered. It's probably apocryphal like everything else about Israel, but I just read that the religion originated in the eleventh century and is based on the claim of Al Hakim, Caliph of Egypt, to being the reincarnation of the deity.

Everybody has gotten into the act. I left Mona with the ibex, the desert goats of the Old Testament and, like the kid I remain, made for the high ground. I was astonished by all the running water and the dramatic contrast of reed and rock, which I imagined were sandy wastes. This was the desert of Moses, where the sight of the hardscrabble relinquishing water was a miracle, a sign of God's approbation. Long before coming to Israel, I could understand how enough miracles paving the way could incline the compass-less, hapless wanderer to the idea of ordination. Providence was not restricted to Rhode Island. My own roaming nose has been a divining rod; and if God isn't my copilot, I would never have gotten off the ground.

From a secluded cave that looked out on a spring fed pool, a winding path took me to what must have been considered a wonder of the world to anybody trudging up that sandblasted trough that stretches to Serengeti. Taking me back to Africa was the crowning glory of the not-so-distant Judean Hills as underwater streams fed by centuries of rain emerged near Dodim Cave smothered in Adiantum. It was nothing less than miraculous that, from the most forbidding mount, sprang forth a carpet of fern and moss, and every crack and crevice was damp with the breath and seduction of the tropics. Not far away on dryer ground was the "Apple of Sodom."

It was by these trickling cascades that David who was in hot pursuit of Saul passed up an opportunity to slay the king as he stood pissing, when the falling water prompted him to follow suit. Not caught with his pants down, but still in a vulnerable position the king lived to see another day. If this story is to be believed, David elevated gallantry to new heights. In any case, there is no question about Tony taking a leak and living to tell about it, though I just barely dodged a busload of tourists hot on my tracks. But their tour ended here.

Above the waterfall, a winding trail leads to Ein Gedi spring. In the filigree shade of a sprawling acacia, this oasis is by noon the most inviting place in the world. I know nothing of the Song of Songs, but rising above the gurgle of water you can hear the song of the Arabian babbler and the more subdued music of the black wheatear. Interrupting the short bursts of melody was the ominous rustling of reeds, elephant high and thickly clustered. The warning above the reserve entrance flashed before me—leopard. Its presence here would be highly unlikely at this time of day, and I even had doubts about their existence in the area, supposing that talk of leopards was touristy hype or bait. The leopard sign was as indicative of leopards as the nearby elephant ears were of pachyderms—I thought. Still, as the furtive sound persisted, the word leopard was transformed into the image. Unprepared for the reality, I approached the towering thicket. Curiosity killed the image of the cat.

A tunnel had been hacked out of the reeds and, on all fours, cats' paws, I made my way through the undergrowth. The strange sounds seemed to be coming from everywhere, the rustling drove me crazy as I emerged from the hollow to see a colony of hyrax scampering over the reeds like a litter of kitten. Adaptive buggers, these 'rock badgers' who make their homes in crags and are related to elephants no less.

Below me was a watermill looking like some ancient chapel. Above me was a Calcolithic temple that commanded an ethereal view and invited the most subtle sacrifice. Undisturbed, the hyrax noshed away on the tall grass. I followed the trail that leads to the Israelite fort, but soon petered out with little inspiration beyond attaining an even higher altitude.

I made for David's Spring, with the memory of David's Well in Bethlehem. A long walk to a dry dead-end far above a Dead Sea this time, and my canteen on empty. But I was rewarded with a herd of ibex that were literally engulfed by their big horns.

Sun sinking into the Moab, and I knew the warden would be worrying more than Mona. Ron, I think his name was. At least he knew I would not be sitting on my butt. Ron drove us back to the Field School where Mona and I moved into a professor's shabby quarters, our new home until he returned from Jerusalem.

The volunteer overseer would not be returning from duty until Monday evening, so morning saw me filling up at Ein Gedi Spring bound for Nahal Arugot. On the southern border of the Reserve, this brook would take me inland as far as I dared to follow it to its hidden source. The mouth of this snaking stream is easily accessible, and hordes of school children were frolicking a good length of Arugot. A matchless oasis, the sculptured walls of the Nahal worn smooth by floods was strewn with towels and beach paraphernalia and unlikable children. In solitude I heard the Song of Solomon, but tomorrow's soldiers rent the desert stillness with the cacophony of Coney Island, and my approach was viewed as apparition and aberration. After truth, the greatest casualty in Israel beyond life has been the casualness of peace. The adults were more mindful of their Uzis as I made my way up the gorge. I came upon a group of officers on a field trip, and the Nahal became a time tunnel as these young men were the beach boys I had left behind on their blankets—still in a group, the last drop of individuality squeezed out of them.

By evening I was back at the reserve entrance being interviewed by my prospective boss. I could be a warden if I drove the jeep and would be on call twenty-four hours a day. The young man assured me that the Ein Gedi Kibbutz was plagued by a leopard. The big cat took the little cats and whatever other pets or chickens he took a fancy to, and the reserve needed somebody to track down the elusive animal. Leopards feed at night, of course. And, of course, there was no pay. The environment was so low on the list of priorities that Ein Gedi would hire a hobo before they paid a qualified man to be a warden. However, I was game as long as I didn't have to drive. That's why the laddie is a tramp and we were compelled to walk away from Ein Gedi.

16
Massada

We got off to a late start. Before heading for Massada, I wanted Mona to see the waterfall. Leopard? Mona thought we were dealing with a pink panther, and she knew the Peter Sellers for the job. Why couldn't I walk? Little of the reserve could be covered by a jeep, and leopard or no, Ein Gedi needed a warden on foot to patrol the trails. Once again, I was at the side of the road musing about a lost career opportunity.

Waiting for a lift, I looked up to the holy cliffs we had just left. It is the western wall of the Great Rift Valley, the likely route from Egypt of the Essenes' creed—as Judaism was influenced by Babylonians, et cetera. The Magi of Persia magically became the "wise men" of the Bible.

Is it poetry or history that "baby" grew out of the birthplace of Western civilization, just as the Sumerians gave us summer (in the summer of our lives) and the word play—belief in the "word" itself. Especially the four-letter ones, which made the comic Lenny Bruce notorious, led him to his death by authorities at a low point in our f***ing civilization. But wise guy Lenny was the personification of his line, "Jews are like everyone else, only more so"—more than he could know—to the extent that their religion, body and soul, was a mosaic that had less to do with Moses than the Magi of the East, rootless as the magic mushroom that shaped the Israelites, especially the Zealots of Massada, like Lenny Bruce on a bad trip. The Zealots were as different from the Essenes as light from darkness, a good trip from an overdose (what Lenny died from). The Essenes were the people of light, living the essentials of life.

A young, pleasant Eilat-bound European couple were giving us competition. Pooped as we were, we observed the first rule of the road and advanced a distance to a suitable post, rather than backtrack a few yards, giving the young Germans first crack at a ride. Evidently, we had age going for us, a reversal of yesteryear. Now the warning is, don't trust anyone under thirty. A middle-aged man passed up our fellow travelers and pulled up to the side of the road. The friendly Israeli was going to Dimona, so we passed up Massada that towered above us to sleep in New Zohar, hopefully in the moshav. It is the site of Sodom or Gomorrah. The moshav was almost named Gomorrah, vetoed because of its shady history and the shame associated with it.

With changing morals, the settlers realized that the name Gomorrah was a selling point, even if the Biblical city is said to be under the lake. When the Irish sailor Costigan was forced to drink from the Dead Sea, he hallucinated (and maybe he didn't) and claimed he saw the fabled Gomorrah under the water. To which one may have reasonably asked, How are things in Loch Gomorrah?

We were in New Zohar by dusk, just ahead of our German friends. Later, in the restaurant we debated whether we would use the camping site where bedding would be provided, when the Germans walked in and walked out, unable to afford to sleep on the grounds. They said they would sleep in the bush that borders the Dead Sea.

The owner of the tiny restaurant was a chubby bundle of nerves whose idea of a good joke was violating the Sinai ceasefire. At the time of the Yom Kippur War, he was a sergeant near the Egyptian border who drove the UN peace team mad with his commands to open fire on the enemy to alleviate his boredom.

The insane former sergeant phoned Asaf when he learned we wanted to work. Asaf, who has a melon field, came by in a battered pickup truck. We could help his Bedouin helper plant seeds on the Dead Sea shore. Our prospective boss was really a nice guy, balding, calm, gentle and compact. He and his wife Rose, a graduate of UCLA-Berkeley, lived in a book-lined concrete block that was tastefully furnished. The handsome pair, with their children, seem the ideal couple and more American than we are—which is really an understatement.

Asaf maintained another house for his workers. Mona was not so happy about the bedroom being occupied by a napping Israeli, but the young man was a jovial character who soon left the house. The living room had been converted into our bedroom. When the worker returned, passing by our sleeping quarters, we thought about our grape picking days in France. This oriental Israeli could have been the Algerian who passed through our room on the way to his. Those were the days, my friend, we thought they'd never end...and they haven't, to Mona's chagrin.

We walked into the Arizona night. Outside was parked an ambulance donated by Ira of the Bronx, New York. We stopped by the restaurant for some coffee and listened forever to the UN nemesis curse the weather, which he claimed was keeping the tourists away from this grand canyon. Israel—this strange marriage of the American and the Middle East—not quite consummated. The American Jews who colonized the West Bank were California dreamin'.

When we left the restaurant, our psychopathic friend assured us the tourists would turn up for the winter holidays.

Next door to the restaurant was the moshav grocery where I bought a can of carrots laced with one or two string beans for two American dollars. My raised eyebrows and rising temper elicited the justification that the goods had been transported from Beersheba, a good fifty miles away. The sullen oriental waiting on me had the air of an exile, but this desert Siberia wasn't really that far from civilization's more reasonable prices. Again, we went down memory lane reminiscing about the time we bought a can of string beans with nary a carrot in Juba, which justified a king's ransom, being in Sudan. Again, the contents of the tin would be our fare, and Mona was talking about writing the Cammarata Diet Book.

I wished she would write something. Her journal was as lean and mean as I was. Searching for something more descriptive than the date was like finding string beans in our can of carrots. Lean pickings lent themselves to the desolation of a desert settlement. There is no desolation like a desert settlement. Especially when you juxtapose this Fort Apache to the Bedouin camps it has replaced, the exotic tents that could be shifted as easily as the Saudi sands from whence these wanderers had emigrated. Settling where roots did not take easily, Israelis, the new transients were as disjointed as the homes that housed them. Concrete blocks were hot in summer and cool in the winter. Considering the Dead Sea locale was a surrealistic attempt to create a suburbia—that metaphor for modern life that Israel projected. Desolation, dislocation and disappointment seemed the lot of these colonizers. Yet another example of the unfinished look in an unforgiving land.

For Asaf and his wife, their books were a more effective buffer against a hostile world than the barbed wire that covered a good part of the Dead Sea shore. Rose seemed more out of place, without a trace of an Israeli accent. She seemed more Eastern European than anything else. Was she really an American? She could have been a high-powered professional, a New York career woman whose energy instead went into mothering and caring for a hard-working husband. The Land promised nothing but hard work. We went to their place for dessert and that easy conversation that establishes compatibility.

I really waned to make a go of this moshav for a few days, but wanted to see Massada first. Sowing seeds would prove to be a seminal experience in a Dead Sea shore, something to write home about, so Asaf had my promise. No sweat, our host said, we would be their guest. No way, I told him, and I meant it.

In the morning we hitched a short ride to mini-Miami. Wanting to catch the Massada bus here, we went into a coffee shop to get the departure time. She was not busy, but the young woman behind the counter informed us that this was not a bus station, not that there was a bus station within miles where you could acquire information. None the wiser about the schedule, but we gained some insight into the Israeli attitude towards service. We tramped towards Massada until overtaken by a bus that took us to our destination in twenty minutes.

From the road, there is little to distinguish Massada from the pristine palisades that stand back from the sea. There is just a trace of a cleft in the cliffs that give Massada the appearance of a great ship. Herod's bow directly above embarked into space.

To many Jews, this was another Wailing Wall, a place where Jewish history and spirit reached a kind of watershed that came to symbolize their will to survive—or perish—on their own terms. Historically and geographically, Massada is a scene out of Hollywood.

As much as Massada meant to Mona, it was getting hot, and she was so tired she almost remained at the foot of the massive plateau, which was the last stronghold of the persecuted Zealots. The almost mandatory cable car was a frill, a not-so-cheap frill, ten shekels one way. Mona worried if we would have enough left to fly home.

I took the high road that skirted the Snake Trail to the top of Massada. It followed the cable car, which I cursed as the invasion and intrusion of nature and history. My little-known path led to the north, but I assumed that, if it didn't peter out and leave me in the middle of nowhere (so often the case in Israel), it would take me to the top.

Taking my chances, I followed my ancient Roman nose and set out on my circuitous route that soon passed by sandy enclosures with little piles of rocks that turned out to be the site of General Siva's camps. The Romans had used the stones to hold down their tents as they hacked the path I was now climbing out of the cliffs. I began to worry when it seemed the trail was taking me to Ein Ged, but then it rose more sharply.

The heat was becoming uncomfortable when I found myself a few yards from a convenient cave. Were there still Dead Sea Scrolls to be found? Like the goat herder who came before me, I simply sought to get out of the sun and maybe look out on the lake. Camel humps shaped by centuries of eroding rains and a merciless sun and sky yielded the ethereal turquoise of a Dead Sea that turned out seers and sulfates, inspired by the poetry of at least one old salt. There is nothing like the light and dark contrast of a sheltering cave with a view. The walls of my Qumran were blackened by a thousand fires. In Bedouin fashion, like man down the ages, I sat on my haunches over sand grayed by eons of charcoal and recent goat turds. The only sign of an Arab.

Avanti. Now the trail turned precarious, and the craggy incline directionless. Not a signpost. With a little trial and error that could have proved fatal, I was soon back on the war path and the approach to the Roman assault ramp, which made for a hardscrabble climb. Before me, the soldiers had piled up enough rocky earth to raise them to the level of breachable walls. The rest is history.

The Zealots, like the less fanatical Essenes, believed in the liberation of the soul, but were only too willing to shed the bonds of mortality, theirs, and like the later hashish-eating Moslem zealots, non-believers. Some of the writings seemed to confirm Josephus' account of the siege and the Jews' self-destruction. As Flavius put it, voluntary martyrs "bared their necks to the blades of the charitable executioners." As the story goes, a handful of women and children survived to tell a story that Roman historians overlooked.

Whether the Zealots died preferring death to slavery is not as important as this symbol of resistance that is reinforced by the Israeli army's swearing-in ceremonies atop the ancient fortress. Curious counterpoint to the Super Deluxe Five-Star Bar-Bat Mitzvah on Massada arranged by travel agents. The Bar Mitzvah is not in the same boat as the military, as the latter is sworn in with the Old Testament in one hand and something more serviceable in the other, a Uzi, I believe.

In any case, the martyrdom of Masada (the s is optional), sticking to your guns seems to speak of a suicidal pride on this West Bank in this compelling age of compromise. And was self-destructing pride any more noble two thousand years ago? A slave had a chance to free himself. What were the sacred scrolls or religion if not to enable us to transcend our servitude?

As the Roman Legionnaires neared the northern flank of the fortress, they must have been awestruck by the imposing perspective offered them. Not only were they under Herod's palace that jutted out into the azure like a high and dry Titanic, but above the columned bow holding up the heavens was the bulk of the great rock massif. While viewing this colossal castle in the air, General Siva and his men also looked upon an inland Mediterranean and the steep escarpment of Jordan. It is from the north that one captures the full magnificence of Massada.

I must say this was one of the more esthetic thrills of my life, if I can use such a limiting word for this incredible blend of history, geography and the crowning glory of archeology. But for all this beauty that belied a significant massacre, a mass murder of the fervent Psalmists, there now was the all important element of surprise. When I set out on my trek, I had little idea of what lay ahead beyond those déjà vu inducing pictures that we carry around in our heads. Like the unvarying view of the Taj Mahal that photography has recorded for posterity. But outside the grounds of this Mogul Mecca, a road that runs parallel to the Taj takes the intrepid to a river, so that the traveler can look for the all-important perspective on the other side of the picture. An exotic seascape where others only see a hoary mausoleum, ever so symmetrical.

Again, serendipity won the day. Ignorance is bliss, but there was an extra bonus in all this. My stealthy assault of Massada had afforded me a gratis entrance because the ticket booth was off the back road some distance from the ramp. I got that old feeling like sneaking into the Center movie on a Friday night. But Israel's perennial and precocious youth soon brought me back to what was becoming an all-too-familiar reality. Had I not seen the youthful hordes exiting noisily from the cavernous hall under the palace, I would not have known of its existence.

It is only alone that we go back in time. I waited for the kids to be out of sight and sound and assaulted the ramp itself and then victorious, set foot atop the citadel. Less sure of myself than Siva, however, since there could have been a ticket-punching Israeli waiting in ambush for the unarmed Quixote (aside from my penknife temporarily confiscated by soldiers in Bethlehem on Christmas Eve). I arrived safe and sound when, as if out of Moab, a wave of foaming tourists washed over me. Boys and girls of American persuasion, they were more revelers than travelers who looked for the soda fountain in this authentic Disneyland. It is to the Israelis' credit that they did not succumb to commercial pressures to soak the tourists at Israel's greatest attraction. It was probably logistically impractical, where the air was so rarified I expected to be paying for it.

In fact, the water was on the house. Lack of water could have posed a health problem for the notoriously unprepared tourists. Rewarded with a taste of desert thirst. Packing a canteen which I filled from one of the giant jugs, lent a touch of authenticity to the pagan siege of this Zealot sanctuary.

Nearby, practically above the ramp, is a synagogue reputed to be the oldest in the world. At the time of the Roman assault in 73 AD, Massada was already a century or two old. The synagogue is a small, simple meeting place of which only the walls remain. Open to the sky and all that lay beneath, this window on the world was more inspirational than all the stained glass in Chartres. Of course, that great Gothic cathedral is another high, and I'm mixing apples and oranges.

An adjoining room once housed Ezekiel's bones. Ezekiel's actual bones? The sign set me to pondering an explanation. Was this some cryptic message, a divined revelation like I Ching, dice, or had the prophet's bones really been carted around for several centuries like the sacred relics of the Catholic Church before being deposited here. In fact the bones were brought here by monks.

I found an ecstatic Mona and hurried her over to the synagogue for a look at severed roots. By the strangest synchronicity, Mona happened to be wearing her Acropolis t-shirt, stranger still because she had pinched it from Kibbutz Snir on the Golan Heights (a bonus she said), even though we had been to Greece's Massada earlier in the year. And now I mix lemons with grapefruits, as the Greek Mecca is but a smog bound anthill compared to the Jewish Acropolis. Ridiculous and sublime, our world has become as absurd as a bicycle built-for-two. Everything was connected, and what's more, mine was the wheel of fortune from whence all spokes and quotes radiated. This speaks of paranoia, except the totality of my experience, its magnificence, filled me with the Zealot's sense of omnipotence.

Massada was a city that boasted of two of Herod's palaces and even a bakery. The promontory is several football fields wide and probably had a wheat field. Yet it was only in the fourth or fifth century that some Byzantine monks built a chapel upon Massada's rubble, serving their Christ for God knows how long before it was abandoned to the elements. Located in the middle of Massada, the chapel wasn't rediscovered until the end of the nineteenth century.

There wasn't much to mark the ruin of the chapel, just some crumbling walls and an actual window that opened on the Holy Land above the Dead Sea where the east bank caught the day's falling shadows.

The total picture that is Massada is so much more than the sum of its parts that I was soon a Silas Marner parting from Mona to count my esthetic coins in the sanctity of privacy. As if sailing the ocean I descended this bridge for Herod's bow and the indulgence of "selfish" pleasures. Few tourists climbed down the stairs to this pleasure palace, which left me alone on the bow of a ship, leaning, merging, flying over the precipice thrust into the infinity of space (more like an ocean voyage than anything else). These royal digs with their faded murals were no more a palace than the Jordan is a river, but diminution only added to the general enchantment. It was that time of day when such clarity, pregnant with spirituality, gives birth to a bible or a Navajo blanket in that other Arizona where the natives also thought themselves to be chosen. We all are if we choose to be.

Time had flown on the most pleasant breeze, and most of the tourists with it. The people who remained behind would camp out and catch the sun rising over the Moab. Sunrise at Massada ranked with a sunset at Key West or camping out on Machu Pichu in the sixties, or sunrise at Nimrod, Turkey, but nobody camped out there. Most of the tourists at Massada would sleep in Eilat or Jerusalem. Watching the last cable car glide down to the parking lot, I wasn't sure where we would sleep. We did little sightseeing snaking our way down to the Massada road. My way and the highway as my genius for genesis merged with my passion for exploration and a challenging climb became a piece of cake. The remaining cars allowed us to go our own way. Panic set in when one of the southbound Palestinian vehicles (the same as yesterday), a van loaded with workers, passed us up. Its occupants waved cheerfully as we frantically signaled them to stop. Sadly, not kosher. Presently, a gentleman stopped and whisked us off into the dusk and our settlement at Sodom, or Gomorrah, passing up a yuppie youth hostel under Massada.

That night as we talked to Asaf we expressed our surprise about Israeli irreligiosity, the atheistic kibbutzim. "As a matter of fact," he said, "there is a religious commune down the road" run by a Jew who believed in Jesus. Jews for Jesus, we thought. Could this group be led by the "two nice Jewish boys" (self-proclaimed) from New Jersey who crackled over the airwaves every Wednesday night. I think it was. And why shouldn't Jews be for Jesus if you removed the Christ from Christianity. These guys were really a couple of jokers, but an interesting addition to "Family Radio." Asaf didn't know if the Jordan Valley guru was in any way connected with the Jerseyites.

Whatever, much to my ire, Mona was determined that this would be our last night at Newe Zohar. I really wanted to plant watermelon seeds, and a "promise was a promise." Not to be confused with a "Turkish promise," though you might expect in a promised land so long under Ottoman control that a word wasn't always its bond.

"I'm sorry, Tony, but I can't sleep under these conditions." In her diary, Mona noted, "Tony felt really bad about not working for Asaf—

seems sincere, well liked by everyone." Unpretentious Israeli was really something to crow about, and I was particularly upset because it was the kind of thing we were doing with regularity, and I wanted to cut the crap. But Asaf understood. "Not all Americans like to sleep with strangers." We were welcome back at any time, the room would be empty in a couple of weeks. I assured Asaf we would only come back to work. It was a deal.

Morning found us playing it by ear when we got a ride with a man drilling for water in the arid Arad. The precious liquid was still being piped a couple of hundred miles. In no time, we were passing the Dead Sea Works, the ugliest incongruity in all of the Great Rift Valley. This gothic antiquity—vampire—is sucking the sea dry while water is diverted into little pools for its "salts." The Dead Sea treasure-house is the largest dollar earner in Israeli industry, according to the Jerusalem Post, though I would imagine that's not counting arms sales. Almost two million tons of potash is extracted annually. Magnesium will be a big dollar earner, and mineral-based industries in general provide employment for thousands of workers in the Dead Sea area. But a hi-tech future is in the works, before the sea runs dry.

I was reminded of Canada's northwest coast where only tourism (little appreciated) with its big bucks would save the land from deforestation. Only tourism will keep the Dead Sea alive. But will enough Germans leave Greece's sun and Skol for a Tote Meer super tan. What the Dead Sea really boils down to is guns or suntan lotion. Because when you're talking potassium, you're in reality talking gunpowder. I'll bet my bottom shekel that some of the more exotic minerals are being shipped to the nearby nuclear installation in Israel's Nevada.

17

Red Sea Blues

I was hallucinating or talking to a barefoot Englishman who had just materialized out of the east like some mad Magi following his star. We were somewhere between the Dead Sea and the Red Sea, or the devil and the deep blue sea, when this lanky lad, bent under backpack and dangling boots, came up a side road with that certain look about him. The young Englishman no sooner greeted us when he went into a great harangue about the Israelis. He was a volunteer at a kibbutz near Jordan and had been compelled to pay for a broken window that he claimed was not his doing. The barefoot contester went so far as to say he got the strong-arm treatment.

In any event, the Englishman was furious and he left the kibbutz a poorer man than when he arrived. I seem to recall he couldn't leave the kibbutz until he had enough coupons coming to him to cover the damages. That or he owed his soul to the company store.

Ever so gingerly, we took our leave of this bad news, sympathetic as we were. Everyone was going to the end of the road, route 90, and we wanted to be on good terms with this psychopath on our path. Chances were, we would meet again, and he barked after us, "See you in Eilat."

Obviously, the sun was past its zenith. Pronto, an oriental truck driver transporting baking goods to Eilat overtook us and gave us a lift. I had not been counting on going directly to the Red Sea. It was another one of those forgotten goals that came suddenly to the fore, and I wasn't prepared for its immediate realization.

In 1968, our thwarted attempt to get to the Red Sea via Sudan was one of the greatest adventures of our hardly sedentary lives. But the closest we got to the almost mythic sea was the neatly printed notation over our Sudanese visa, "Port Sudan abroad by ship." The visa was stamped over the Ceylon immigration endorsement from the year before that was affixed to the extra pages added to this ancient passport that I still carry around for good luck—and direction. The railroad to the sea was washed out that year, and we went overland to Cape Town instead, sailing up the Nile to Juba whence we traveled with an army convoy to the Uganda border, living on tea and English cream cookies, after we'd run out of those string beans...I felt like I had passed life by.

I had my spear gun with me that year. A skin-diver traveling to the Red Sea in those halcyon sixties was engaged in the penultimate peregrination, and I realized the fish speared might be necessary to keep us going. I couldn't imagine what Port Sudan would look like, and that was part of the lure, but Eilat...I had seen the handwriting on the wall, could imagine what it was like, and doubted I would like it. Getting to the Red Sea these twenty years later was a circuitous route indeed and only as an afterthought, after all.

Not only was the world in my pocket, but it had shrunk to the size and soul of New Jersey, and there was little room for serendipity. Most of the Bedouins had been exiled to Beersheba. Down one of the side roads we had passed, in their stead was a most curious Jew for Jesus who, as it turned out when we finally crossed his path, was really from Miami. Eilat, compared to Miami (I forget by who), was not what I expected either. Nothing in the world could prepare me for this former Turkish police post. For, driving towards the center of town, we found ourselves running parallel to the airport runway, the geographic heart of the resort and its most popular restaurant. Across the street from the airstrip, in letters that could be read from the air, the restaurant advertised, "All you can eat for 10 shekels." Which really ain't bad, but, oh, this horrid homogenization from sea to shining sea.

I guessed we were on the wrong side of the tracks. On the other side of the airport the better hotels just off the eastern end of the runway served as a kind of control tower for aircraft that could just as easily land in your bedroom. Like all the fringe settlements in Israel, Eilat was squeezed between Jordan and Egypt and had been chose for its strategic position. The fast growing resort sprang up around the airport. The runway, a kind of boardwalk, began just off the beach gardens where blond goyim pulled weeds and otherwise maintained patches of greenery. In their own land, this work was relegated to Arabs, but in the land of Arabs, who were mysteriously absent, manual labor was the lot of Europeans (peons) without a pot to piss in. Earlier, Israelis who were a little better off had slept here after being disgorged from the Tel Aviv bus, rather than sleep in the control towers.

Three thousand years after King Solomon welcomed the Queen of Sheba to these coral shores, the King Solomon Hotel across the road was attracting another kind of royalty. The Europeans on their pampered package tours demanded to see their favorite TV programs and had compelled the hotel to install a satellite dish. But Israel has brought a divided Europe together in that there are few Israelis living here, and the barefoot Europeans wait upon the well-heeled, a little existent phenomenon in Fatherland.

The mayor of Eilat, a Rafi Hochman and something of a Koch man, revealed "yet another plan for a high-class urban neighborhood. In the first stage it will have 500 luxury residences..." The mayor already "has a list of would-be residents from Los Angeles" and said that "an additional list of South Africans is in the pipeline." What will ultimately "put the town on the map is the $30 million international sports and training complex..." The politics of Israel promise to remain complex. However, Israel won't become the Nevada it was destined to be until the wheelers and dealers of the Dead and Red Seas float their casino schemes past Israel's legislature.

We took a bus past the navy base out to the Coral Beach Reserve to see about work. Just ten years earlier, I was a professional lifeguard not too far from that other Miami, and this did not seem like too unreasonable a quest, but there was no work. Across the road was about a mile of fenced-in beach and too much like what I expected, so we pointed our thumbs in the direction of Sinai. Incredibly, the bakery man who had made a delivery in Eilat was now heading towards Taba, near the Egyptian border. Our friend could not speak any of my languages (neither could I), but even if this obliging Israeli could understand me, I would not have been able to tell him where I wanted to go.

He did know we were Americans, so the truck driver disgorged us at a home away from home, "A million miles away and just ten minutes from Eilat." We had followed our star to the Five-Star Aviya Sonesta, "For all of you who want the very best. The very most. Make very sure..."

Brushing the day's dust off ourselves, it was Dr. Jekell and Mr. Hyde time. High time, with the sun setting, to go into my "travel writer" routine. I don't think I ever felt or looked more disoriented in all my born and aborted days, and Mona, who wasn't exactly a Queen of Sheba herself, wouldn't tell me what I smelled like. Yet, before you could say Jackie Robinson, a waiter was offering us a couple of drinks, and I was unblinkingly quaffing them both. The yellow colored cocktails were the welcome drinks that were included in the American Tour package. Not in a million years imagining how we came to be standing in the lobby of the Sonesta, the waiter assumed we were part of the recently arrived group milling about the receptionist desk.

Mona felt like a thief and was afraid that we'd have to pay for the drinks. The piña colada, Sodom screwdriver, or whichever, was just what the doctor ordered and eased me into my new role—in Israel. In Turkey, such hi-jinks (travel writing, not quasi gate crashing) had kept our heads above water. I got on the house phone. Fifteen minutes later, a charming young lady with a green and cream Sonesta folder filled with hotel information appeared in the lobby. My guarantee to put the Taba Sonesta on the map of the world not withstanding, I could not persuade the assistant or promotion manager to extend us more than a ten percent discount.

We walked over to the public beach, right off Nelson's Village, to a "special" holiday oasis run by a Jewish cowboy. I left Mona outside the thatched entrance and combed my way up the coast to the border, picking up russet stones along the way. The "Red" water reflected the ochre colored Sinai unevenly sloping seaward. Somewhere in that harsh and hauntingly beautiful hinterland was Mount Sinai. I'd been to Egypt, but the closest I'd gotten to Mount Sinai was the New York hospital. It hurts to think how close I was to that pinnacle of peaks, where God speaks, but money also talks and it was out of the question.

Block out the mountainous backdrop, and the public beach is a scene out of Key West. A mixed bag of tourists and Israelis watched a vermilion sunset. The sign read "no camping after dark," but like Key West and points west, Taba had the air of an endless summer at the end of a road, though it was a little chilly now. For an eight dollar Israeli exit fee and an Egyptian entrance fee of six, there was an endless beach beyond Egypt's flapping flag.

In the dark, we piled on an Elat-bound bus, passing the border checkpoint without a hitch before debussing near the Yigal Camping or Holiday Village. (Israelis can't make up their minds about names, as well as spelling, giving us something in common.) Ygal (the i is optional) Camping is a cluster of thatched huts perched on a promontory overlooking the sea. If the owner wasn't interested in my recommendations, his was a price we could afford—and with pleasure, as for the first time we would bed down without being encased in concrete. The owner hadn't yet arrived, so I had to deal with an airborne Dutchman who ran the village for him. He was a Van Gogh who'd gone Gauguin, staying on a year or two longer than he'd planned, a kind of burgermeister to the mostly penurious German clientele who didn't know Mexico from Israel—or Tahiti for that matter—and couldn't care less as long as they got their tan. For less, and the cold beer that the Dutchman served, none of it Maccabee.

One pub-crawling snot-shot was an "entertainer" living in Tel Aviv. I realized I couldn't distinguish a number of Israelis from your most arrogant Germans in that disturbing symbiosis that is Israel. Years removed from the provocation of the concentration camp, surviving in the collective unconscious, I seemed to be witnessing Primo Levi's observation that "power was sought by the many among the oppressed who had been contaminated by their oppressors and unconsciously strove to identify with them."

It was this identification that I found most oppressing about Israel, as only the strongest Israelis would transcend their history—given the geography. Was it not inevitable that the Arabs would become the latter-day Jews? Black South Africans. American Indians. In the American West at least, in territories usurped by the white man, there were Indians selling their trinkets. In Eilat, the Bedouin boutique was operated by our Dutch friend who was selling more than booze and blankets.

One look at the owner Adrian, and I knew he was not painting the town. As he steered every conversation towards Jesus, I was in good stead when I produced my translated-into-German article about St. Francis and my stay at his Carceri above Assisi. More lively articles and letters of recommendation later persuaded the owner of the holiday complex to give me a crack at producing some publicity. We could have an airy hut for the night if I promised to write a badly needed full-page ad by noon. Was I supposed to write the thing in my sleep? I asked. That was my problem. His sister understood English better than he, and she could write the ad if I was not satisfied with the arrangement. Somebody's sister was writing the Sonesta's stuff.

Pap is a piece of cake for the poet, and by the time I fell off to a sleep slightly delayed by the grunts and groans of our more audible neighbors, I had written the plug in my mind and had only to scribble down in the morning some cheesecake about a romantic hideaway under the Red Sea stars. Better known, I did not add, as the Gulf of Aqaba. This alias might induce some readers to make unpleasant connections and remind them that this is not the safest place in the world.

The sun was only mast high when we were at the Coral Reef Observatory talking to Jerry Ramberg. This unlikely character from Brooklyn couldn't believe I was from Queens. Neither could I. I wondered what he was running away from. I just hope I haven't given his secret away, because anybody looking for him would expect to find him in Miami, where he would be trading in his marine observatory for Davey Jones' locker. If Jerry wasn't a quick change artist, he was a stranded advance man for the late Meyer Lansky.

And if Elat was a little bit of Miami, Ramberg was still a fish out of water. But I josh. This likeable Ramberg had been living in Elat for four years and went on about how much the Israelis loved Americans. He recommended we check out the Peace Café, which he said was a scene out of Hemingway. Whatever that meant. I'd been on Hemingway's trail for years. By 1968, down the road and up the river from Juba, the approach to Kilimanjaro boasted of a YMCA run by Hindus.

The observatory was almost worth the price of admission, which I really do not recall paying—speaking about quick change artists. Either Jerry let us in free when I convinced him I was from Queens (though I'm not sure what his job was), or when I waved my expired Writers Union card at the ticket attendant and mentioned my ad that also included the observatory across the road from Ygal Camping. The observatory immediately transported me back to Florida, where I'd spent more time than I care to remember hovering over the Palm Beach reef like some deflated blow fish. A clown fish who had lost his colors. Reefer madness.

The coral in the Red Sea is incomparable, but here, as in most tropical waters, it is fodder for the perennial parrot fish. Bermuda, Palm Beach. I don't know where I hadn't seen these ridiculous rainbows. But Mona's enthusiasm over the bird-beaked fish reminded me how commonplace can become the most exquisite creatures if seen often enough. The parrot fish is but a comical interlude or interloper in the phantasmagoria of fan and brain corals.

It was time to get our feet wet. With my diving or face mask, we headed for the reserve. There wasn't an inch of reef you can see without paying an admission fee—unless you were a determined travel writer. I waved my Sonesta folder, and we entered the beach on the crest of my crust. Of course, we could have climbed over the fence, but the tourists inhibited Mona. Poverty aside, I make no apologies for such egregious ingress. With the Taoists I believe the sun and even the sea would not rise without my love and affection. In a more serious vein, I think the earth's inheritances should be gratis for its deserving inhabitants. If we lovers of the cosmos don't coax the sun out of its lair, we at least keep the world spinning.

There is an undersea trail with markers, but above or under the water I take the less traveled path and was burned by a stinging coral that mesmerized with the fatal attraction of a fire. This reef, with its 20-pound parrots, is a Dali-esque jungle or limbo that separates the desert of the land from the one beneath the sea—and it grows where the twain meet. Proliferates with angel fish, zebra striped, and wrasse, black and white. Queen angels of royal purple vie with emperor upon the spiny globe's stage, and camouflaged lion is not the king of the beasts.

Alice egressed from this baroque wonderland as blue as the queen angel at the lower depths. A little watercolor I picked up with my scarlet fever as a child. Showing all the signs of nervous exhaustion, half century old symptoms were resurfacing...but where will the poetry end if it was dictated before I was born.

Greeting us at the door of the Bedouin Village was the young burgermeister himself. As Mona continued her climb up to the hut, Adrian, dark eyes burning like some one-eared impressionist of the last century (whose irises went for about $50 million), pulled me into the wine garden and, without warning, sat me down and asked how I stood with Jesus. Jesus

Christ, I thought, hadn't he read my article about Saint Francis. Wasn't that good enough? Was my publicity piece too naughty? Or was this springing upon somebody on his last legs a knee-jerk reaction with these Jesus Freaks.

I imagined we were on good terms, I replied, also indicating I took a broader view of religion—and not necessarily a Christian one. I might as well have been speaking about devil-worship, as he became the spitting image of Saul when lightning struck. When Adrian went on about his inspirational walks in the desert, I think he was really putting a mirror up to my face, since I've never known a zealot to be spiritually moved by nature's artistry.

What disturbed me most about Adrian's proselytizing was my sense of déjà vu and inadequacy, or rather the appearance of it. My vulnerability incited all manner of assault, but I'm as defenseless as a Venus flytrap and am nourished by others' transgressions. No matter where I went, there was an evangelist lying in wait, ready to push me over the edge—and catch me. Catch as catch can.

For a number of years now, I have looked like I was on the verge of falling, but if I haven't already fallen and been stomped underfoot, then old sailors just fade away. My most memorable encounter with these John the Baptists occurred in northern Brazil, in a missionary camp in 1976. Again, I was at a literal end of the road after months of travel, broke and practically a captive audience...but read my Spirit of 76 or my Journey to the South if you'd like to know how that one turned out. Now, I simply walked away, remaining unconverted to this or that cause, stumbling seeker after the ultimate cause, but in that unguarded (Goded) state that makes me prey to those who would make me pray—not that I don't in my own Way. The Tao of travel.

Adrian pushed a Bible on me. "Read it."

"I can't take this from you, man."

Adrian wouldn't take no for an answer, "Don't worry, I have lots of them."

We left the Bible behind in the hut. That was too bad for a couple of reasons, the least obvious being that Mark Twain never got this far south. Some days later, when I picked up the Post and began reading about a Dutchman saving souls in Elat, I thought I was reading about Adrian, until the article went on to describe an older man, one who'd been in Elat for maybe seven years. An original turned out to be a disciple. But whence the Dutchmen and their wayward wards. The Dutch, because they represented Israel in countries where it did not have diplomatic relations, enjoyed special privileges in the Holy Land. (And I guess the Israelis greatly appreciate the assistance the Dutch gave the Jews during the war.) Yet Elat was kind of like northern Brazil, where you can wake up one morning and discover you're up the river without a paddle. And the Israelis exploited these young unfortunates for all they were worth—a few shekels.

Taking our road show to the Caravan Sun Club Hotel, opposite the coral reserve, I immediately went into my spiel. Luckily, the manager was not in the market for my services, as this looked and sounded like (with an accent) an English Fort Lauderdale during college week. I checked out one or two more sophisticated hotels, but I could not convince the managers that a free-lance wasn't exactly a free lunch. Didn't they want "the very best, the very most." Where could they find such professionalism east of Queens.

18

Claude and Claire

We learned that there was a kibbutz outside of town and, after a late lunch, our thumbs pointed in its direction. We weren't five minutes into our routine when we found ourselves the guests of Claude and Claire who were recently arrived from Switzerland and driving an expensive rental car. We had met our match when it comes to odd couples or improbable pairs. Claude was a hyper "diplomat" who looked the Arab playboy, unlikely in Palestine. Apologetic to a fault, apoplectic, he was lean and loony, apparently leaning on coke. What were we doing with this crackpot who narrowly missed a car? What was he doing with us? Buzz. Claire, older than Claude, was a little spacey, but respectable Swiss and not lessening my suspicions.

If they hadn't already determined we were a couple of demented Americans, what better way could security conscious Israel curious about our movements put us under surveillance than to team us up with these off-the-wall "tourists." Could the government really believe we were harmlessly knocking about, knocking on any door—without an ulterior motive. Fresh out of Adrian's Godly grasp, I couldn't see what attraction we held for these hedonists. It wasn't as if we were that glamorous, a song and dance team that sailed up Africa twenty years ago when I earned enough in a month to travel a year for us both. If I haven't mentioned it already, Mona was the young Ava Gardner following her star. I could understand why Stan the White Hunter was only too happy to give us a lift—that lasted three days and included boiling water, prepared by his porters.

We had barely warmed the seats of their Avis when Claude invited us for a drink. Did we know a nice place? I mentioned the Peace Café. We wound up on the opposite side of the runway and, of course, there is no cross-town traffic. It seemed like we went halfway up the Arava before we could get around the airport and back into the general area of a café as elusive as the name might suggest. We circled around this hodgepodge neighborhood, where Claude would suddenly stop and sputter out our destination to startled pedestrians in his French accent. His first query was in Hebrew, so I was now wondering if we were dealing with an Israeli playboy, but he assured us they had simply memorized a few phrases before coming to Elat. Finally, we collared a frightened jaywalker who replied, "You must mean the Haifa-Haifa."

Haifa-Haifa? Once was not enough? The café was across the street from where we stopped. I could not believe Jerry had recommended this glorified hot dog stand. Had he been homesick for Brighton Beach? This street was as nondescript as the Brooklyn hinterland—off the water. Maybe LA with a bit of tropical bucolic clutter thrown in for good measure, but infinitely preferable to sterile settlements starkly naked against the desert.

Claude could not believe this was the object of our search either and asked a man in a wheelchair if this was the Peace Café. It was indeed the Peace Café. A couple of European street cleaners were enjoying a beer. Did Haifa-Haifa sound more classy than Peace Café, or did the stammering idiot who changed the name fear that Peace sounded too subversive for well-heeled Israelis out slumming. Peace had been bad for business, evidently; while Haifa-Haifa had that New York, New York, ring about it. Maybe the new owner was from Haifa? We didn't stick around long enough to find out. Claude returned to his car to get a sweater or something warmer, and I thought it was time to check out a kibbutz before, in the spirit of things, I got drunk.

Our friends decided we would all go to the kibbutz together. In fact, they had been thinking about staying at a kibbutz also. This was going too far. Then I realized they thought we were guests at the kibbutz. When we explained, they took our situation in stride.

"We would do the same if we were on the road so long," Claire assured us.

That was sweet of her, I thought, a consoling lie.

But it was already dark, and getting to Elat Kibbutz proved to be a nightmare. Somewhere north of the airport we were in the industrial zone going around in dizzying circles when Claude experienced post-traumatic stress or something similar.

I was ready to approach a couple of characters outside a warehouse when Claude began to relive an unpleasant episode in Uganda and told me to stay put. He had been on assignment as a kind of peace broker between the rebels and the government. Returning to his hotel one night, several armed men stopped him.

I never could follow any of Claude's rapid-fire monologs for very long, but he was clearly in a panic and shivering violently by the time we found the kibbutz. We stood around the lobby or the ground floor of the elevated chow hall and debated our next move when Claude ran out to his car to search for his sweater again. He found that and now was compulsively combing a plastic bag that never left his side, double checking, triple checking for an unspoken treasure.

Claire assured us the papers were mostly "junk" and that Claude should throw them away. What was not junk concerned me, but I was a bit of junkman or collector myself and was even more disturbed that I always seemed to be meeting the most disparate, desperate, people and seeing a side of myself. The man I was, the man I would be...though I can't say in what tense I related to Claude.

Was another mirror being held up to me? Was it just a matter of style? I was afraid our stressed-out benefactor would—at best—blow any chances we had of remaining on the kibbutz and suggested that our Swiss friends leave us to our fate and we would contact them in the morning.

The volunteer overseer was unavailable and we were directed to a member of the Israeli youth group who had assumed that responsibility. Bright and vivacious, somewhat attractive, she was surprisingly human for all the gung ho indoctrination that had preceded her entry into the kibbutz. The young lady belonged to a group that was being groomed for a permanent place in the kibbutz. This was a kind of alternative to the misfits who seemed to be the kibbutz mainstay. She shared a small room with four other girls whose cots lined the wall.

We were able to have a dilapidated room for the night. A broken window provided excellent ventilation. The broken lamp and holes in the wall had no utilitarian value. Was there never a handyman about for the perennial state of disrepair? Were repairs the province of the mostly excluded Arab in the Jordan Valley kibbutzim? Were there no Jewish jack-of-all-trades? Or would they not take time out from their cash crops and factories for the inconsequential volunteer? This less than benign neglect made the sterile seedy, but it was in a perverse way preferable to spooky-clean concrete.

Over breakfast we got the bad news. We had had little sleep last night and didn't want to worry about where we were going so sleep tonight, so we were ready to work. But our fate had been decided by a member. He read our Snir letter and was sorry to let us go, as he would be needing volunteers the following week. Why didn't we stay in the area? He wrote a letter of introduction to the head of Kibbutz Yotvate, about twenty miles up the Arava, that needed help now.

Blame it on battle fatigue, but the pink stained mountains that swept down the Gulf of Aqaba were mesmerizing. Because of its elevation, Kibbutz Elat, which was a good two or three miles north of town, provided the best view of the strategic waterway and was an ideal site for a guesthouse.

We got a ride to town with a bus driver who was of the mind that he should have been behind the wheel of a Cadillac. He probably had his fling as a New York taxi driver, but that road usually leads back to Israel, and all roads lead to Elat. There were as many taxi drivers in Elat as there were in Taiwan when Vietnam was good for business, though the Taiwanese were a lot more aggressive and nearly ran you down to get your attention. If you were too quick for the bastards, they would toot their horns until you were singing "Auld Lang Syne" and cried "Uncle."

Though we told the bus driver we wanted to get off near the Galei Hotel, he couldn't be bothered with telling us where to get off. Instead, I told him where to get off. The hotel was easy enough to find, as it couldn't have been any closer to the runway.

Claude invited us to join him for breakfast at poolside. It was a tasty Israeli wine that seemed to challenge the authority of the exercise instructor, who was hopping around the pool chiding the sunning Swedes into action and ultimately in good spirits chastising Claude for his choice of juice. This barefoot drill instructor in his padded boot camp with docile tourists playing their Simple Simon and Claude babbling on was really too much for me to handle after the sleepless night on the kibbutz.

I had to urinate. The bathroom was closed at the pool, so I went down to the beach to see about a restroom, but the Israelis, like the French, seemed determined to make going-to-the-bathroom a cottage industry.

Everything had its price, especially near the marina, with its Rhapsody in White and the like. I held my fire until we arrived at the Last Refuge, which looked just that. But with that weathered look, it had character and was strategically located for freebie forays into the coral reserve, provided you could swim around the fence that bordered the diving center. No problem, as we Third Worlders like to say.

We did consider staying at the reserve beach, but the ranger on duty didn't buy my travel writer's number and insisted we pay several dollars each to go on the beach. Claude observed the altercation and ran to the rescue. The ranger asked me who he was.

"Who is he?" I incredulously repeated, as if Claude were King Hussein himself on a peace mission.

"Who am I!" Claude more demanded than asked, and got into the act. "Who am I?" Claude repeated, less sure of himself.

"Yeah, who are you?" the ranger coolly inquired.

"I am Swiss," Claude replied in his Arabesquely French accent.

I don't think a declaration of Dutch citizenship would have helped our cause. I was half hoping he would break out a diplomatic passport. But instead, we just cracked up like a couple of sailors on a long delayed liberty.

The Last Refuge was really made to order, and it was a pleasant dive, indeed, the haunt of more conventional sailors. Claude befriended an African deckhand whose ship was at anchor in Elat—though most of the marine traffic seemed destined for Aqaba, just beyond the King Solomon Hotel. Israel had been getting enough ships calling at Elat to consider digging a canal all the way to the Dead Sea Works, but the constant threat of war kept that idea on the back burner.

Claude seemed a candidate for shanghaiing. But the plot thickened—this potpourri of improbabilities—when I realized he was talking to a countryman or a reasonable facsimile. Claude originally hailed from Mauritius, ancient Mauritania, I believe, or five thousand miles away Malagasy. Wherever. His mother remains there, and if I followed his convolution correctly, he wanted to buy her property in Elat. But I'm not buying any of this, and I think Claude is a tossup between a rendezvousing bagman and a clever real estate agent on the trail of a couple of eccentric Americans who might be in the market for a plot of desert. Maybe the rangy Mauritanian is who he says he is. At least, it explained the Sheik of Araby look and the French accent.

Writers who lead uneventful lives like to say, you can't make this stuff up, a cover for fabrication. My life is stranger than fiction. But I was relatively unknown and mused it had been arranged to keep it that way with an encounter I really couldn't make up. Yet, Israel was the land of the impossible. If this Last Chance Café scene is something out of a Hollywood movie, why believe the uneasy truths about the rest of Israel that make up so much of my book. But the issue is the courage to publish. Obviously, my fantastical style doesn't encourage belief, but did that stop people from believing in other theatrical testimonials about the Holy Land these thousands of years. And why shouldn't this be a scene out of Hollywood? The Texas range, a movie city on the hill above us, was making Matzo Ball Westerns. Nearby was Mandy's Chinese restaurant that served up chop suey and leftover shibboleths. With all this fracturing fragmentation every place seemed like the disembodied movie set on a great sandy lot. Israel, a work in progress running out of time and space.

The Swiss Arab had driven me into the sea, and like the Navy Seal I had almost become those many years ago, I penetrated the territorial waters of the reserve, skirting the English scuba divers and turtles to surface a less than royal purple, not long after, shaking, rattling and rolling to keep warm.

Storm clouds gathered. Elat, Eilat, any way you spelled it, I had it. It was already drizzling when I convinced Claude and Claire to get the show on the road and keep ahead of the rain.

The athletic diplomat ran for the car and was sideswiped by a young woman who knocked Claude to the pavement. He bounced up, quivering and cursing the girl in French. He accused her of deliberately running into him, but with his plastic bag once again in his grasp, he gained possession of himself. I was pained by his vulnerability. Whatever Claude was, I had ruled out his being an Israeli. Though we'd seen what happened to...

We had decided on visiting, what was for us, the convenient Timna Valley. Claire insisted Timna was on their itinerary anyway. I would like to think that Mona and I provided a kind of therapy for them and projected a joie de vivre, a carefree couple that would turn him around and neutralize his demons.

We were little prepared for the ensuing deluge, but when it rains, it pours in Southern California, and we rode up a flooding Arava on the most improbable of arks. That our captain would see us through hell or high water spoke of a charity beyond belief or a saint on performance enhancing mushrooms.

Even a nation of master spies lacked the imagination for the creation of a Claude. Maybe we were the only show in town until the discos opened. We sell ourselves short.

This was the boondocks, and what was Claude doing in an Israel with few loose ends, indulged like royalty in one of the best hotels. Then again, we had only seen the more Spartan side of Israel (Jerusalem was already a dream), and perhaps there were some legitimate off-the-wall characters bouncing around the carpeted lounges of the Arava. My doubts and this absurd blend of the bizarre and the Byzantine took me back to Palm Beach. My personal journey was complete when we drove up the Timna Valley jeered on by the most portentous claps of thunder.

The enchanting canyon was desecrated by a manmade lake as outlandish as the London Bridge that spans the desert wastes of Arizona and done in the same exhibitionist spirit. Insult was added to injury when we discovered that the Barnum behind the improbable puddle was none other than our West Palm Beach landlord, the man who tried to have me evicted from his Viking Arms (and legs, as I used to write in the bulletin). Yes, as we were to later learn in the December 5 edition of the Jerusalem Post, the developer who made the desert "blue" was Milwaukee lawyer, Avrum Chudnow, who wouldn't be content with his ruination of nature until the ancient copper mines of the ochre colored canyon were literally mined by an army of tourists. One of the most beautiful archeological sites in the world, replete with Egyptian and Midianite rock-drawings has been "blue-printed" for the Holy Land's answer to Disneyland.

Claude became one of Mark Twain's Innocents Abroad as he scooped up slabs of Timna sandstone to brighten up one of your less staid Swiss homes. But mostly, he talked non-stop—about as out of place as an artificial lake. If the rain hadn't confined him to the car a bad part of the time, it's likely he would have made off with chunks of a two-wheeled chariot drawn by ibexes. Actually, it was the ancient miners who carved the scenes of men and animals on the rocks, probably in the spirit of magic. The supernatural sculpture was heightened by the mask of Hathor, goddess for the Timna temple. I have no memory of it, but there is a drawing of a pharaoh worshipping Hathor, possibly Ramesees the Third,

So you must wonder why the Jewish National Fund of America was charged with the task and has nothing better to do with its money than minimize the contribution of ancient Egyptian culture and extract and destroy all the natural beauty by wasting millions of dollars on this grandiose scheme to turn the desert green with dollars. What can man possibly do to beautify a Grand Canyon? It may be good PR for the puerile to tout the conquest of the desert with a lake it can ill afford to maintain, but the site is doomed to revert to dust before the ink is dry on the rest of Chudnow's schlocky plans.

Between the dreams of developers (a lawyer no less) and the schemes of the military up the road, Timna's most popular tourist attraction becomes an ominous symbol. A curious double-edged sword, as the Mushroom, the fungi-shaped rock, becomes a replica of the magic root and impetus behind ancient civilizations. But it is also a shape of things to come if we don't become one with nature and our neighbors. The nuclear alternative seemed to hang over us. And you can bet some radioactivity was raining down upon us, beyond nature's acceptable dosage. With the weather turned upside down, the stage had been set for an end-of-the-world scenario. Such an unlikely quartet—the cascading rain that stained the delightful colors of the desert black.

To remain in the car was to drown in Claude's stream of consciousness, and I was literally driven up the wall of the canyon to ponder the wisdom of leaving my wife with these imperfect strangers. At least, the rain made the lake plausible and would delay its evaporation.

A question that began to nag me was, where was the Bedouin and his perennial camel?

We were on the road to demonic Dimona (southern environs). Actually, Claude and Claire were all for—"no problem"—driving us up to Kibbutz Yotvata, only fifteen miles up the road.

"I always wanted to see a kibbutz," Claire said.

The disco wouldn't be open for hours, and what the hell (or high-water) we were in a desert lark, ark. What was a little water between friends. Sticky wicket, but endangered species had to stick together.

As we left Timna Park, we came upon a posse of Israeli cowboys tall in the saddle. The riders were from a nearby kibbutz and all but corralled by Claude who, like most men, become small boys before big horses.

In a torrential rain, we disembarked at Yotvata. Not a soul in sight, not a sign of life. Upstairs in the dining hall, I collared a man preparing the tables for the Shabbath meal. A phone call and Bernie materialized out of the miasma. It was bad enough that a character like me had to deal with this refugee from the Big Apple, but Claude vouched for me and got into the act. He told this Tony Curtis clone from Rockaway (or was it Howard Beach) what a great person I am. If that wasn't the kiss of death, he dug into his plastic bag when I shooed him away.

Streetwise Bernie smelled something not kosher on the menu. But it was dark and dangerous out there, with deluge and delirium. Everything was closed but for some distant kibbutz, and this son of a gun from Brooklyn—or was it Queens—was telling his landsman, maybe his long lost father stranded in a flooding Sinai, to take his traveling circus elsewhere.

I asked and pleaded how could he do this to us. On the Shabbath, no less. The three of us were on the verge of a physical or nervous breakdown, and the critical fourth who was doing the driving, his nose in the bag, had already gone around the bend.

Not to worry. Bernie assured us that a camping site down the road was open, and in any case, there was no room for us. Without so much as a cup of coffee, he sent us on our way. The camp was closed and we had never seen a more terrible rain.

A famished Claude, who stoked the ashes in his burnt-out stomach and shivered like hell, drove on until even he was persuaded to pull over to the side of the road. The rain let up and, still pointing north, we pressed on until we arrived at Grofit.

Kibbutz Grofit was home to many Americans. Claude or no, Snir was the magic word. Not only did I have the letter of recommendation, but one of the guys we spoke to in the chow hall lounge knew Joel, the first Joel (and the angels did say), the American who was in charge of us picking avocados for one or two days—also in the rain. Joel had spent several years in Grofit before he tired of "Southern California" and went up to the Golan Heights. Oh, how I rhapsodized about the bespectacled fellow from Pittsburgh. No, Philadelphia, our new friend corrected. Yes, yes, of course, Philadelphia, the City of Brotherly Love. He was like a brother, a son to us, but this guy Bernie...I explained. But Israel was a contradiction.

Joel's friend told us not to worry and certainly we could eat here. He fetched the volunteer overseer who was an older man sympathetic to our story, another singular mensch. We were invited to share the Shabbath meal with them. Mona and I would be able to spend the night, but Claire and Claude would have to leave after supper. More volunteers were expected tomorrow, Mona and I would then have to be on our way. For the moment this was our monastery in the desert, its doors open to all.

Claude went for the wine like an Italian monk. Our Swiss savior had acquired a justifiable thirst but was unaware that spirits was not the standard fare and called for more. He was unaware that the meal was on the house and the so obliging English girls with their bottles were not guests. In an unprecedented move, the overseer brought an additional half-full bottle to our table. Of course, it was just what the doctor ordered for the wayward pilgrims. Claude made up for whatever bubbles the white wine lacked, and we were all simply ecstatic that such a day could end so ideally.

Even Friday's chicken had been replaced by ravioli and roast beef, not bad. If this multiplication of loaves weren't miraculous enough, Claude had turned rain into wine, and the world was one.

The overseer who took time out from coveting a young blond could have been a maitre d' at the peace brokers' favorite trattoria. Claude responded in kind, got up from the table with his hand on his wallet, and asked for the check. Unlike your more conventional monasteries, not even a contribution was suggested.

A year later, we received a Christmas card from Geneva from our friends whose names in my book will be changed for diplomatic reasons. I considered changing our names to Bonnie and Clyde. I now realize Claude was a soul brother and that, for the grace of God, go I. Regrettably, I had a problem keeping my own head above water and could not help him.

19

The Original Hebrew Israelite Nation

The rain had stopped, and we wished our Swiss friends Godspeed, with a promise to call in the morning. Claude extended his compliments to the chef. I must say if the meal was the exception to the rule, the room was standard fare and only an ingrate would elaborate. We slept, and a palace couldn't better serve our needs.

After breakfast, we had a good hike down to Route 90 where we were joined by the usual soldier. Two other soldiers had just gotten a lift. This inquisitive chap was serving his time at Kibbutz Grofit, and he was going to spend his day off at the kibbutz two miles up the road. I asked him if Israel soldiers ever marched. Were we under surveillance or the morning's entertainment?

Either way didn't wash, and we made tracks before long. Not only would we leave the driving to someone else, but we would let our benefactor determine our destination. If he or she was driving due north, we would seek out the Jews for Jesus before returning to our Dead Sea friends further up the road. If the driver turned left and went into the Negev, we knew of a nature reserve and had some vague recollection of a kibbutz associated with Ben-Gurion. The name held magic for Mona. To any idealist over forty with a selective memory, the former Prime Minister was the embodiment of George Washington and Pope John rolled up into one. The latter with a green thumb.

The Negev road just up ahead saw little traffic, and Dame Fortune would be pushed only so far. The first driver to stop was going a couple of miles with the soldier we had deserted at the bus stop. Yes, he knew about the Jews for Jesus, and the way he vilified their leader, I thought he must be a saint. The driver knew him back in Florida and said he stopped believing in Jesus last year when his wife left him. I stopped believing in the Jew for Jesus when I learned this character is from Miami. I would have been more comfortable with the idea of a defector from his faith being from

California—but a Messiah from Miami? We left the car with the soldier and they disappeared in the desert.

In due time, the strangest lift carried us away. The couple was driving up to the Negev plateau and immediately returned to the canyon, leaving us off at Kibbutz Shizafon like babes left on a doorstep. Near the Sinai border, it had been a small military post, but now resembled a sixties commune inexplicably plopped in a nether land so desolate that even the buzzards stayed clear of it.

Yet, a loose bunch in their twenties who were happily grab-assing greeted us outside the dining hall. A girl who had just spent her summer in Brooklyn with relatives invited us into the Quonset hut type affair for a cup of coffee. It never ceased to amaze me, this easy ferrying between New York and this Staten Island, a seemingly smooth transition from Brooklyn to kibbutzim. Like changing your clothes, but the farmer's garb just didn't lay right, kind of like a tree growing in Brooklyn. Not a hayseed in sight. The real miracle behind the desert blooming was girls in bloomers. Water did the rest.

The Arava was the place of agriculture. Shizafon's nineteen members did their farming in the valley below and cultivated mostly out-of-season produce. Above, as one writer said of Labrador, was the land God left to Cain. Poetic but not descriptive. Labrador was lush compared to this rock-strewn moon, but I went off into a bareness that was barely relieved by a wadi or two where God-forsaken roots were hardly stirred by last night's rain.

We were to sleep in the children's nursery, though apparently there were no children about, despite the suggestive, even inspiring, masterpieces that hung from the walls of the diner. All the paintings showed a loving mother and child from various periods and cultures in history, and it seemed a sure bet that this psychological love affair would bare fruit. The kibbutz movements relied heavily on kibbutznik offspring to replenish the ranks of their mostly transient workers.

A large mattress was provided for us and was sufficiently comfortable resting on the Turkish tiles. Indeed, when an attractive young lady came up with a beer, I could have been the last of the Pashas. The beer turned out to be artificial, but the sleep was sound enough.

This foreign legion had never seen volunteers, but we became the responsibility of a one-armed man who suggested we go to Sde Boker. Not only was this the kibbutz that became home to Ben-Gurion, with a famous field school nearby, but the woman who recruited members there had helped in the development of Shizafon. We must be sure to send their regards to Brenda.

Wasn't it time to be a member, I thought. Really, we were expatriates in spirit, and I'd had it with my own country, which was no better than Israel. Our things were in storage in New York. Nothing was permanent anyway, and a member told us we would have a better chance of being accepted. We looked reliable, and what better kibbutz for an idealist than Sde Boker. Ben-Gurion was older than I when he went to Sde Boker; while I was old enough to be the father of every volunteer I had met. I was psyching up for my new role.

After breakfast, we called Claude and Claire and, at least for the time being, closed that chapter in our lives.

It was still cool, and we were raring to go, as prepared for any eventuality as the Reverend Pike. My thumb was held as high as the Statue of Liberty. Mona was about as moveable, but with a little prodding and a short ride, we were deposited at the Sinai turnoff. The junction boasted a bus stop and the omnipresent soldier, at least partly in uniform, the impressive part.

I thought back to turkey where we would see armed soldiers in the least likely places, as if they were guarding the very rocks themselves. Out of uniform, this chump's Uzi became more menacing, and Mona got the creeps. The problem with continuing on was that, to the pack-minded Israeli, this Pikeish behavior was almost an effrontery. Walk? Where? But before we could desert our post, an American Israeli bore down on us and we jumped aboard—with the soldier.

Our driver, still in his thirties and a diver living near Haifa, had just checked out the Red Sea and was now heading for Mitzpe Ramon. As I looked up the town on my serviceable tourist map, the man strongly suggested and practically chastised me for not having a better map of Israel. He added that there was a good map of Israel available for fifteen dollars. I said I didn't think Israel was that large. I didn't dare say I could see Israel itself for less. I knew where this yuppie was coming from, California as a matter of fact.

He said he helped National Geographic explore Cesaerai. I thought that such a knowledgeable fellow could help me identify the desert acacia. I had been seeing it all over the country and asked this subterranean what the story was and did I have the right label.

"How should I know? I went to school in California." He had been in Israel since 1962, and I hope he remains there, the oceans of the world aren't big enough for the both of us.

In about an hour's time we slowed before a great divide that had all the colors of Timna, but without the staining rain, and then mindful of Twain descended the grandest canyon. The driver couldn't say enough and waxed lyrical about the American West, and here it was like the American counterpart, mostly devoid of the indigenous inhabitants.

Mitzpe Ramon was yet another concrete mess without benefit of trees, acacia's filigree, to fill the empty spaces. Yesterday's strategic outpost sits on the northwestern edge of the Makhtesh Ramon and commands (in the truest sense of the word) a view that almost ranks with our own Great Crater. Israeli Druse occupied the observation dome, which almost replicated their imposing hats.

We thought, what a great place to work. The woman at the information desk said it was entirely possible. We were directed to a back road that would take us to the nature reserve's recruitment office—via Maryland. This tedious stretch of tarmac had been funded by Governor Mandell, whose dedication plaque was another reminder of the placenta that stretches across the sea.

We weren't parked by a Bedouin workman very long before a nature reserve jeep driven by a Frankenstein in uniform stopped to whisk us off to the headquarters. For all practical purposes, it is run by the military.

The young director seemed as impressed with our name as he was with our letter from Snir. "Is that an Italian name?" He loved Italians.

"Why?" I asked.

"They've done such great things."

Mussolini's invasion of Ethiopia, I wondered. But I kept this upbeat and produced my credentials, amongst which was a letter of recommendation from Canada's National Parks system. It was obvious I could be a boom to tourism and would do great things with my pen for nothing. I was in love with that most exquisite expanse of desert below.

However, the director's banal buttering up was followed by meeting with a woman in charge of house cleaning and maintenance who lived in a nearby bungalow. She tended to her child, and they helped themselves to a disconcerting bowl of fruit that remained out of our reach. When I realized I was being groomed for the position of domestic, I whipped out my Sonesta folder with a flourish. Was this woman unaware of my Italian name? Look at this letter from the Moroccan government, in French no less. Look, look, I'm a writer.

No dice. There wasn't even a leopard for me to track down. We would get five shekels a day, with which we were to buy our own food, to be cooked in our own apartment. This complex of cottages just back from the canyon's rim was the most tasteful housing arrangement I had seen yet, but we were to be no part of it.

Frank drove us to town, to an apartment block that was something out of the Eastern Bloc. One concrete cubicle after another that was so totally dehumanizing that it was Totalitarian. No physical or spiritual connection to the canyon, no place for a free spirit within these constraining corners chipped away by vandalism and neglect. We were to live in a communist slum. More drab. We remembered Moscow in summer, the trees at least giving a softer edge to the new sections of the city.

The hulking chauffeur couldn't open the door to our apartment. While he went off to get another key, we were left to shiver on the dark stairwell that was festooned with overhanging electrical wires. This dangerous decoration was a foretaste of the spaghetti we would be eating. We went down the cement steps to see if we could focus on something more pleasant than dangling wires. Our building was on stilts and there was a bird's nest where there should have been an electric bulb. Thank God, Nature abhors a vacuum.

We should have smelled a rat when Frank let us into the flat and we saw the living room lined with cots. Our room was what you expected it to be. I bought our food in a dismal grocery that from the outside looked like a prison cell. At least our apartment didn't have bars on it. I put away enough dago red to send me straight to bed.

The following day we were allowed to rest up, psyche up, before actually working. Mona stayed in bed, while I went with Frank to headquarters before walking into the canyon.

I asked about the cots. Well, yes, he said. Sometimes guests who we would be cleaning up after slept in our apartment, but that was no concern of ours. After all, we had our own room. I remarked that this was not part of the deal. While I was at it I added that, though I was a beloved Italian, neither I nor my Jewish wife could live on spaghetti. I did not know that anything else was prohibitive, except for the beans I'd had for breakfast. For good measure, I threw in that my wife wasn't happy with the accommodations.

"Where is your wife?"

I seized on this opportunity to escape and retreat from our commitment. "She is sick in bed," which was at least half true, as Mona would be with me if all was well. "And the heater is broken."

"No problem. You will get a new one."

As I retreated out the door, the director called after me, "You and your wife will work tomorrow?"

"If she is better. Will you teach her how to clean a house?"

Below me spread the beckoning chasm, 1200 feet deep, 25 miles long, and 5 miles wide. The crater pales before our own, but this is the gateway to the Wilderness of Zin, the Holy Land of Moses. More technically, the crater, as it is called, is a cirque. Not even that is accurate unless you go down there on a holiday in the tourist season and then it is, indeed, a circus. A cirque, if I may get geological instead of illogical, is carved out by a glacier and remains frozen poetry. At this point, I was still looking for signs of a meteorite, thinking that this was how the grand gorge came to be known as a crater. But then many Israelis were not as fluent in the newest language as they were in one of the most ancient. A crater was cosmic, more mysterious, and more likely to suck you into the bowels of the copper earth.

The weather was cool and threatening, but come predictable high water, I would still have my day in the desert. Again, I was disoriented by such undesert-like climate, although one sage brush has said that the desert is a cold place with a hot sun. But the sun was nowhere to be seen, and this was so out of character compared to those brain-baking days in the past that had their part in burning me out. My cranium was a crater. Before Timna's deluge, my only experience with desert floods was in the Nubian desert, the actual periodical washout of the tracks to Port Sudan. But that was another lifetime, and I could never truly enjoy the desert summer because of the heat. A wet desert was as much an anomaly as a cold day on the plains of the Indian subcontinent, where incidentally upon my arrival, it rained for the first time in four years. It seemed that my nose not only divined water but made it as well.

And where was that desert fixture, the fly? Mind you, I wouldn't change this day for anything (not yet, anyway), but I'd come to feel that discomfit was associated with romantic places, the price one paid for forbidden fruit. Like coming down with the clap or Montezuma's Revenge. The most exotic waters harbored sharks; so naturally, since I felt so wonderful, I felt something out of whack. Not to worry, as darkening clouds piled up. It was the price I paid for solitude.

If skies heavy with gray kept the tourists away, there were more violent intrusions into my meandering meditation. As my stream of consciousness followed a not long dry wadi, jets screamed overhead and sonic booms were a precursor of the more natural thunder that followed me up this crooked trough. Foreboding exploded into anger and distracted me from the consequences of rain, as I dwelled on that insult to the soul that streaked towards Sinai. Was there anything more corrosive to the spirit than noise?

The skies opened up and I scurried like a badger into a cave that just barely sheltered me from the downpour. I shivered in my prenatal position and would like to say I was born again, but I just went on asking why, why must irony be my way. It was as if the gods were telling me that things weren't as they seem, after years of trying to fix labels on a universe whose essence is change and contradiction. It was the eroding rain that gave this canyon its color. Life. Uncovered the color from beneath the bleached surface of things. I had no bones with that, but just when I was beginning to need it, I was denied the comfort of familiarity and the security of a reliable scenario. That was when things really begin to change.

I was forty when I went into Argentina expecting to see pampas, but saw more llamas in the high desert than I had seen in all of Peru. The boundaries we put on life are no less arbitrary than the borders of countries.

But I stray from the desert, this low desert, generally the more predictable environment and most conducive to the vision of the prophets. The woodlands could cloud the vision and mire you in a muddied present. In the luxuriant tangle of the crowded forest with everything connected was paranoia's most nourishing nursery. How much easier to skip like a gazelle over the hardscrabble of the desert.

It is no accident that the visionaries remain nomads, rolling stones who gather no moss and evade the dense undergrowth of the cluttered mind. Now I must believe it was no accident that I unwittingly followed in the wake of Moses, open to the unlimited horizons that stretched up the length of the desert floor. Desert flood in my case. Cammarata, the rainmaker. "But judgment shall be revealed as water, and justice a mighty torrent" (Amos 5:18), God's rebuke to Moses before His Commandments.

The rain let up long enough for me to find sanctuary in a man-sized cave above a Nabatean campsite. By the third century BC, these Aramaic speaking people were creating a great civilization, in communities that predated the arrival of the fugitives out of Egypt. Enough speculation? I hoped a jeep would come by, but it was becoming apparent it was time to call it a day. I turned back, not entirely sure of my bearings until I homed in on a radio tower that I would normally curse. The trek back dissolved into a trudge in shoes unequal to rain or even rock at this stage of the game, but my Turkish jacket kept me moderately warm. If I had my choice of carrying it in the heat or wearing it in the rain, with my Navy watch cap, I gladly opted for the downpour.

By the time I climbed out of the crater, I looked like something the leopard dragged in. Yet, I was studiously ignored when I entered the office. Of all the pompous poops I'd met, these nobodies took the cake. I was not to partake—but learn my place. I had to ask for coffee, and the birthday cake that was being passed around was never offered to me. Letters of recommendation not withstanding, I was accorded all the dignity of a domestic. It was the moment that mattered, and if I could do the work that no Israeli would, then I was just another Arab. And Mona? A woman's place was in the home—cleaning it.

If there weren't enough Bedouins around to do the dirty work, a most unusual occurrence had guaranteed the Israelis their lumpenproletariat, or underclass. In the seventies, waves of American Blacks emigrated to Israel and most of them settled in the Negev. I was unaware of this exodus and was taken aback by a Black with a pail and squeegee climbing the hill under my apartment block where I had walked after being left off downtown in the rain. This man was a Negroid as Jericho's stoop laborers. His outfit bore some resemblance to the robes of the sons of the desert, but blackness aside, he struck me as not being entirely kosher and not of Israel. Was it that loping gait of the camel, a cool that spoke of soul that made me suspect. Or was it the tools of this man's trade that placed him beyond the pale. I think what really aroused my suspicions was when he took a short cut, that hint of individuality that stuck him out like a sore thumb.

With a little effort on my part, our paths crossed on the side of a desolate hill in a dreary drizzle.

"Hi," I said.

"Hi," the Black man replied and slipped into Hebrew. But he'd said enough to indicate he spoke my language better than any Israeli.

I asked the graying man where he was from.

"Cleveland." Initially, he couldn't believe whence I hailed, but was convinced when I rattled on about the crater. He told me about his pilgrimage to the Holy Land. "I've been here twelve years."

"Holy Moses," I replied. "What's it like for you living here. Are you all together." They came under the umbrella of the "Original Hebrew Israelite Nation." "Jesus."

"Listen, man," he said, "we speak Hebrew. We are Hebrew." His name was Gershon, having taken on a biblical name.

I wondered how all this washed with the government.

"The government is trying to deport us, but we're the original Hebrews. Moses, Christ, they were all Black. We have as much right to the land as any other Jew."

I asked how they all managed to avoid deportation.

"We lost our passports."

"Yeah, but man, I can tell you're an American..."

"Don't matter, nobody can prove I was an American."

If his walk gave his nationality away, his beatific features and inner calm were not common among Americans of any color. That open expression that can encourage persecution and the other side of paranoia. I asked Gershon how he was treated.

"The people are okay, but it's a racist government."

And fascist, I added.

He heartily agreed in Hebrew. "They are gonna treat us good? Look how they treat their own people."

Did Gershon mean the ghettoized Falashas who were brought to Israel from Ethiopia with great fanfare and are still in periodicals like the Readers Digest being played for all they are worth. Or did he mean your average white Jew who broke his back to get by. Not everybody bought the Israeli dream. Since Gershon was in the country illegally, as the Law of Return did not apply to American Blacks and the uncircumcised, he had been compelled to circumcise.

Hustling, he could make ten shekels a day cleaning windows.

"Ten!" I exclaimed. "I only make five."

"Five!" he shouted. "Nobody can live on that. You're kidding."

"I swear," I regressed, "and we don't get paid until we've been on the job for two weeks. At least we don't pay rent. How do you get along?"

"We help each other out. We have our own hospital and school, and our spiritual leader runs a restaurant in Dimona." It was owned by the Original Hebrew Israelite Nation.

I hope they're not vegetarians, I thought. The Krishna gang was big on veggie restaurants.

His description of the Hebrew guru fell short of a living God. "Israeli agents have already tried to kill him. They underestimate him. They don't know who they're dealing with."

Hare Krishna and a happy new year.

Welcome to the club. Until we got onto the omnipotence of the leader aside this Golgotha, a subject that seemed to be building up to a crucifixion, I was moved by Gershon's humanity. But now it seemed his tranquility was born of unquestioning faith in just another fellow. I wondered if this spiritual leader was another Moonstruck demigod whose will was the way for people who had lost their own. Was he another Moses crying out in the Wilderness of Zin? Or enterprising restauranteur. Everybody was getting into the act, but as far as I was concerned, the Messiah had already come and gone, and he happened to be Black. Martin Luther King's message was the most valid, the most relevant for peace on this earth.

I didn't know where Gershon's guru was coming from and maybe he was what he appeared to be to Gershon; but if the government was persecuting him, it wasn't for religious reasons. Why then? Were they too much of an embarrassment to the government, even perceived as a threat, with the American Blacks' growing empathy for the Palestinians? Was the guru showboating to increase his standing among his followers? Was I to believe the American Moses was too much for Mossad? It was more likely that the government was content as things stood, since the Original Israelites conveniently filled the gaps left by the dispersed Bedouins. Somebody had to do the menial work.

I was disappointed in Gershon's deification of his leader. It was like needing an icon when the idea is to believe in the unknowable. But people wanted answers, ultimately denying faith and nullifying fate. Too bad, I thought, because grizzled Gershon with those patches of white looked so much more the patriarch than the pink-skinned punks who only spoke the language. They kept the bathwater and threw out the baby, but dressed quasi Mid-Eastern, he looked more authentic than the Shillucks on their own Nile turf who, for all their feathers and primitiveness, appeared as if they were on their way to a costume party the moment they put on sunglasses, receding into the twilight world of the future.

More proof the promised land is a state of mind, as people who belong will take on the proper appearance. A believer had no need to plant the symbolic tree. His roots were in the very air he breathed. He was in his promised land.

"It's beautiful," he said, and it was compared to Cleveland.

I asked him if there was any possibility of Mona and me getting together with him and the group. The thought of warm company and some decent food appealed to me, and I knew Mona would go for it. But we had to wait until about seven, and so I stopped by the grocery for a bottle of mercifully inexpensive wine. By the time the appointed hour rolled around, I was as loose as a wheel myself. So cozy, romantic, the idea of going out was not so much unacceptable as impossible. Karamazov had "repaired" our heater. When he first gave us the heater he told us it had to be kept on low or that we would blow a fuse, so we only had one coil lit. But now that it was fixed, I was transfixed by our double-barreled fireplace. Our rickety electric heater held all the magic of a fire, if not nearly as much warmth.

I don't know which disturbed me the most—breaking yet another promise or at least going back on my word—or the knowledge that we were missing out on an incredible experience. I mean, these were "roots" with an entangling twist, because the African experience was a lot closer to the Holy Land that say Rabbi Kahane who is centuries removed from the prophetic spirit. Israel was but a spur on the side of Mount Sinai and Ethiopia was a lot closer to the Holy Land than Brooklyn. Or as Mort Sahl used to say, "Is there anyone I haven't offended?"

I hoped I hadn't offended Gershon. It was downhill all the way to his place, but I knew I would never be able to make it back up, which maybe wasn't such a bad idea. I told Mona we'd see Gershon and his friends tomorrow.

But she said, "I'm not going to stay a minute longer than I have to in this dreary place."

This was a word, dreary, that I had never used before.

"I'm so disappointed. It's horrible."

"Just let me work one day. We don't want the police on our tail."

She was convinced guests would be moving in with us the following night. "No."

Karamazov came by in the morning to see what our plans were and was as dismayed as I. Another curious character, this tussled-haired rascal who was married to a Moroccan a third his age, and now he was doing a number on us. French was, of course, our lingua franca, and the conversation went something like this.

"If you leave, you have to pay rent."

"Then I have to go to the bank to cash my travelers check."

In the meantime, he checked out the walls for any holes we may have left behind in the event we had hung some paintings. Unlikely as that was, how do you deface the faceless. Absconding the den of inequity, we made for the border of the Original Hebrew Israelite Nation.

As Gershon had said, their city block of two-story apartments was distinguished from the other buildings by the smoking chimney. Did no one else have heat? It snowed in Mitzpe Ramon. I forgot that everybody gets by on electric heaters.

Just as we were ready to enter the first apartment we came to, we ran into a black munching on a candy bar. He had Gershon's serenity and was friendly, but he was on his way to work and pushed on after I pumped him about the Nation's leader.

Gershon had already gone to work, and it was only after this man was convinced that we were a couple of eccentrics who actually knew Gershon that he opened up. Again, I was struck by the man's innocence and vulnerability. Ultimately, gullibility. The need to believe had become an instinct for self-preservation, a loser's self-effacement that finally says, I can't make it alone, and follows the most debilitating defeats. I'd been there, but thank God, I'd been able to stay clear of Jim Jones…and his Kool-Aid.

It was Sde Boker or bust. Downtown, we chanced upon a rustic incongruity that turned out to be an empty youth hostel. The small wooden building most likely had been the Turkish police station once upon a time. A cluster of trees pinned down this memory, a kind of oasis to see us through the razor's edge of Mitzpe Ramon.

Industrial Zones One, Two, Three, on we trudged, watching the cars pass us by until I became a very loud voice in the wilderness. Calmed by the slowing car going our way. It was Dostoyevsky at his best. Unfortunately it was Karamazov, accompanied by another man, who called out and apparently informed us that the jig was up.

"What are we going to do?" Mona whispered.

"Plead insanity," I suggested. I stepped lively and cried out, "I can't hear you, qu'est-ce que vous dire?"

Karamazov repeated, "The bus is the other way." He pointed towards town. "The bus doesn't stop here."

The car turned around. "Au revoir."

We plodded on and wondered when we would be beyond the Third Industrial Zone.

Across as eerie a landscape as anything I'd ever seen, a Bedouin woman, covered from head to foot, glided along with her goats against a backdrop of giant domes and towering smokestacks. The old lady was the disconnected thread that ran the length of the land, and one life wouldn't touch the other in a million years—for all the illegal settlement. At least, some nomads had fallen between the cracks of society.

Yes, the Negev could have been Nevada or, more accurately, Arizona. Because the old woman in traditional garb was really a Navajo. All of this was in actuality a replay of the American dream, the winning of the West. A slide show. Those ghostly gargantuan installations on the horizons could have been the nuclear power plants near Dimona, which was the closest city, a distance covered in two days by Moses in the canyon below one of the plants. Not forty miles as the vulture flies to Mamshit. In all of Africa, I'd seen "civilization's" stragglers. This apartness was not most apparent in South Africa. I remember well the segregated Maasai of Tanzania as they still retained their independence.

20

Sde Boker
or
Welcome to Sun City

"And the wastes shall be builded and the desolate land shall be tilled...and they shall say, this land that was desolate is become like the Garden of Eden." (Ezekiel 36:33-35)

"And the children of Israel...came into the Wilderness of Zin...and they assembled themselves against Moses...strove with Moses and spake, saying...why have ye brought the assembly of the Lord into this wilderness, that we should die here, we and the beasts. And wherefore have ye brought us out of Egypt to bring us into this evil place..." (Numbers 20:1-5)

I could never dream how close route 40 came to taking us to South Africa, even if the friendly Israelis who'd given us a lift in no way resembled our African rides. They were three or four young men, nice enough to let me out of the car and briefly survey the Nabatean city of Avdat above the Byzantine caves just off the road. A week or two later, I went into the canyon and ascended Avdat from the rear, employing again (when I should have been working) General Siva's approach to Massada. But more about that later.

Not a twenty-mile drive from the twilight zones, the road skirts an exhilarating canyon and the Ben-Gurion complex that looks out on the misted mesas. It was these archeological tabletops in the great banquet hall of Zin that drew the prime minister here to feast his eyes. Beyond the Institute for Desert Research were rows of vegetables, followed by the framing orchards of Sde Boker. I could not see or smell the immense chicken factory. Almost gone were the original "Cowboy Fields" (as Sde Boker is translated from the Hebrew) that had attracted the first pioneers to this unfriendly frontier. In his "hut" bordering on the kibbutz, we could see the pistol-packing prime minister's weapon—and compass—without which he never ventured very far.

I hoped we had arrived. Serendipity, it seemed, had never dealt us a better hand. I saw no options open to us beyond an uninviting Europe. We had spent a Siberian winter there a few years back, and I lose friends as easily as I make them. We were so determined to be accepted that we were credible recruits. I could forget the situation in Israel, but I could not forget the situation in the US and my own problems with the government...but that's another book. After Mitzpe Ramon, Mona was taken with this place with renewed hope in that old dream.

Brenda's office was beneath the chow hall. A personable PR type who hailed from Scotland, she could appreciate why we might be seeking a new life. Brenda said to become a member was a bit more complicated than just coming in out of the cold, since there was probation, et cetera. On the other hand, the persimmons had to be picked (there was a more forbidding reality in store for us), and who really gave a damn about formalities—this was the southwest. The driver, maybe in the spirit of his calculated cruelty, had said we were too old to become members, as candidates must be of child-bearing age. True or not, there were few retirees in this part of California that was a regular youth culture. Yet, as Brenda was quick to point out and I as quick to milk for all it was worth, the intellectual Ben-Gurion had tended his sheep here, and the gritty Zionist had a good twenty years over me.

And wasn't I an idealist, ready to write some PR stuff about Sde Boker, pap to persuade tourists to pay for the privilege of picking persimmons where the desert first bloomed. I would package the place as a health farm.

Brenda may have snickered, but I did have our Snir letter and had just given her the regards of an old comrade back at Kibbutz Shizafon. She was delighted with her catch. Mona and I were a couple of honeymooners being shown our cottage. A bowl of fruit beckoned to us on the coffee table, a TV that worked, and a spare room with gymnasium lockers that separated a mattress with its wonderful potential for workouts, from the kitchenette and the inspired bathroom doorway. This had been Tony's pad, distinguished from all others by the sign he had so proudly carved over the bathroom door. It read 4U2P. And what if you wanted to take a shit (SHIT), I later asked my namesake and childhood clone. A cozy patio, plants—and to top the whole thing off was the Israeli flag that fluttered from our roof. Talk about setting roots.

Tony was the volunteer overseer and not bad as South Africans go, or even as Tonys go. He was more a bore than a Boer. Yet, though we were not technically volunteers, we would be overseen by him night and day, since the South African's new pad was across from ours. If we were under surveillance, Tony treated us with a certain amount of deference. I think our age threw him for a loop, this husky youth who was apparently close to his parents. His father was a doctor in Cape Town, our destination when I was about Tony's age. I had, through some strange alchemy, gone back in time to the tip of South Africa. After traveling the length of Africa, I was no longer as broad as the Boer, but almost as blond. Tony was, of course, Jewish, as were most of our friends in Cape Town.

We joined the other pilgrims at Ben-Gurion's hut. There isn't that cult of personality in Israel that has George Washington sleeping about as indiscriminately as Don Juan, but Ben-Gurion is more than a distant father of the country, though shrunken to the size and value of a dollar bill. He lived stoically in the comfortable book lined home with enough memorabilia to make the hut the respectable museum that it is. A curious photograph shows Ben-Gurion in a fez, a de rigueur concession to Ottoman rule when he was a young man.

We befriended David, who knew Ben-Gurion and now looks after the hut. He also gave talks to the busloads of tourists that were always on hand. Today, most of the visitors were soldiers stretched out on the grass who listened to the caretaker reminisce about the almost mythic "prophet." As it turned out as despised as the Spinoza at the side of his bed amongst many of the kibbutzniks.

I cut across some of the cropland and made a valiant attempt to visit the futuristic Institute at the edge of the plateau. But my sense of esthetics got the best of me and I wasn't within a stone's throw of the center before I'd been driven into the gorge to mark the beginning of my love affair with the wilderness of Zin. But that's not entirely fair. It could have been worse, those buildings that are in back of the gravesites, but my eye is as fragile as the ecology.

That night we were introduced to a Californian, Richard, his Israeli wife and kids. They were watching TV when we stopped by for coffee. I don't know if Richard retained any of the idealism that brought him here, but I think the Israeli reality had left him sad and bitter, taking refuge in an inadequate irony.

I silently resisted an inexorable fate and could not really relate to the tall and lanky man. We shared more than disappointment with our countries, adopted or otherwise.

Rich had also undergone a stapedectomy. His earlier deafness had led to at least a part-time career in teaching handicapped children. Now he was a fruit picker, sometimes thinking about those wetbacks he'd seen back home.

In the morning we'd all be picking persimmons. This succulent was not among the crops listed in the booklet Brenda gave us. Nor was the new tape factory that put Sde Boker in the red. Most of the kibbutzim were in the red in more ways than one, but you said "communist" at your own peril.

On the walls of Richard's apartment were photographs of Blacks he had taken on a recent visit to New York. I would later wonder if this was a calculated attempt to appear integrated and shake the Sun City image, for it seemed Brenda was choosing our friends, and Mona had already gotten bad vibes from Richard's wife who was sullen, but otherwise attractive—too attractive to stay at Sde Boker any length of time. She worked in the kitchen, and who can blame anybody on mess duty for having a chip on their shoulder.

Sde Boker's biggest orchard is the peach, irrigated by the ancient Nabatean method, leveled terraces that catch runoff rain. Most likely, it was the peach trees that were cut down, because there were not enough pickers available. Help could have been bused in from Gaza, but this blooming desert was not for Bedouins. Rubin, an American member, said that to bring in the Arabs was to assent to the Arab's claim on the land. Of course, they would expect to be paid.

Potatoes are a large crop. One of the best photos I've seen of Israel is an aerial view of the cultivated land with the beautiful Nigal in the background, the much lower ground of Zin in dramatic juxtaposition to the peopled plateau. Made into a poster that reads "The kibbutz experience," it could also be titled California Dreamin' because there are no Bedouins or camels in this picture. It hung above Brenda's desk, and I wondered how many American volunteers had been hooked by that one in the sixties and early seventies. Judging by the response, it seems the poster's circulation is limited to the youth agencies of Northern Europe and South Africa. South America was sold on the idea of the West Bank. For Mona and me, California Dreamin' will always be that poster of an American rig in a French truck stop just south of Paris—in that winter of our discontent. Ah, it's never been all that bad.

A stunning autumn day with the sun on the horizon and the frost on the persimmon. Most of the fruit looked okay, but was supposedly damaged by last week's hail, and the bulk of this freckled orange succulent (only when very ripe) was meant for the insurance man. Still, it was necessary to pluck the fruit with special pruning shears, cutting the stem at the base of the persimmon so that a protruding stem would not damage the rest of the thin-skinned harvest when exported. This was confusing at first, since the idea with the Golan avocado was to leave the stem intact. But Snir was fast becoming a dream.

It wasn't until I had a few buckets under my belt at about eight o'clock, when the sun was at a more generous angle and my arthritic fingers were thawing, as the icing on the cake was melting, that Jack be nimble, Jack be quick, I could have jumped over a candlestick. I'm always gung ho on opening day so that nobody is suspicious when I take sick and disappear later in the week. Of course, I couldn't be too fast when every other ripe persimmon went into my mouth. A chubby American member, Sfen, said they had had to open one guy's stomach because he'd stuffed himself and his intestines would not pass this fruit with very strange chemical properties. I could imagine the ingestion of too many ripe persimmons would have the opposite effect.

It was easy to justify removing my nose from the grindstone, when we both would have been more in character helping out the Sandanistas. If I wasn't already an anti-Zionist, Rubin got my Irish up the very first day when he joked about sending poisoned persimmons to the Sandanistas. Obviously, he was anti-communist. If a kibbutznik wasn't Red, Rubin was at least ruby.

The volunteers who knew where their bread was buttered buttressed Rubin with laughter. They seconded the motion. As one English boy said, "It's good coming to a kibbutz. We can eat again."

For some of these dubious Byrons who came here via Greece, Israel was indeed the Promised Land. They were promised nothing, and they got nothing beyond food and cigarette money and maybe something left over for a bottle. In Greece, in lieu of drachmas, they were left holding the bag. I'm not sure if they even got food for their labors.

This type of rip-off was rare among grape pickers in France. Wherever. The British are an enterprising bunch and as long as they have enough blood corpuscles running through their veins to pass for plasma, they'll get by. One bloody waif who was caught short in Greece about fifteen years ago actually returned to Britain on a pint of blood, which I believe he had sold for twenty dollars. Talk about blood money.

Stranger things were to happen in this very strange society. I have said that I wish I could desist from reporting (using the word loosely) the incredible facts. It's so much easier to be facile, but truth has always been my downfall. The most shady of the English volunteers who proudly wore his Sun City t-shirt kept apart from the Kafirs of his own color. Sun City is after my time, but it seemed that in all those dark places of the world, it has always been more a question of caste than color. Blacks may one day have equality, but there will always be the economical "nigger"—and those of us beyond the pale every government's victim. In the USA, South Africa and Israel, we are in a no-man's land—an Animal Farm.

To the editor of the Jerusalem Post:

Sir, It is incredible that at a time when the whole world is moving away from relations with South Africa, a delegation of Israeli municipal officials should venture forth on a mission ostensibly to study the manner in which municipalities operate in South Africa. Why South Africa? Why should Israeli municipalities want to study a system of government which practices institutionalized racism and is among the most oppressive in the world? How will such a study benefit the people of Israel? Does Israel consider emulating South Africa? Will they also study the operations of the Community Council's vigilantes and the violence and mayhem they wreak on the people whom they allegedly govern?

Tel Aviv...Esther Levitan

But who was studying who?

Alon, also from South Africa, had been here for sometime and was in charge of agriculture, the overseer of overseers. There seemed to be total acceptance of this arrangement on the part of the British. All in a day's work.

I said to one kid that he looked like he might be more at home working in Nicaragua.

"Nicaragua, are you bloody mad?"

Was it that this caste or class of Englishman, unlike the Germans, simply couldn't afford to go to Nicaragua, or was it that the German youth were more idealistic? At least one Englishman answered that question. There were no Germans here.

Rubin also looked like the kind of guy who would have helped the Sandanistas at another time. If they existed twenty years ago. But then, he said he loved Israel because he didn't have to worry what his gentile neighbors thought. Was he serious? Mona never felt this way. Was he justifying his defection by saying he could only feel at home here, because Rubin from Long Island was just too hip. Hypocritical and had something of Babylon about him like that other gerrymandering-Rubin, a self-confessed masturbator whose revolution was skin-deep. He wore body paint on his way to the brokerage house. Don't all revolutions end there?

I agonized over Richard's raison d'etre. As we picked the persimmons, we kicked Rubin's remark around. Richard claimed he was unaware that there were international work brigades who assisted the Sandanistas. "You mean, like during the Spanish Civil War?" he asked.

I guess there aren't too many Americans who know that foreigners of all ages were harvesting the coffee beans at their own peril. I hoped that bringing up the Spanish Civil War and all that conjured up about the Lincoln Brigade and the Jewish volunteers involved in that noble struggle for democracy was a subtle way of telling me where his sympathies lay.

Richard could have been another Linden who was murdered by the Contras while working on an engineering project. Linden, also Jewish and a little younger than Richard, would have preferred putting his idealism to work in a just Israel. Could such a Jew survive east of Tel Aviv? If Richard's pain was political he was being torn between tribal loyalty with today's diseased dictates and that universal sense of justice he imbibed with his mother's milk but could not satisfy.

Of course, that was probably a lot of crap. Richard dismissed idealists as "communists" in that tone we reserved for rapists. His contempt was as sad as ludicrous when one considers what a kibbutz is. I hoped this party line was for Rubin's consumption—maybe a way of feeling me out, though I tried to avoid rocking the boat to keep afloat this winter. I had to keep cool, so I didn't blink when he answered my question about the six-day workweek.

"You get used to it."

At least he didn't tell me that he liked it.

Sfen was the most obvious joker amongst the American Israelis and his lack of subtlety almost had disastrous consequences. I guess it was the third day in the orchard when we were sitting around a pile of our pickings, polishing the persimmons and culling the "exportables" from the less than "excellent." Sfen lost control of his forklift and ploughed into us. Luckily, the crates that were stacked up like a kind of stockade took the brunt of the bulldozing, but I had to help free a volunteer from her pinned coat. Sfen was more shaken by the accident than anybody else, but the "defective" forklift reflected a fuck-you attitude that Fodor Guide apologetically puts forth as macho.

Sfen was a nice enough guy, but he was more moron than macho and, like the rest of the Israelis, driven to distraction. He helped me to pull the girl out of her coat before the lift moved any further and Alon cursed Sfen. Sfen gave the effete South African tit for tat and placed all the blame on the forklift. The conversation became more animated, but the girl who was now free of her coat shrugged off her near mutilation with "This kind of thing is always happening to me."

I didn't need any more encouragement to get back up into a tree. With that extra surge of adrenalin, the persimmons came into a more flattering focus. At the moment I couldn't recall seeing these luscious works of art outside of a famous Chinese ink on paper entitled "The Persimmons." It is a somewhat somber abstraction for so lush and lively a fruit that is freckled by a smiling sun to the hue of a setting sun.

That night, the Shabbat eve, we'd been assigned to sit at the same table as Alon and his wife from California. I wondered if it was the political climate or the weather that had brought these people to a place so much like home. Alon even had a touch of Hollywood about him, if you can picture a mincing Paul Newman. The South African looked like the actor, but there was something affected about his walk and that strong and silent style that was just a little pathetic. Imagine a consumptive Newman exuding a kind of English ennui. Yet in all fairness to the man, I think the decadent aura about Alon was as much a physical characteristic as it was a personality disorder. Symptomatic or caused by the contaminated air that he breathed as he worked with an indiscriminate amount of toxic insecticides and fertilizer. We were studiously ignored by this odd couple.

Maybe it's because the old surfer can't get by without making waves. I had already complained about the school children who were bused in from Beersheba for the persimmon harvest and trampled all the bottom branches that were laden with fruit. I suggested a more effective way of reaping the trees. Obviously, any advice coming from a cotton-picking character like me didn't sit too well with Alon.

Mona and I were seated across from his more responsive Cape Town cousin, and he was drinking as much wine as I. Enough for me to wax nostalgic over Table Top Mountain and its cloth of cloud forever slipping off this most picturesque of plateaus shaped by two oceans.

Unassuming cousin on an extended holiday was now the kibbutz dentist and the most engaging driller I'd met anywhere in the world, including India, where the wrong tooth was treated with a manual or foot operated drill, no less. We discussed what stress was doing to my teeth and how I had just lost a filling in Turkey, and would he please peer into my Dark Hole of Calcutta—on company time, of course. With pleasure, he said, but I would have to make the appointment with Alon's wife, who promptly and illegally denied me treatment. She retained some of her capitalistic beliefs.

I went into the canyon Saturday and Sunday. I just can't get used to working on Sunday. Sunday is my youth, my day off, our day in the park when we lived in New York. However, Mona opted for persimmons this Sunday.

I went to the orchards with her (does this sound like Chekhov by any chance), as usual in the "cattle car," which is really something out of Tolstoy. The chassis was rigged with benches and towed by a tractor. The early morning breeze was biting, but a never more contented serf had something up his sleeve.

When we broke for coffee, I complained about diarrhea, which nobody who had observed my eating habits could doubt, and slinked off into the desert like an injured fox. Nobody was suspicious about the canteen hanging from my side either, since I disdained drinking from the unsanitary plastic water jugs.

Nor did I appreciate the absence of cups when I put away more water than wine. Richard was amazed by this aberrant imbibing. "You drink water in the winter?" The water reeked of plastic no less.

By ten o'clock, it was light sweater weather. The pockets of the Air Force jacket issued to me when we checked in were stuffed with what I hoped were enough provisions to see me through a frigid night, should it ever come to that. Slung over my shoulder as I traversed barbed wire and green crops, my jacket made a convenient backpack, until I simply let the hood hang from my head.

In twenty minutes I was beyond the "experimental farms" and landing strip and fast approaching the upright railway tracks that are strange but starkly beautiful totems celebrating Nahal Tsin. The Wilderness of Zin. Picasso couldn't have more artfully marked his way to the canyon trail, and I must say never has a guidepost been less obtrusive and maybe even enhanced by nature's design. Not too many other times have I set out on an adventure more buoyantly, boyishly, a happy hobo who rode the rails rooted in the canyon's rim. One needs inspiration, instinct, to get by, because there was nothing marking the way down or up except the Picasso-esque totems at the plateau's edge as the trail petered out.

More rain the night before left in its wake the sea-like sweep of the wadi. Like a pristine beach at low tide was the desert's debris of driftwood and uprooted reeds, bulrushes, overturned rocks, even shells, including Bedouin clothes washed away in the flashflood. Continuing up the wadi and below the field school, I discovered the water-warped passport of a Dutch girl under a layer of silt, her peeling photo barely intact.

The wadi, rippled and rolled smooth like a Japanese rock garden in places, froze my footfall. Nature had created a clean slate, and I would not disturb this sea of tranquility in miniature. However, further on, I could not help myself. Before me, fashioned by time and circumstance, lay an early Picasso, a head with Black African lips. An ancient-modern sandstone that I put aside to retrieve on my return. I took a good hard look at my surroundings and my position to the barely visible tracks that stood on air (actually upended rails that became artistic markers for the trailhead) and my way out of here. Rarely do I backtrack, with the devil taking the hindmost, but I did want to take back this piece of desert sculpture.

I followed the ancient watercourse away from the field school and considered the fate of the Dutch girl who had lost her passport. It had a recent issue date. Had she come here to work at the kibbutz? Had she survived the flood? Just a few hours ago, the raging torrent would have been a few feet above my head. Pools of clear water remained from the flood that had inundated and swept away the toppled tamarinds much taller than myself.

Near the waterfall off the trail to Avdat, I found a flowered skirt. These clothes were little better than rags, but they were somebody's wardrobe. I was thrilled that somewhere in this canyon nomads had survived the military juggernaut. What to do if I ran into them?

Alisha, a lively but laid back member who had offered me his detailed map, had assured me that I would come to no harm if I showed no fear. "Never let them know you are lost. Make them think you belong wherever you are."

I remembered running into a Masai warrior at the bottom of the Ngorongoro Crater, who laughed when I materialized out of the bush. This day I looked a lot more ridiculous, so not to worry. If God looks after the fool, it's because he incapacitates potential enemies with laughter. I had a lot in common with Jewish comedians. Though as a spaced-out traveler, I am less a comic than cosmic. And that's not meant to be funny.

The sun was so warm and bright in its ascendance that it was difficult to imagine that, if only for a minute, the wadi had been a raging river. But it made the world of difference between the canyon and the upper desert. The difference between the engaged psyche and the hardscrabble surface of everyday life. It's in the exposed depths that we find the color and continuity that the plateau with its cultivated lines lacks. All is a bland desert without those streams of consciousness that nurture the Nahal of our existence.

Wadi way to go.

21

Off the Wall
or
Guess Who Came to the Ben-Gurion Centennial

I turned the Dutch passport over to Brenda. Damaged as it was, it would fetch a pretty shekel on the black market, but I assumed it would reach the proper authorities. She did not know the owner but said she might be able to do something the following day when she went just down the road to the Ben-Gurion celebration.

"Oh, Brenda," I said, "think of the mileage a travel writer can get out of this event. And I can use the holiday."

"It's not a holiday. We have to work here, but I'll be representing the kibbutz."

She did think it was a good idea that I accompany her, however, and I was excused from work.

Ben-Gurion died on December 1, 1973. He had been born October 16, 1886, and we would go to this memorial on December 1, 1986. In the morning, Brenda stood at the Sde Boker bus stop cradling a bouquet of flowers. With her was a young man from the kibbutz. They were the Sde Boker delegation and paying their respects with flowers, as more important representatives would honor Zion's lion with flowery words and store-bought wreaths.

Brenda's bouquet didn't meet the specifications of the ceremony. The man who had eschewed formality could only be honored with a regulation wreath fit with a stand. And so, Brenda and the young man disappeared with the official in charge of the wreath laying. This gave me an opportunity to wander about the gravesites of Ben-Gurion and his wife Paula. Simple slabs of stone.

As an international cemetery buff, everywhere from Russian to pre-Columbian, I can say with some authority that no other burial ground opens on a more dramatic panorama. In back of the twin graves was a whitewashed building that almost takes fight, a place to be launched into the hereafter. A small semicircle of bleachers looked on the burial site and the Nahal gorge beyond. To be visually carried such a grand distance speaks much more of a sunny cremation than sepulchral gloom. Such a place, this promontory, has the promise of eternity. The only Promised Land.

On the south side of the memorial park were mostly green grounds. Some of the irrigated grass was not unlike Ben-Gurion's little sheep meadow that Richard contemptuously dismissed as a publicity stunt.

I let myself get lost in a mixed crowd of celebrants who listened to the expected eulogies. Each speech was punctuated by representatives of the various organizations present placing their wreath at the foot of Ben-Gurion's final resting place. All of this Hebrew wasn't going down very well with me, until Sde Boker was called and I felt I belonged, as Brenda laid her newly acquired regulation wreath alongside the others.

Sde Boker had really become something special to me. Thanks to David—also the prime minister's first name—Ben-Gurion had become more than a disembodied shock of white hair. The caretaker had some books about Ben-Gurion, the only literature on the kibbutz about the man being honored. Even with allowances for apocrypha, I had begun to see why kibbutzniks were hostile to the Prophet of Zion. One of his biographers, Robert St. John, wrote, "To him the people of the Bible are not dusty historical characters...he knows them better than he knows most of the ministers in his last cabinet." He was always speaking about the redemption of the people and the land, quoted now in the speakers' notes. Language was no barrier when an Israeli soldier sang a stirring song that left me close to tears.

Ever mindful of an opportunity to hike, I stayed lost and gravitated back to the gravesite when most of the crowd had melted away and I presumed Brenda gone. As jubilant as a boy before the Grand Canyon was Congressman Art with his aide, before eternity posing for posterity. Or was Art a Senator. I don't recall the tag. Anyway, he would have a nice photo for his constituents.

There was talk about the dedication of a wall. It was for the benefit of the international high rollers, many of them Americans who had been helicoptered out to the kibbutz landing strip and chauffeured to the ceremony. I thought I heard the booming voice of Shimon Peres. Anxious to hear what was being said, I walked up a small flight of steps to the side of a memorial building and eyed the blue-ribbon audience curiously.

Neither Ben-Gurion nor I went in for frills, and the canteen that hung from my belt was the epitome of desert informality—and my Boy Scout preparedness (in winter no less). If that wasn't suspect, my Amnesty International look and those gentle but accusing eyes were offset by a bombardier jacket.

A concerned policeman who wondered what kind of mission I was on tapped my canteen to determine if I carried anything stronger than water. Satisfied I must be a thirsty son of a bitch, he asked for my passport. "What's this, you got your passport in Turkey?" he asked in a tone as accusatory as interrogative, as if I had a part in the recent bombing of the Istanbul synagogue.

It was of no consequence that Turkey was an important ally of Israel. I now realized how peripheral I was to this inner circle into which I had wandered. Being the only Original Hebrew here, uncircumcised pecker not withstanding, I was being persecuted for my originality. In Third World situations like this, I usually cry out for the American Consul, but he was probably sitting a few feet away mumbling, "Throw the bum out."

I stood my ground and my voice rose with every syllable as I asserted, "I'm an American journalist." I felt silly about the declaration but silently cursed the unoriginal scribebags their politically correct stories. Any Reaganite who sat in the makeshift stands would have sooner thought me the resurrected Che Guevara than a card-carrying journalist. It was with a mind towards any untoward interrogation that I had brought along my Turkish letter of recommendation that I now flourished like the Magna Carta.

Now more suspicious, the policeman asked me, "How long were you in Turkey. Why did you buy your passport in Turkey?"

"My other passport expired."

The American Consulate in Izmir, Turkey, wasn't exactly the black market, but I was just too unkosher a product to pass inspection, and I was whisked away from the assembly-line personages to be questioned by a cop better versed in such matters. "Where is your pass, your tag?"

I'd gotten so strongly into my journalist shtick, with the post-traumatic stress of ancient arrests, I'd almost forgotten I was a quasi delegate from Sde Boker. We had been admitted to the gravesite with no questions asked, carried along with Brenda's flowers. I said I came here with Brenda and that I worked for Sde Boker.

"Brenda? Brenda who? You're from Sde Boker?"

I'd gone from being an unlikely journalist to a dubious kibbutznik, and the policemen wondered which was my more outlandish claim. Both were totally off-the-wall.

Meanwhile, plaques were being affixed to the wall that bore the names of rich South Africans and Canadians who were mostly from Montreal and had contributed substantially to the Ben-Gurion Institute. In appearance like a handball court, the dedication wall nevertheless hinted at the foundation of the first temple, symbol of a failed dream.

An inscription that quoted Ben-Gurion read that Israel would be remembered for its morality, rather than its scientific achievements. But even Israel could not produce enough whitewash to pull that off. One day soon flashfloods would be borne of the Arabs' pent-up rage, like the winter rains filling every wadi in the land.

I caught enough of Peres' speech to get the general drift, the Ben-Gurion dream of the desert blooming realized. At a great cost in lives and money a patch of green had been maintained, but the real stakes were with the soldiers and one of the most destructive crops of weapons the wilderness has ever known. Even the less destructive armored vehicles left terrible scars on the canyon floor and set the stage for a situation as bizarre as it is symbolic.

With the forced exodus of the Bedouins and their camels, a major source of food for buzzards when death stalks the dromedary, the prized birds have gone hungry. It took a lot of meat to keep that seven-foot span of wings flapping, and now it is only through the largesse of the field school that the desert sentinels get their fill. Food is brought to their favorite perch above the canyon, but it seems there is more a blight than a bloom on the land when vultures go hungry—as well as the indigenous inhabitants who must fend for themselves.

Airborne, the great scavengers are a marvelous sight as they glide on unseen currents, the equal of any creature in God's eyes. I was somewhat incredulous about the Israelis' affection for these gargoyles atop the cathedral of Zin devouring their sacrificial animals. A good three miles northeast of the kibbutz, I once got within a few feet of one of the birds perched on a ledge. He opened his wings and was aloft, as effortless as any phoenix rising.

Page two of Tuesday's Jerusalem Post showed Prime Minister Shamir's affected frown as he laid a wreath during the memorial ceremony. Under the photo, President Herzog, who was also present at the Centennial, was quoted as saying, "Peaceful coexistence between Jews and Arabs as Ben-Gurion envisioned it is vital" to Israel. Lest any right-winger making an association get the wrong idea, the following week the Jerusalem Post showed Prime Minister Shamir, as he grinned from ear to ear and aimed his Uzi at some not-so-hard-to-imagine enemy at the new Herzliya shooting range. The cute caption read, "The weak won't be harmed." Though admittedly, "We are not zealots for egalitarianism." Would that they were.

A Ben-Gurion celebrant, Yitzhak Rabin, former and future Prime Minister of Israel and Nobel Peace Prize winner, was soon to be assassinated by a right-wing Israeli whose light prison sentence spoke to the government's true intention regarding peace.

22

In the Wilderness of Zin

As I left the din of inequity, I was out, or rather, inward bound. However, a busload of children beat me into the canyon. Oh, these all pervasive precocious ones had me wondering if all these group activities were meant to instill a sense of camaraderie, safety in numbers for the future band of brothers. As my gorge rose before this flashflood of humanity (another bus was on the way), I sought the high ground, dismayed that this desert was made familiar and turned into a communal experience and was preparing the youth for less playful excursions into the wilderness in their later years. Always uncomfortable and fearful, they occupied the people who were the living spirit and extension of the land. The desert.

Above the first waterfall are Byzantine caves that look down on a stream fed by the higher second cascade. This lush pocket of trees and shrubs is a hidden paradise that at one time must have been Nabatean and unknown to the Romans. Later a ravine of recluses, it was one of the more curious surprises the desert would unveil with a little searching out. I had to overcome some fear before I ventured out on an ill-defined path, actually a ledge that led to one or two of the caves, an earthen door opening on Capodoccia and much of Asia once occupied by the Spartan aesthetes. Monks in retreat from civilization who sought the solitude that could reveal God—if you didn't plunge into the valley below first. Were the anchorites like anchors hauled up to their hermitages, or were they more athletic than I. My God, how many thousands of men gave up all for their God in those first centuries following the Messianic message.

Obviously, there was something beyond words in all this. A remarkable faith that allowed oneness with the elements, the elementary that would endure and be rekindled in a Saint Francis. And didn't yours truly, if I may name drop, spend some time at the Carceri.

I looked out an earthen window on the dark shadows that filled the canyon, as a more obtrusive invasion was underway above me. Like the rock badger, I emerged from my hole and incredibly watched women in Gypsy shoes and the most pedestrian clothing with entire families climb down the ladders hacked out of the cliff. This was the only way out of the canyon, unless a basket was lowered or I backtracked. So patiently, I observed the painfully slow descent until I feared I'd have to spend the night here in a cave and tried to go up the down staircase and probably bump into Erma Bombeck herself.

"What's your hurry?" a member of the tour cried out. "Wait your turn."

About a mile south of the parking lot, in the direction of Avdat, I stumbled upon a Bedouin encampment. The tent appeared empty with cooking utensils carelessly lying about and was nestled amongst tilled but tired mounds of earth. There were signs of a pickup truck that would truck the produce out of here. I strained to see inside the darkened tent, but only the pots and kettles spoke of recent habitation, which was good enough for me. As long as I didn't hear barking, I was happy, though I really didn't know what to expect from the Bedouin.

I wasted no time climbing a ridge, from which I spied the ruins of Avdat and the surreal stacks of Mizpe Ramon beyond. Here and there, I could see pockets of cultivated earth of illegal farms irrigated by rainwater alone. Adding insult to the injury of this concealed cultivation the Israelis claim that this ancient method of farming, thought to be "mythical was borne out by their experiments at Sde Boker." Public relations notwithstanding, it seemed the desert has been blooming since time immemorial. Or at least since the advent of Avdat, or Abdah, named for the Nabatean King Obodas.

I remained on the high ground and had managed to avoid the road and the ticket booth. I now peered into the ancient city's incredible cistern. That perennial center of desert life, the artificial oasis that was your original piazza, endured through Byzantine times. Eventually, Christianity destroyed something that could never be replaced. The Nabateans lost their art of pottery making and writing script and ultimately lost their essence. But in its heyday, Avdat was a great way station for travelers journeying to the east.

The remains of a substantial church faced west. Below it are caves that, from the road on the first day when I passed this way, looked like any old holes in the wall, but upon closer inspection took me inside the head of an early Christian. I had to step down into a cave and found that my way was lit all the way to the rear of this abode of Abdah. Caved out of the earth was a kind of bench. As I sat in the bowels of the city for a glorious five minutes, I was bathed in sunlight, Sistine. Evidently, the caves had been shaped with an eye towards the setting sun, a desirable thirty-degree angle that brought warmth with light and solar energy that converted a cave into a chapel. The light was as spiritual as it was utilitarian.

I didn't have much time before dark. Thumb extended, I jogged along the road, Sde Boker bound. Two boys and four camels passed me heading for their encampment. So much for the Bedouin pickup truck and the million miles that separated the two cultures that shared this bit of desert and their reasons for being there. Within a few minutes, a friendly Israeli and his daughter were driving me to the gate of the kibbutz.

Militaristic societies produce few loners. Only once did I see less than a busload of people in Zin and they were never far from the road. So I was surprised the following Saturday when I encountered three teenage boys miles from the Ben-Gurion complex. I was scrambling down the crumbling wall of the canyon in another race against the encroaching darkness when one of the boys called out to me. It was late and I was returning to the kibbutz and left no doubts that I was a man in a hurry. Of purpose.

I thought it strange that one of this trio shouted, "Are you lost?"

I looked up at the questioner and shouted that I was not.

But the young man was insistent and with some urgency warned I was going back the wrong way.

"But I came this way," I said.

"We know a short way. It will be dark before you return if you go that way and you'll get lost."

They were learning to be guides at the field school and said they knew the desert well. One young man had a two-way radio, and I thought, why not go back with these guys. I wanted to go back a different way anyway. Earlier, I had tried to trail blaze and headed in the general direction of the field school. But I finally decided to go back the way I had come when it looked like I was going into a cul de sac.

They would not admit it in a million years, but it was soon apparent the intrepid trio was lost and, like misery, wanted some adult company. Especially since we had to skirt the Bedouin camp and the two idle men on the ridge above us could have posed a threat. As an adult accompanying high school students, the chances were I was armed and my presence guaranteed safe passage.

The youngest boy reminded me of myself and blurted out what happened to his parents' car when they were here a couple of weeks ago. He caught himself painting a less than idyllic picture of Bedouin acceptance of their condition and quickly changed the subject.

Little news came out of the Negev, and how would it sound that displaced Bedouins showed their displeasure by smashing windows? Admittance of imperfection was unpatriotic. Nor could the young Spartans show fear. Under the averted eyes of the Bedouins, the boys charged down a gully letting out war whoops that fell somewhat short of blood curdling.

I remembered climbing up the Ngorongoro crater at nightfall with two Maasai warriors who insisted on accompanying me because they really feared for my safety. The Maasai who were hardly older than these boys coughed and grunted like lions, claiming this would hold the nocturnal cats at bay. It is likely that imitating lions bolstered their courage. It did little for mine.

I didn't get into the act now, but in the wake of the sinking sun, adrenalin, following the most splendorous light, felt rapid cooling of the desert and my own crystallization.

Up and down we went, without benefit of compass, if I recall correctly.

The youngest boy asked me how I was doing, and I could honestly say it was the closest I came to social climbing. This engaging lad, my alter ego, inquired if I was an explorer. I told him I wouldn't go that far, but on the other hand, I'd gone much further.

As we raced the receding light, the boy pointed to desert flora, exotic bushes and shrubs and explained their properties. Was he going to be a guide? No, this was just a course he was taking.

It was already dark when we reached the bottom of the canyon, and one of the boys radioed our position. Awaiting the arrival of the jeep, we spotted some girls heading our way, who we were soon picking up and checking off the driver's list. Like everybody else, I should have registered before going into the canyon, but that would have meant going a couple of miles out of my way.

In a few minutes we were at the field school, and I fended for myself and wended my way through the blackened fields, not unlike a blind drunk, a half moon for a lantern.

But what was this fire lighting the fields before me, raucous laughter, rumdum welcome. Hadn't I heard something about the volunteers having a barbeque? I was near the volunteers' shacks and the perimeter of barbed wire. Dumbstruck myself, I had a little adjustment to make.

On many mornings this seemed like the wilderness of din, an infernal noise coming from the canyon that sounded like an airport. But by the time I would arrive at the edge of the abyss, all was bliss. The buzzards had been fed, and I was following one trail or another that was reclaimed by nature before I got very far.

Today, I was following a wadi in the direction of the railroad, and by early afternoon my meandering had taken me to a low mesa. The tell (tel) tale circles of stones were Mosaic in the most literal sense. High enough above the wadi, unwashed and untouched by periodic flooding, were almost intact pages from the Bible. Up ahead, I could see a factory, one diabolical works or another. Impelled to return to the kibbutz, I took a trail that seemed to lead out of the canyon. Trial and error took me into a gorge that I prayed would wend its way up to a ridge within my reach.

Climbing up what had to be the most spectacular cascades a few days earlier, I vaulted polished boulders, bolted up vaults of geologic treasure, illogic measure. Why? A solitary boulder at the edge of the sand lot across the street from where I lived in Queens, left by a receding glacier—a gift I cherished and climbed, reinforcing my yang until life's yin wore me down, as it did these smoothly sculpted boulders I scrambled over.

I knew there was a jeep track that skirted the rim of the plateau, but where was the edge? I was like a drunken boat riding the waves, mounting a ridge only to plunge into another ravine and laboriously climb back up the crumbling earth until, eureka, terra firma.

In my race against the sun, I was beginning to panic a little when a gazelle sprinted before me and a few seconds later was pursued by a wolf.

I was told later that what I saw was highly improbable, yet less improbable than my life.

In any case, these magic moments dispel panic, though I might have considered what could have been my fate had I injured my ankle, and the wolf who eventually gave up on the gazelle tracked less nimble footed prey, as unlikely as that was. I was so grateful to be on the wretched road, but now I had to decide whether I would follow the longer route to Sde Boker, littered with an interminable number of fist-sized rocks, or try my luck by slipping under the barbed wire and see where the wadi that snaked in the direction of the kibbutz actually went. I didn't need any more surprises, but in fact didn't know what the jeep track had in store for me beyond stones.

In the morning I had walked along that track for about a mile, before going off the deep end. Still putting my faith in the least traveled path, I slid under the barbed wire and trusted that any Bedouins I might encounter would be the perfect host. There would be no idle kettles at this hour. By the time I was upon the water catchment site and the long abandoned arid tangle of vegetation, a silvery moon had become my main source of light. There was no more magical sight than the thorny bushes that marked my way. They were transformed into tiny Christmas trees by white snails that clung to them like adorning bulbs. They heralded the Christian holidays. I would have my white Christmas, after all.

Christmas was nostalgia and a long pagan link back to my past. The childhood joy of the Christmas trees arriving in Queens, "joy to the world," toys for the world, carols and, of course, the first snowfall—after "dreaming of a white Christmas." A year down the road, there was a pleasant nip in the air, a lone spruce decorated with falling leaves and a dusting of snow. It is my burning bush. It commands me to love. Nature and what is true. The memory it holds (without the tinsel), that old feeling, whether religions intended it, is what it's all about—beyond the obfuscation of nation, temple and church.

23

Sticky Wicket

Within a week, with the help of the school children recruited for that purpose, we completed the persimmon harvest. Brenda's real interest in me was then apparent. The tape factory needed a man for the four a.m. shift, four to twelve. Placing more pressure on Tony, the South African who worked in the factory, was the fact that he had just lost a Finnish boy to the hospital. A two-ton roll of tape from Taiwan that was waiting to be transformed into countless rolls of Scotch imitations had fallen on the boy's legs.

Unsure of my reporting time, I came to work a few hours late, complaining to my boss about this little surprise that had been sprung on me. My phlegmatic friend was apologetic. His buddy had gone to the States for a couple of months, and he was now working 25 hours a day, sort of filling in for him. He needed me. I indicated my aversion to noise, plainly obvious, and the impossibility of keeping up with the conveyor belt. My job was to cull defective tapes from the line, give them a patch-up job, and stack them in the corner with the manual forklift.

Tony S.A. gave me earmuffs to muffle the racket, but it wasn't that effective and I found myself starring in another Jackie Gleason skit. I tried to explain to him that I was an idiot-savant, and patching up pseudo Scotch tape bound for Patchogue, or was it Babylon, Long Island, was crap beyond my capacity. I was, after all, a writer. He bought that and had me paint the sides of the platforms the forklifts slipped under.

If I was a kibbutz misfit and Tony was over tolerant of my shortcomings, Mona was now working in the laundry and to Sde Boker born. Mona made me worth their while, at least for the time being, and Tony got me a job pruning.

Such a peaceful occupation sounded ideal, but Israeli ingenuity had transformed what I hoped to be soothing work into a nerve-wracking pursuit that had me climbing bare-limbed trees. The saws and shears were power operated and plugged into a generator that was hauled by a tractor every few trees and was my idea of an arboreal nightmare. Forget the laborial. Alon by now bordered on the homocidal and tried to make me as miserable as possible, though piling up the pruned branches and making them accessible to the tractor that would cart them away wasn't all that bad. But this barbaric assault of the trees wasn't even cost effective.

Assisting me in the cleaning up operation was a stereotypic cockney, a street urchin of the first order who Alon liked to bait. This other South African would ask of the retarded lad what he did in England. It was a question many members put to him and to which he replied, "I was a cinematic engineer." The joke was for this unschooled unfortunate to explain that he actually operated a movie projector.

He bad mouthed Tony S.A. and was only too happy to fill me in on the barbeque the other night. "He made a damn fool of himself. Drunk! Never saw anybody so drunk. Threw up in the toilet."

I could only tolerate a day or two of this and was again badgering Tony S.A. for a more suitable job.

He felt terrible about the injury the Finnish boy had sustained and blamed himself. "The kid was in this great pain, his legs were crushed, I don't know if he'll ever walk again. All he could think about was that he would be forced to leave the kibbutz." Tony had already made several visits to the hospital in Beersheba and said, "I don't want these kids to think this place is a prison. You want to write, okay, see if you can do something with this." He gave me the information and indoctrination sheets and said, "Humanize this."

Putting a Madison Avenue twist on things wasn't what the kibbutz needed. Most of these kids didn't feel like they were in prison, but they had been conditioned to feel like they were volunteering for the military. Like boot camp, the kibbutz demanded you go the distance. The work clothes issued were a kind of uniform, and the esprit de corps of volunteers breached no failure. So desperate to remain on the kibbutz, the boy was like the soldier who tried to prove himself at the front lines. He got his Purple Heart, but to return home before he honored his contract was like shooting himself in the foot.

A guy I knew who couldn't complete boot camp considered shooting himself in the head. To many of the non-English-speaking kids, the kibbutz was a challenge not unlike the Krishna cult, which at least in Italy appealed to the novice's sense of macho. When I tried to leave the cult that, believe it or not, was housed in Machiavelli's former palace outside Florence, a Krishna kid accused me of cowardice. Here I was old enough to be this punk's father, and he taunted me about not having the stomach to stick it out. "And what are you going to do, go back to fornicating and drinking?"

Page three of the information sheet read:

Drugs. Drugs are forbidden. It is kibbutz policy to turn over to the police any person or persons involved with drugs. Work. Volunteers work eight hours, six days a week. The kibbutz can ask a volunteer to work on a Saturday. Status. As a volunteer conform to rules...if you remain for 4 months you are entitled to a new shirt and underwear. After six months you receive a shirt, pair of trousers and pair of shoes. After one year on the kibbutz, your status will be brought up for renewal or change....Leaving the kibbutz: When you decide to leave, you must obtain the signatures of people in charge of the store, laundry, library, and office. Only then will the treasurer pay you money due you. You must return work clothes, boots, bedding, library books, and collect valuables from the safe.

We hope you enjoy your stay with us!

It was agreed I would humanize the information sheet on company time and forthwith is my Zin inspired alteration:

Shalom (there wasn't so much as a shalom in Tony's version). Welcome to Sde Boker. We are pleased to have you as our guests and will make every effort to see that your work-holiday here is as pleasant as possible.

Exactly what is a kibbutz, you may ask. In these times of great transition the answer to that question is open to debate. A paradise it is not. "The Cowboy Fields" is not a scene out of "Dallas" either. If Sde Boker is not a deluxe hotel, we do make available to you all the amenities of a health farm. Free! (I wanted to be one up on Tony S.A.) Fresh air, though you must take the necessary precautions in a desert climate, and a wide range of outdoor activities....Just outside our backdoor is the gateway... kaleidoscopic canyon that is home to leopard, ibex...spawning ground for the world's great religions. This is truly God's country...but if you can't get high on the scenery, back at the kibbutz there is a volunteers' bar open on designated nights. Moderation is the word.

We trust the diversions we provide will cushion the culture shock of living in an Israel so buffeted by the winds of fate. If some of us seem to have gotten up on the wrong side of the bed, and often after only a few hours of sleep, we also write from right to left. To you that may seem backwards, so we ask you to put yourself in our shoes and meet us halfway—it takes two to tango. Accept our limitations and we'll try to accept you with all your imperfections and together we can work towards making this a better kibbutz.

We are open to new ideas (I gagged on that one). Use the suggestion box in the liaison's office. Thanking you in advance for your cooperation, Tony (of South Africa—actually, Tony from Queens).

Blame it on nervous exhaustion, but my tongue was not entirely in my cheek. I still saw hope, but as things rapidly worsened, I decided that even an ex-copywriter could not participate in a whitewashing that is a page out of Fodor's. Politically okay. And it took me some time to produce this drivel, as I can't write when I'm on the road and I won't write when I'm close to nature. So I wrote a word for every mile I walked, pausing to jot down a word or two whenever a bolt of lightning illuminated my way, in the Wilderness of Zin. Guilty as sin.

In the interim, the kibbutzim were combating volunteer disaffection on another front. Posted on the bulletin board opposite Brenda's office was the copy of an article that appeared in a Beersheba periodical. It explained the differences between Israelis and non-Israelis, the misunderstanding that exists because of misinterpretation of the respective lifestyles: "Volunteers were really suffering from culture-shock. They think Israelis are rude and arrogant when they are actually justifiably proud."

I didn't understand how you could separate arrogance from pride, but the article went on, "...non-Israelis took offense because they were too formal. They should not be offended." Two columns compared Israeli characteristics with the more uptight non-Israeli traits. "Non-Israelis should not feel insulted if they are ignored." In other words, if nobody says hello to you, that's your non-Israeli problem. We never heard anybody say "excuse me," "ma," or whatever was the acceptable substitute. Fodor's Travel Guide made an issue of Israeli rudeness, offering line-jumping as an example, but this is par for the course in the Third World, the subway, and the least of Israel's pathologies. Actually, their curious behavior is out of this world: You are watching TV and a kibbutznik changes the channel without so much as a glance at you. This is the "pride" of America's south, a sharecropper compensating for his lousy station in life by taking out his frustration on the first "nigger" who comes along.

Kibbutzniks traffic in ambiguity, so that you don't know whether you are coming or going. Reinforcing the volunteer's insecurity and sense of inferiority, he or she reaches an impasse and remains on the kibbutz. But there is never any question about the kibbutzniks' contempt for the Arab. It is so unreasonable that it must be seen as a never articulated cry for help and was tearing Mona apart. Yet it brings Israelis together.

Sde Boker was a beginning for Mona. She forgets easily and was happy to be here. I hoped this would be her "roots" experience, that something that laid dormant in the States would find nourishment here. Give my wife an opportunity to move out of my shadow. We'd spent so much time together these last few months, and now we were pretty much going our separate ways. But what could have been an opportunity for the reaffirmation of her Jewishness...Mona's Diary:

Dec. 6th, Saturday. Felt strange to have breakfast with Richard and Alisha and not go along with them to the orchard. Beautiful weather. Cottage reminds us of Palm Beach. Very peaceful sitting in garden—secluded—good to be away from everyone, ideal place to rest and read. Tony C. says way of life on kibbutz not socialism but totalitarianism. Last night, volunteers sitting separate as usual from members—strange not sitting with them. Don't know where I belong here.

English language library a mess, books dusty. Member said only open half hour per week.

Dec. 8/9/10/11. Ironing all day. Tony refused to return to factory. Belgian lady invited us for coffee, as well as David and his Wife. Richard the only members house we've been to. Tony said kibbutzniks are quite ignorant, she said they don't have time to read. Go into army when young. Tony ironing in the laundry with me. Can't believe it. Last time he ironed something in the Navy. Letting everybody know what a waste this is. Thinks they're trying to humiliate him into returning to factory.

Dec. 13th, Saturday/14 Sunday. Friday night dinner with volunteers good change—good to be with gentiles—relaxing, being away from everyone. Brenda may change our rooms. Volunteer from north of England wearing his Sun City tee shirt. I was asked by David's wife if I was Jewish—again I seem to be more accepted when I say I'm Jewish. What a strange feeling—you're almost made to feel different and think about being separate from the "Christians." Never had this feeling in America or any other place (maybe South Africa, almost amounts to same thing—black and white, making you feel you are something rather special). It's a very uncomfortable feeling—always reading in the paper "the Christians, the Arabs." I wonder if they realize how unhealthy it is (of course, I try to think where they are coming from). Brenda sounded as if she took in two stray cats—I think I worked for everything I got here—there have been some restful days which I desperately needed.

Tony S.A. talks about bus to Bethlehem for Christmas. Hope we are still here.

Dec. 15th, Monday/16 Tuesday. "This is our home," they always say—Brenda said because of feedback she was getting we would have to leave—Alon & wife really belong back in S.A. Seems they are running show—Alisha didn't acknowledge our "hello" this morning & some people really making it uncomfortable for us—Brenda referred to Ben-Gurion as "right wing" hated kibbutz life & lived very much apart from it, although he was on premises. (Her response to Tony's charge that Sde Boker not living up to its reputation.)

It's good to be out of laundry today—think if I ironed another shirt I would go mad—Leontyne Price singing "Ave Maria" and girls in laundry lowered radio—don't think there is an ounce of culture in their life. I mean the members. Belgian woman (her daughter member) said they also would like to be in orchards, but not true. Tony referring to kibbutz life like Hare Krishna—getting up at 4:00 am—everything planned—no time to think—only about job. All Alon said to Tony yesterday was, what are your plans, when are you leaving? Tony said wants to be buried alongside Ben-Gurion.

Alex, Jewish, from Canada, volunteer, hope not so naïve to get caught up in this. Seems like Alon and few others really make decisions. Tony S.A. said he didn't know we had to leave. Tony C. says he wants to get out of Israel before he becomes anti...

Thank God for the enclosed garden, birds, trees.

Dec. 17th, Wednesday. Leaving Sde Boker this morning, but couldn't find Tony S.A. so read and relaxed. Will probably leave tomorrow—it's getting more and more uncomfortable eating in dining room—not talking.

Mona has been talking about the Holocaust, pogroms, and asking me why all the suffering has led to the oppression of others. And maybe that's the answer, a suffuse of suffering. But Mona wants a justification for the centuries of Jewish pain, there has to have been a good reason for it. I can only say the Israelis muffed it, like the Americans, and basically for power. Pride. The pride before the fall. I think of the Snir seer in Golan saying the Jews didn't need a God now that they had a country. A bad weather friend. The Israelis may have forgotten the covenant, but God didn't.

Brenda's last words to us (regarding my freedom of expression) were "This isn't America, you know."

24

The Tents of Sham

The Messiah.

I did not go to Sde Boker in order to be a token symbol to the Israeli youth. I came here because I loved the place, I loved the courageous men that dared establish a settlement in the heart of the Negev, I loved the working of the land, I wanted, while I still have enough physical strength to return to working the land and to actively participate in making the wilderness bloom, in which I see the highest of human dedications. I did it for myself out of pleasure and love...

We were waiting for the bus, and I was reading one of Ben-Gurion's letters, when out of nowhere a Bedouin came sidling up to the Sde Boker bus stop. He was the most unkempt Arab I'd ever seen. The Israelis, waiting for the bus that would take them to the "Bedouin market" where they might rub shoulders with the man, now made the air palpable with their displeasure and discomfort. The brown-skinned man was a Black in the pre-Civil Rights South, an embarrassed intruder who'd spent the latter part of his life eating humble pie. To the ire of the Israelis, I bade the middle-aged man to sit down next to me.

Immediately, I was immersed in the smoke of last night's fire, a thousand fires before that. Though one didn't have to smell the man to know how he slept. That not unpleasant scent took me back centuries to the communal fire and the original kibbutz, or camaraderie. This son of the desert went further back than that, salt of the earth, clay from which we all sprang, texture and tint of sandstone, face the wrinkles of a wadi after the rain. No, he was made of more substantial stuff, a coil of copper mined on the opposite side of the grand "crater" and fashioned over a fire. An Arab. I was consorting with the "enemy."

If the smoke got in my eyes, I'd also been brainwashed. A good minute passed before I took them off his hand and didn't concern myself about what his loose clothing might conceal. With the contagion of Israeli hostility, I had inherited their fear. But the Beersheba area (where the bus was going) was the most dangerous for hitchhikers, and we didn't ride a mile before we were resuming our post at the side of the road, with ample reason for caution. We weren't courting danger, but by thumbing, we would cut many miles off our journey—be spared two or more bus rides and the money that went with them—when we only wanted to get on the other side of Zin. We hoped to spend Christmas with the Jew for Jesus. The son of Noah, Shem, easy to confuse with sham.

Maybe it's a sign of encroaching sanity (God forbid) that I feel compelled to explain such a cavalier or knightly (Don Q) approach to travel. Once you've had some luck hitching, it seems like the logical thing to do. It's also addictive. While that element of danger can't be much greater than flying or at least hang gliding. And of course, off course, there is no more adventurous way to travel. It is such a break from the ordered routines of the world that every encounter is of the third kind, a world fraught with destiny and dementia—magic. Even something as pedestrian as walking along the side of the road holds the wonders of exotic exploration. Just as the ancient Chinese said, you can't see the flowers from the back of the horse. I see the flowers and the nitty gritty from the side of the road. The gateway to synchronicity, connections far beyond coincidence and understanding. We cursed or blessed seekers who have had a taste of the other side, or one ride too many.

But you aren't going to ask a chameleon his color, an atom its shape. You really want to know about Mona. How a middle-aged woman can play Sancho Panza to the man from La Mancha, but even that won't play in Peoria any longer. As incredible as our mode of travel is, rarely, very rarely does anybody ask us what the hell do we think we are doing or going. Is it a matter of blending into the scenery, some block on the part of the driver, the Good Samaritan's saintly penchant for minding his own business when he (par) has just allowed a couple of strangers into his car. Usually, they don't want to embarrass a poor man, never dreaming it's more a matter of preference than poverty. Are you going to ask a man who is talking to himself why he engages in such insane behavior? Yet curiously, no one ever asks if our car has broken down. Rather, it's as if we had a rendezvous.

It is the unquestioning acceptance of the driver that has encouraged me to follow my nose. In that day's whirlwind circling of the Negev incline me to believe something extraordinary was in store for us. This side road that ran parallel to route 40 was not the easiest road in the world to hitch. Probably the only vehicle that would stop for us is the one that happened to be going our way, a mobile workshop, a converted bus operated by two dark-skinned Jews who exuded a boyish enthusiasm about the US. From then on, it was gravy with maybe a little gravel. Left off at the Dimona junction, we got a lift from a hip but uni-lingual truck driver who dipped into the canyon and passed within a few feet of dubious mining operations before depositing us south of the Dead Sea Works.

We hadn't walked a hundred feet down route 90 when a driver headed south stopped for us. Did he know the Jew for Jesus? Did he! And his demeanor changed. "You want to work for him? You can work for me."

About twenty minutes later, we were let out of the man's car where a dirt road led to the Wilderness of Zin. Nothing prepared us for Orvot or "Water Skins." It had been a Turkish outpost before the Mandate, and now trailers like covered wagons formed a semicircle about the outcast kibbutz. From the road we could see the small hilltop headquarters, now topped with a tall antenna, but still looking turn-of-the-century.

As we reached the perimeter of the mobile compound, an elderly Norwegian emerged from his trailer and smiled a big hello. Not a Jew for Jesus, but an old-fashioned Christian who had heard about the renegade Jew. The jovial Norwegian (I could see this place would be full of paradox), curious about this oddity and on a tight budget was "helping out around the kibbutz." "The Rabbi is sleeping, but you can look around if you like."

Orvot or Ovot, although it is also the site of an archeological dig, seemed to be deserted. Disconnected. A helter-skelter welter that whispered abandonment and had something of Charles Manson's digs about it. The Norwegian introduced us to his wife, and we stepped inside their trailer for a minute. California Dreamin'.

Presently, we met the "Rabbi," a Mr. Perelmutter. He was a short, squat, squinting fellow with a practiced handshake. I was about to cry uncle, when that former Nazi out of the "Producers" or "It's Springtime for Hitler and Germany" thrust himself upon us. His name was Peter, and he babbled and bid us welcome as if directed by Mel Brooks himself. Although bareheaded, I will always picture this hapless soul in a Nazi helmet. Indeed, he carried on about the war, and I really do not think Brooks could have created the babbling penitent or his squat savior in Hasidic curls. In the Wilderness of Zin, mind you! The Rabbi sent him on his way.

Like a fat cat, the Rabbi watched my every move. "How did you come here, why did you come here?"

I said we needed work and that we heard about the Jews for Jesus when we were in the US. I told him how disappointed we were in the other kibbutzim and how great it was to find a spiritual commune.

"What did you hear about me?"

I really hadn't heard much about him, and the worse the better. "I can appreciate your unpopularity."

Even in less hectic times, I'm brain dead by four in the afternoon, and I am that classic fool who will not learn from experience. If my memory didn't fail me, I would be without faith, and where would I be then. Certainly, my experience dictated that I be suspicious of any messiah, but I'd also become superstitious and wanted to believe. Still, there was something special about Israel, and this much I knew: If there was a messiah, he would be a pariah.

Paranoia would be par for the course, the concomitant of persecution, and in that respect at least, the broad man in the tight jacket filled the bill. If a Ben-Gurion had feet of clay (were the Arabs supposed to evaporate), he was, after all, a politician first. There had to be another Moses or Christ in this Terra Santa who was not a Holy Terror. Enter Perelmutter.

And if I could not see the S. J. Perelman behind the Hasidic curls or peyos, I'm a sucker for the all important exception to the rule. I did not tug at the Santa Claus beard, but accepted the comedian at face value. The idea that this Jew was another Jesus living on the fringe was too much to resist. It appealed to my sense of poetry and justice after the endless cycle of cynicism, and I chided myself for being so judgmental. This explained my sense of destiny, portent, disappointment leading to a storybook ending that would make it all worthwhile. Oh, yea of little faith, I was ready to buy Perelmutter lock, stock and barrel. Though generally repelled by lard, I was like St. Francis before the leper, knowing God was where we would not go.

If there was another Jesus—no matter how gross—walking about, it seemed only right he would be a persecuted Jew. If Perelmutter hailed from Florida, wasn't I tested by fire there also.

But I had made the Rabbi paranoid. He asked, "What do you have to do with the Jews for Jesus."

"Just listened to them a few times. I thought they were a couple of affable yentas."

"They have a holocaust complex," he said, elaborating.

But I wasn't sure I followed him. Something about setting themselves up to be victims and reinforcing the Christian mindset. Ostensibly, at least, the New Jersey Jews for Jesus wanted to bring Jews into the Christian fold. But Perelmutter wanted the Christians to take responsibility for the holocaust and, via this guilt trip, lead them into the Jewish fold and appreciate that Christ was a Jew. Presumably assuring acceptance.

So far, so good, Christ without the pomp and circumstance. The Rabbi was really a first century Christian. This seemed more honest than the "two nice Jewish boys" Mona and I had picked up on our AM radio, who really wanted Christians to see the common ground. In my more Machiavellian moments, I half suspected that the comedy team that arranged tours to the Holy Land mollified Christians at the bequest of the Israeli government. In the face of a rising tide of anti-Semitism, the Jews for Jesus project the desired persona. The Jew as the eternal mensch, rather than a part of a nouveau military machine with worldwide tentacles—perhaps extending into the very tent of Shem himself.

And speaking of Machiavelli (Hare Krishna, Krishna, Krishna, Hare...), all that has befallen me and Israel since leaving that beleaguered country inclines me to believe that the "Elders of Zion" conspiracy theory that is held by the right wing whackos is also a creation of Mossad. How better to discredit an idea than identify it with the whackos, enemies, and exaggerate that idea beyond belief—with more than a kernel of truth. What is confusing is the very real anti-Semitism of the disenfranchised lunatic fringe, while the big money right, the Ivan Boeskys, are Jewish as well as Christian (and Krishna) and inseparable from the machinations of the Israeli government, the essence of the military-industrial complex. Which you better believe includes publishing.

Whatever the Jewish Jerseyites were up to (and they weren't

converting Jews to Christianity), Perelmutter was more ambitious in his schemes. He lent me his Tents of Shem, Vantage Press, 1980. Most of the biographical note on the book jacket was blocked out, but it seemed that Simka Pearlmutter, the author, was reared in Boston before absconding to Florida where he became a lawyer or worse—if that's possible. Reading between the lines, I could see that Simka (his Hebrew name), Pearl of the desert, had been in the kibbutz business a good dozen years before returning to the US and going to New York with his revelations—and incriminations. Almost a nonstop diatribe against the Christian tribe. Recounting in his book the Christians' many crimes against the Jews, Simka stated that the only way they can atone for their sins is to follow a Jew, worship a Jew, Christ-like and chosen, and the most likely place to find this fellow, squat and squinting, is in Tents of Shem.

So, this born-again Jesus, also the King of the Jews, though he now labored under a crown of thorns, his "Water Skins" had been a regular money bags. At one time as many as a hundred followers of the "Messiah" of Zin or Yesuva, labored with him. Part of Simka's shtick was to escort pilgrims to the nearby spring and bless the water. Instant holy water. Ever thirsty for the bizarre (now I understand what happened to Melville), this idea of a modern Jesus or Moses also appealed very much to northern Europeans.

But if the Yesuva of Zin had fallen on hard times, the word hadn't reached Finland yet. Two Finnish girls who had recently read about Simka in a Helsinki religious magazine were gathering up the irrigation tubing and helping the messiah close up shop.

I asked Simka what was going on, and he told me that the government was confiscating his kibbutz for some obscure reason. He had been ordered to stop farming three weeks ago. Now that I think about it, he did not legally qualify as a kibbutz operator because the land wasn't legally his. But Simka said that it was and he had a right to do as he wished, though I also seem to recall that when his membership fell below a certain level, he was not entitled to kibbutz assistance. Simka was contesting the government foreclosure in court and said he would have a decision by Sunday.

Any enemy of the government was a friend of mine, and Simka got a sympathetic ear, even if he was something of a "Rainmaker." The sheer chutzpah of the man grabbed me, and his book before he went off on the deep end—even then—was well written and even reasonable. Christians do owe the Jews, and if we compensate Blacks for the exploitation of their ancestors, why not affirmative action for the Jews. For, if you couldn't find your way to the Tents of Shem or the Trailer Camp of Messiah Yeshua, almost any Jew would do as a guru. So my wearing the pants in my relationship with a Jew didn't sit too well with Perelmutter because he really did write that Christians were obligated to submit to a Jew. But then, marriage is really submission no matter what you're wearing, so I guess I had fulfilled my obligation, in spades.

Maybe it's because the Mormon image sticks with me that I seem to recall Simka saying he would not go peacefully. He did say he was under constant surveillance, and I could only wonder what he had done to incur the wrath of the authorities to the degree that they threatened to take his two boys, according to Simka. They were a sickly pair. As confused as I was, I did commiserate with the man. Tragedy did outweigh absurdity. Whatever he was, he did stand to lose everything. He may have been a Pasha in payos, but he was in pain and had my support—mostly because I thought his persecution stemmed from his acceptance of Jesus. It was more likely that he was interfering with the archeological site. Or fooled no one about being a Jesus freak.

Actually, if Perelmutter didn't exist, the Government Office of Disinformation would invent him. Pandering to Christian pishposh, it persuades pilgrims to see things the Israeli way. Conveniently, Jesus is the magic word, as in Megiddo or Armageddon giving the Fundamentalists what they want to hear: Apocalypse, now. Or at least salvation, in the Wilderness of Zin.

Dinner was a bizarre affair with Simka sitting at the head of a C-shaped table dispensing benediction before we dug in. Strained, strange, but the Finnish girls managed to giggle. Simka's boys wouldn't eat. Their father tried at least to push a sweet on them. the mother remained in the kitchen. I thought of one of the more depressing monasteries that take in guests, but here there was no picture of Jesus or any sign of the cross.

Outside, I asked Simka if it wasn't unusual that a Hasidic rabbi believed that Jesus was the Messiah. He replied that in their heart of hearts the Hasidim believed this. Was there a twinkle somewhere behind that rabbinical beard? But even Henderson the Rainmaker didn't know the dark continent of the Hasidim. I didn't take into account that they had their Messiah returning to Jerusalem on the back of a white ass, while the more imaginative fundamentalist had conjured up a Captain Marvel. Apparently Mona and I were such an innocuous pair that Simka could chance us meeting his parents.

First, Perelmutter showed us around like a proud father. Overlooking the Turkish buildings was all desert, he said. There weren't even birds here before his arrival. I commended him on his appreciation of ecology. Our tour was interrupted by Peter who jabbered how much we would like Orvot, but Perelmutter shooed him away like he would a misbehaved dog. I noticed his boys weren't very tolerant of the shell-shocked apostle either, but it was well past four, and all suspicions suspended. At my most vulnerable, I could easily relate to the repentant German. I couldn't get into the shoes of his master, but they were opposite sides of the same coin. Simka had yet to lay that bombshell that would flip the coin.

Simka pointed out his parent's trailer that was near ours, and then we were on our own. We demurred, but Perelmutter said, "They don't get many visitors, they'll be happy to meet you."

Peter came running over to us. "The mother is a very nice woman, very nice..."

"Come on, Peter."

On the side of the trailer a sign read, "Donated by the people of America."

Occupants, Floridians. No trailer had ever taken me so far so fast. The inside of it revealed a condominium thick with Florida living, lox, schlock and barrel. New money, Mona said later. No money was more like it. Looking like she had just deplaned, ending her transatlantic or even space flight—so other worldly was her materialization on this oriental bazaar—was Mrs. Perelmutter dressed to kill, her blond hair undimmed by seven or eight decades of not necessarily easy living. I would never dream that the last two or so had been spent in the desert, a good part of the time operating a kiosk outside her son's first kibbutz further down the road.

I marveled at how she had given up the glitter of Miami for this

Turkish delight, but Mrs. Pearlmutter explained they were a lot closer to Elat in the beginning.

I brought up that her son's work was the price she paid for a little deprivation. "You must be very proud of Simka, all he has accomplished. Building his own kibbutz and congregation in the desert." I looked to Mr. Pearlmutter senior who had been smiling throughout our conversation.

"He's deaf. Would you like some ice cream and chocolate cake?"

An unsettling case of déjà vu turned out delightfully disorienting. I had seen it all, but if I was neither here not there, my palate centered me. Like a river of Jesus' wine, the generous portions of childhood were a godsend, yet another miracle in the desert. The Rabbi's mother was no Theresa, however, and I'd have to be entirely comatose not to see through the scam. My consciousness, I sensed, had exceeded the bounds of decorum. Not that Mrs. Pearlmutter was ever less than the gracious hostess, but on top of her bookcase was one of those teasing contraptions that read "Shalom" if you observed it from the right angle. You were "Welcome" if you knew your place. Mona gave her two cents plain:

Dec. 12th, Thurs. Kibbutz Ovot…hardly any people around—many signs reading a Settlement of Congregation Messiah Yeshua. Strange group of people—don't think they know what Simka is all about—Norwegian admitted as much—Peter really wacky—took our soap—some mumble jumble about it. Simka showed us his synagogue—told us he did all the work & also put in electricity, water, etc. His wife cold, doesn't say anything. Norwegian lady seems nervous when setting table—when offered to help she said no.

Met parents—mother bleached blond…

25

Sodom and Gomorrah

From Mona's diary:

Dec. 19th, Friday. Hitched to New Zohar—think Asaf surprised to see us again—anyway, had no work & somebody staying in apartment—Moshe wanted 20 IS for camping, no food. Asaf drove us to good hotel & deal was only for 25% discount (room at $53 plus 15% tax—almost did it, but Asaf came back for us). Strange again back to hotels—everyone dressed up—entertainment. Children making a lot of noise in lobby. Asaf knows not much money left—mentioned Arab shelter where sleep occasionally—says safe—good workers. Says Texas like this. Shelter hovel. Make deal with owner of Dead Sea Hotel—Asaf knows him—won't cost us anything. Once Youth Hostel. Room once communal bathroom—fixtures removed. Shades of Turkey but cleaner—Arab managing place.

Asaf told us what he knew of Perelmutter—about 2 years ago 80 people plus one of his wives all up and left one day by bus—seems he was telling who to marry who—really becoming a dictator—didn't build anything on land—not so much as put in electricity or houses. Had another parcel of land first—something about map (secret) indicating where spring was. Many people looking for this place—amazingly Simka finds it. Said when he came to Israel Messiah would come there—then when he had to move—said Messiah will come to new place. Not Rabbi—smells of Jim Jones. Asaf laughing.

Mona joined in. But the joke was on us.

A beautiful sunny morning. The hotel is also the site of the Dead Sea Museum. Just outside our room overlooking the lake is the dinghy or rowboat of one of its first navigators. An unfathomable coincidence, as I've been reading about Herman Melville's voyage to the "Levant." The greatest American writer who ever lived and no mean sailor himself. Yet, like Mona, the author of "Moby Dick" was tapping out an SOS of dots and dashes as he floundered on the Dead Sea shore. In synch, Morse code was my medium as radio...operator when I was in the Navy. Now I'm just an operator.

But here's old Ahab himself going off the deep end: "Ride over moldy plain to Dead Sea...foam on beach and pebbles like saliva of mad dog—smarting bitter of the water,—carried the bitterness in my mouth all day—bitterness of life—thought of all bitter things—Bitter it is to be poor & bitter to be reviled, & Oh bitter are these waters of Death, thought I. ...naught to eat but bitumen & ashes with dessert of Sodom apples washed down with water of Dead Sea."

Obviously, the old salt was out of his element—as well as his gourd. So homesick was Melville for more lively seas that even in the best of times, the rolling Berkshire mountains reminded him of ocean swells. But Melville, Twain, a whole army or navy of disenchanted pilgrims would turn over in their graves if they could see the resurrection of Sodom and Gomorrah. Ah, the wonders of advertising and sunshine below sea level—with the miracle of mud. Just up the road from where we were staying in Newe Zohar, cheek to jowl, back to back to old Zohar, the heart and soul, home, bizarrely, of the mystical Kabalistic writings—are frauleins galore floating in seventh heaven. Just off shore.

The cluster of resorts had everything going for it but the soon-to-arrive gambling casinos. Depending on how older Germans looked at it, Melville's abomination was a pleasure or penance, in that strange symbiosis of German and Jew. And mixed feelings. Israelis had gone to the end of the earth to bring back Nazis dead or alive...though most Germans had more than atoned for the sins of their fathers, the guilt card is being played to the hilt. By 1980 the tables had been turned to the degree that *TransAtlantik Magazine* was translating, publishing my essays that American editors rejected—as they have now. I've already sent them portions of this "hot potato."

"Dann liess der Herr auf Sodom und auf Gomorrah Schwfel und Feuer herniederrgnen; und er vernichtete die Stadte und die ganze Wuste...: aber seine Frau schaute zuruck und erstarrte zu einer Saule aus Salz." (Genesis 19:24-26). Quoted from one of the brochures available at the Dead Sea, all of which are in German. But the photos speak an international language and lending itself to an ends-of-the-earth or beginnings-of-earth sensation, the photograph above "Schlamm Packung" informs you in no uncertain terms that the seductive woman, exposed breast, whose back, buttocks and thighs are plastered with mud, is not being turned into a pillar of salz or salt.

Und there is a photo showing a beguiling woman taking a bad, one getting a massage outside the "Beheiztes Seewasserschwimmbad" that features a luscious blonde. Resting above the head of an even more sensual blond is a cluster of "Apfel von Sedom." Housing these Sodomites are the hotels Moriah, Shulamit Gardens, Ein Bokek, all very biblical, but a bit like Baden Baden.

We only had three or four shopping days left until Christmas. We wanted to work at a kibbutz near Jerusalem, near the festivities, and really didn't know where to begin to look.

Melville never got down to Sodom or Gomorrah, but we were soon passing another source of his inspiration, "Barrenness of Judea—Whitish mildew pervading whole tracts of landscape—bleached—leprosy—encrustation of curses—old cheese—bones of rocks—crunched, knawed, & mumbled—mere refuse & rubbish of creation—like that laying outside Jaffa Gate…You see the anatomy—compares with ordinary regions as skeleton with living & rosy man—so rubbishy, that no chiffonier could find any thing all over it.—No moss as in other ruins—no grace of decay—no ivy—the unleavened nakedness of desolation—whitish ashes—lime kilns. Port Esquiline of the Universe."

That last reference to a desolate potter's field outside Rome—and the Judean hills are a limbo with none of the more defined juxtapositions of desert and oasis a little further to the south, but then "spring" was also a long time in coming in that January of 1857. Or it had an early arrival in that January of 1987, as I indicate in my first chapter, the hills a sea of colorful flowers. I know this unexpected explosion of life allowed me to keep my own head above water, and it's interesting to speculate what an earlier spring would have done for Melville's melancholy. As it was, we have two of America's literary giants (Twain, my earlier companion, toured in summer) emerge from a colorless Holy Land shrunken in stature. And if they saw the flowers, would they say there were more in the Berkshires. If they did, they'd be lying.

Encouraged by her similarity of style to Melville, Mona is now putting down more than two or three words a page:

Dec. 20th, Saturday. Left Newe Zohar—bus to hotels—then police car to Ein Gedi—German couple up to field school—bus shelter scribbled on wall "Expect to wait here 8 hours because Israelis are #$&*!??/!!#!!!—wait a few minutes—kid from kibbutz up north dropped us off at Naran (many Arab cars back and forth)—kibbutz depressing—didn't need volunteers—back on road—upset about wasting so much time & where we are—getting late (3:00). Israeli couple picked us up—explained no kibbutzim where they were going—area West Bank—got off at Kibbutz Gilgal, not far from Naran—everyone friendly, seemed receptive (very young kibbutz). Said few kibbutzim in West Bank because of it being Arab land at one time.

26

Bedlam in Bethlehem

Dec. 21st, Sunday, Gilgal. They were willing to let us stay and work (as on other Kibbutzim often a shortage of help). We had to change rooms—put us up temporarily in a small house reserved for guests or people they wanted to—and hoped would eventually join the Kibbutz. Put into a filthy apartment—had to clean up—washing the floors without a proper mop—in all of Israel they didn't have a mop—it was an enormous squeegee—what a mess—trying to even the water out water all over the floor—it was the same way in Turkey. The Kibbutz members decided they wanted us to start working the following day. We were really tired and thought that we might leave and perhaps return.

Dec. 22nd, Monday. We toured the cow shed and were given a pretty good idea about how they were milked and cared for—told that their procedure enabled them to milk the cows three times a day—cows—little more than machines to them. The calfs were taken away almost immediately. Everything economics. In other countries milk was taken twice a day from the cows, yet they were able to perform this task three times—left feeling that I was looked upon in the same way—all you can eat—milk us for all we're worth.

Tony went to Jericho. When the rooms were in tiptop shape it did turn out to be one of the better places we stayed except for Sde Boker—everyone seemed to be genuinely friendly.

Dec. 23rd, Tuesday. Hitched from Kibbutz Gilgal with two Arabs in a cabbage pickup truck and walked a few meters to Hashim Palace—Tony got in with writers card. Waited in Jericho for 1 hour—bus to Jerusalem didn't stop—picked up by two soldiers (one was originally from the States) took us to bus stop—other tourists—mostly kids waiting for bus also. Arab bus came by—Tony and I only ones got on—took us to the Damascus Gate and checked into Knights Palace Hotel—once a monastery—really getting the feeling of Christmas—just a little. Tony says he feels as if he's spending

Christmas in West Palm Beach—hotel has original stone floors—hardly any tourists (20 Israel Shekels for two). At New Gate—several soldiers guarding.

Dec. 24th, Wednesday. Good to be back in Jerusalem again—almost two months have gone by and feel like everything has been a dream. The church bells—so many memories of Christmas—the church bells bring back other Christmas'. One can walk forever and come upon so many surprises. Spoke with night manager of Knights Palace he lives in Ramallah and told me of his brother who left for Canada yesterday—he too wants very much to leave—says he feels suppressed. Left for Bethlehem on Arab bus—station reminded me of South America—more chaotic and dirty—feel as if I entered another country—Arab music blasting on radio—waited an hour for bus to leave. All sorts of religious and non-religious articles hanging up above bus driver—including evil eye—some tourists on bus—children coming aboard selling chocolates, etc. Just a few blocks away but could be thousands of miles away from Jewish children. Entering into Bethlehem—they tried to make it "merry" but decorations poor imitation of anything cheerful—long walk after getting off bus—tourist buses and Egged (Egged bus line—like our Greyhound) don't have to pass through search area—Tony stopped because of his pen knife—soldier wanted to keep it—Tony very angry—called me over and knife given back—more soldiers than civilians—plus other police—saw some people from Kibbutz Snir. Mostly young European kids and young Arabs—very few older people—police on rooftops—kids drinking beer—sitting in groups—walking around—only one group singing Christmas songs. Couldn't get into church—decided to leave after an hour—no one could tell us where to get Arab bus—Egged is not going to old city—only main terminal—double the price. Seemed we walked forever—only Arab cars—number 22 not going back to Jerusalem—started hitching near gas station—taxi with family wanted 8 Israeli shekels—Tony ticked-off—cursing soldier for trying to keep knife—attempted theft, too used to picking on Arabs. Soldier justified saying boy might steal knife off him and stab somebody—When went into Arab store owner claimed no need for all the soldiers—hassle—disrupt Christian holiday. Buses still streaming into city.

Tony getting desperate—suddenly stepped in front of bus—driver stopped—Israel kids said not regular bus but going to Jerusalem and took us to Jaffa gate. Kids coming from outing and happy—bright spot in disappointing evening—awful. Met young guy, asked way to Bethlehem—walking. Soldiers guarding gate—Rebecca refused to pick us up saying people throwing stones—but everything very quiet—few tourists for this time of year. Went to bed—Tony went out, visited Arab social club and church (Palestinian Christians)—later could only listen to music in German church—said peaceful moment at midnight—first feeling of brotherhood since Druse of Golan—wish I was with him—strange, have such good memories of Germany.

Dec. 25th, Thurs. Doesn't feel very much like Christmas—strange when here we are—where it all started—walked to Mount Olive—beautiful Russian church—picnicked in cemetery overlooking old city—beautiful garden outside—Mary Magdalin Church—where Christ was in agony, arrested. Took bus to Rebecca's and picked up our things—only stayed one hour—not comfortable—couldn't be honest with her—everything is us and them—she had difficulty accepting (I think) where we were staying and the way we were touring Israel—kibbutzim, etc. rather than first class hotels—as a Jewish middle-aged woman from America should. Also confirmed Simka's status in Israel but exaggerated things—said he had 20 wives—the talk was small and my feeling for her could only be of sorrow knowing that many Israelis feel that way and peace may never come—she may lose her only son to the Arabs and she can't seem to deal with the situation. As she said earlier when she purchased her condominium and was still in the process of furnishing it when we arrived—it's an escape buying all these things. How strange that I may never have come to Israel if it hadn't been for our chance meeting one year before—a train heading for Canada. Arab man went out of his way to shake Tony's hand when we were back in Jerusalem—Tony thinks he wants to reassure they are not terrorists.

Knights Palace (could Don Quixote resist it, and at a writer's discount at that) is the last place in the world anyone would expect a Jew to be staying—unless she be Sancho Panza, of course.

I'm sure the reader is as sorry as I am that Mona just didn't have the horsepower to continue. She was the young believer who belatedly learns there is no Santa Claus. We were in that state where anger clashes with sorrow. I am indeed the Knight of the Woeful Countenance sallying down the alleys of old Jerusalem. How could it be any other way? Place. My road could only lead to the Knights Palace—the stuff of poetry.

Yet here it stands down a cobblestone street off New Gate entrance to the walled city, a stone's throw (an expression that has taken on a special meaning in Israel) from the Catholic Church's pontifical headquarters, beyond the pale where I looked for a room before being referred to the former nunnery. It would be so much more acceptable to omit those coincidentals that put-off the much too sheltered reader, but then I wouldn't be writing, and this tortured land cries out for the truth—no matter how unacceptable. Like change.

Even absurdities like Mona loving monasteries—this former one near the New Gate that was built after Emperor Wilhelm of Germany had his triumphant entry into Jerusalem. The walls had been torn down at this site, so that the German king and his cumbersome entourage of coaches and horses could enjoy a royal entrance into the Holy City before going on to its holiest Protestant church. It was here, in the Lutheran Church of the Redeemer, the last place in Jerusalem this Jonah wanted to be, where Wilhelm sat on his magnificent throne like a respectable Jesus, that I brought my Christmas Eve to a pleasant close. I regretted I couldn't be with Mona, but I had to get Bethlehem behind me and have my Silent Night before I would get to sleep—even if it was in a decidedly Teutonic ambience. But then isn't German close enough to Yiddish, close enough to the Judeo-Christian tradition—at least to the ear, "Gottes Sohn ist Mensch gebornm ist Mensch geborn, hat ersoht des Vaters Zorn, des Vater Zorn."

Really, I will always remember the redeeming light of that church that night, the stones that held it so perfectly. For me this esthetic illumination becomes the illusion of Israel—seen more realistically the following morning in the light of day as we sat eating our lunch in the cemetery. But this is more Melville's bag—though granted, there no longer remains quite the desolation that fed Melville's desperation, "Wandering among the tombs—till I begin to think myself one of the possessed with the devils. Variety of the Tombs—with stairs like pulpet & c. 'Multitudes, Multitudes' in the Valley of Hinom. Stones about Absalom's Tomb—gravestones about Zechariah's."

The City of the Dead, scene of the Last Judgment is just beyond the (pale, indeed) east wall climbing up Mount Olive and descending into the "ghostliness" of Jehosophat or Kedron, where Jew, Christian and Moslem awaiting their respective Messiahs live in peace. Poetically so, as there have always been more than enough olive branches for the offering here. If the brochure be believed, I looked upon the olive tree under which Jesus sat in the Garden of Gethsemane. Melville found the "penitent" tree very suited to this milieu, and I must say there is something of the agony and ecstasy in this perennial evergreen—gnarled grace, pirouetting to the tune of wind and sun.

Beyond the sacred groves and the "valley of decision" (Joel, the first Joel 3:2,12-16) "the wall of Omar rises upon the foundation stones of Solomon, triumphing over that which sustains it, an emblem of the relationship of the two faiths." (Herman 1857) It is from here that the seer, with the Russian church squatting in the foreground, is afforded the more complete view of Jerusalem. It is upon Olivet that the graceful onion domes are a counterpoint to tortured olive trunks—like Omar, perhaps, triumphing over that which sustained it.

Keeping within the theme of California Dreamin', Olivet also afford a view of the Golden Gate. Walled up by the Turks who feared the city would be taken at this point, the gate remains blocked up today, prompting Melville in his day to say, "seems expressive of the finality of Christianity, as if this was the last religion of the world,—no other possible." But this is the ornately "Beautiful" gate and the resident of Gramacy Park is less charitable when he is at the Dung Gate: "Village of Lepers—...their park, a dung heap." Certainly, much of the Holy City was a horror in Melville's day, but a little spit and polish has gone a long way in bestowing upon Jerusalem its Crusader image. Nor has Golgotha lost its attraction, though gentrification is another kind of garbage and high-rise and high-tech the equal of squalor. Out of place. Today, any antiquity no matter how encrusted with disease is a blessed improvement over modern sterility. If you've been inoculated.

Ben-Gurion, your practical Zionist, wanted to tear down the walls of old Jerusalem and let in a little light, give the town an air of progress. The confining ghetto was too much a part of his collective consciousness, but everything is context and in the light of history the walls are expansive. I spent most of the seventies in the "Palm Beaches" and nothing, to me, was more disheartening than a cloudless sky in winter—changeless weather. Variety isn't the spice of life, it is the essence. But ultimately it was the darkness that got me down—fittingly enough in that bus station beyond the pale, waiting to be off to Bethlehem.

That hustle without bustle in the gargantuan depot, dark, dank and cheerless, the disorienting drone of the desert when I needed something that spoke of some snow and spruce, a carol to be sung, pitched me into the blackest hole. The general din and dinginess of this Calcutta was enough to drive any esthete up the wall of the Damascus Gate across the street, yet I would like to think that the cause of my paralyzing depression lay in the station's location—unbeknownst to me, consciously, just below the accepted real site of the crucifixion or Golgotha. The Palestinian bus depot was just under the last station of the cross.

The Golgotha at the end of the shop-lined Via Dolorosa is then the site of the crucifixion, another one of those touristic traps chosen for their location, while the Golgotha above the bus station, even outside the centuries old Turkish walls, was never financially feasible. Far from the crux of the city, a church of the Holy Sepulcher laden with riches would've been until recently vulnerable to banditry and only of late enjoys the patronage of the more selective bible students. Christ or no, this was the site of many crucifixions, and what better place to feel the agony of the persecuted than in a noisy bus station.

And maybe it was premonition that plunged me into my black pit, the unconscious knowledge that we would be swept along in a sea of Arabs, swirling up to the very gates (electronic) of Babylon, rather, Bethlehem, a handful of tourists bobbing up and down in the young multitude, a Times Square rush hour suddenly slowing to the trickle of an hourglass before the screening doors of Kennedy Airport, me screaming for my wife as the soldiers carted me away because I refused to give up my "weapon."

Passing for an Arab, I was being taken into custody a stone's throw from Manger Square. Mona heard my yelling and quit the women's line where she waited to be searched herself.

"Tell this guy," who was by now a man in civilian clothes on scene, "that you're my wife before I'm kidnapped.

27
Gilgal

Dec. 26th, Friday. Sad to be leaving Jerusalem—picked up our tickets for January 25. The few days here went very quickly and still more to see—will miss the churches. Made reservations for January 22 at Knights Palace—really lucky to have found that place—especially over the Christmas holidays—it was a special place—I really needed to stay somewhere with the kind of feeling—a feeling that maybe—in all the mess—there was someplace I felt I belonged—inside the Arab quarters. Israeli soldiers outside—everything upside down for me. Need to spend more time walking the streets of Jerusalem—inside—outside the Israeli and Arab quarters. Arab station—again waited on bus a long time—same scene as other night—again, shabby attempt at Christmas decorations— Egged bus to Gilgal. Back at Gilgal—went with member up mountain to view David and other members running back to Kibbutz with torch as they did (the Maccabees) after the victory over the Greeks—also the lighting of Hanukkah candles in evening—each member said something in Hebrew for each candle lit. Dinner was the usual chicken and rice, corn and wine for Friday night—sat with Yoni—but very uncomfortable—very difficult to make conversation—I would like to believe it is because their English is poor—most members don't seem to want to get involved—Yoni and his girlfriend seem a little more friendly.

Dec. 27th, Saturday - Jan. 3rd, Saturday. Started working Sunday, December 28th—routine is easy to fall into—especially when you think of being on the road almost every day—again like most Kibbutz we've been on—members not really friendly—was invited for coffee at Yoni's— they fix up their apartments fairly nice—a sense of individuality—working together—eating together—most meals. Picked corn in afternoon—raw corn very tasty—tractor making it unpleasant—putting chemicals into banana trunk after cutting away inside core—Tony not feeling good about chemicals—spent one morning turning on and fixing irrigation of pumelos (a huge grapefruit-like citrus fruit)—also picked the pumelos—very heavy—could hardly carry in sack—then when full carry to bin—break time—peeled pumelo. Worked with David in banana orchard—we met before—he brought table to apartment—young guy from Larchmont—can't decide whether to stay on and go into army—can't make out if he's honest about what he says—or just wants to be away from home for awhile—think he couldn't hack it. Chicken dinner again—Friday—sitting alone—until asked to join couple who had been to States—also picked apples in areas of Wappingers Falls, NY—strange hearing about that place again—first time was in Nazareth. So many times David would come to our table—when we sat alone—did he come on his own—was it suggested to him—I think he felt uncomfortable—started bringing dinner, breakfast to our room—many members did.

Jan. 4-5-6, Sunday, Monday and Tuesday. Hands really hurting from pruning—South American kids sitting around—Sara said "too bad parents didn't teach them how to work"—Tony taking off at lunch to be away from everyone—to eat outside. Back of trucks packed with Chilean and Argentinean kids—coming and going for lunch—kids always eating fast—running for truck—some with food still in their mouth. Tony saw dentist—needs lots of work—raining today (Tuesday) started at nine—finished at 12:00—not at all like Snir when we picked avocados in heavy rain—so tired at night—pass out about 8-9. Hands beginning to really hurt—arm as well—kids as usual doing very little—S.A. kids beginning to talk about the accommodations—little hot water—crowded—perhaps rats. Girl managing pumelos made remark that we all looked very tired and they usually picked until sun went down—They didn't seem to have any feeling—or care about working the kids as they themselves worked. Again it was a reminder of the cows. Invited for coffee after Friday night dinner by next door neighbors who had been to States—she liking New York—he finding it maddening. He remarking Americans were very naïve—they paid for one in hotel than bringing wife into room—other people also invited—spoke about Israelis bombing South Lebanon—said they never gave it any thought—it always went on and it was necessary. We spoke about the religious Jews—Hasidic—and as with all Israelis we spoke with—they said they were as bad as the Arabs. Just as Rebecca saw everything—black and white. Had tea at David's apartment—whatever he was about—he still spoke of doubts—mainly the army—Tony thinks he speaks differently to Americans. It's good having dinner in apartment—not having to make conversation. Tony saw doctor—arm needs rest (Jan. 9)—Doctor said he visited other people from another Kibbutz—also with same problem—Tony felt Iser should have told us to go slow at the beginning pruning grapevines and knowing what it can do to you—but thinks he doesn't care—as long as he can get as much work out of you as possible—not thinking at all about the long run—the cows again—everything in Israel seems to be for today—maybe as an American—well, there always seems to be tomorrow. I want to think that—that they are really more caring. Sylvia, who works along with us is primarily there to interpret for the S.A. kids—made a remark when Tony asked about the Jerusalem Post—she said we could get the paper in Jerusalem—when they can be sarcastic they usually are. It may have something to do with the fact that they think we are naïve—or something to do with needing the Americans—love and hate. Having difficulty writing—hand still hurts a little. Every day now S.A. kids complaining about their treatment—today it's the broken showers—said they knew it wouldn't be like home—or treated with open arms—but sore arms. Sylvia said they are being treated that way because they weren't working—there is lots of goofing off—but I doubt if they would be treated any differently had they had the stamina—it would be impossible to prune without the S.A. kids—for one thing with them goofing we don't have to work as hard—not that I don't want to work—but I do wonder if my arm will ever be the same again. There is a young guy—Israeli—claims he joined the group because he's going to Brazil and is improving his Spanish (they speak Portuguese in Brazil) claims he speaks little Spanish but seems to hold a pretty good conversation. Tony called him a liar—thinks he's some kind of undercover—security—reminds me of a character from Dr. Zhivago—a young communist after the revolution. Ridiculous having kids work so many hours pruning—having never done any physical labor before especially young girls—didn't work yesterday afternoon or today because of hands (Tuesday and Wednesday, Jan. 13 & 14). Tony trying to see again about his teeth—Yoni sat at our table this morning—Tony thinks it was another of their calculated moves—getting more and more difficult to eat in dining room. Every day planes flying above—noise hurting my ears—

hope they aren't same planes bombing Lebanon—every day on the news—Lebanon being bombed—no one seems to pay any attention—soldiers guarding dining hall—didn't see same at other kibbutzim. It seems the South American kids spent something like $1700—but can't buy chocolates in kibbutz store—they have to buy their own rat poison—but Sylvia giving them her pep talk to calm them a little. Other kibbutzim, most, seemed to have many soldiers doing their part of their service on the kibbutz—only saw few here. The bugs started coming out heavy this morning (Jan. 16)—along with hot weather—torture—worked until 12:30 because of Sabbath—it's becoming more difficult because of bugs and heat to do any work—kids have slowed down—if that's possible—because of heat—they mostly sit among the rows of vines—sometimes peeling pumelos—we all get thirsty quickly—the plastic water containers empty—Tony goes to fill some. Today January 19—they asked me how I liked life on a kibbutz—had to lie and say I did like it—they said they didn't and only wanted to rest—were very tired—and looked it. I think they are sleeping eight to a house with one shower and one toilet. These kids from middle and upper middle families putting them in such squalid conditions certainly won't have any of them appreciate kibbutz life (knowing that the members really live very well) or ever want to return. Were told they would be picking fruit—but doubt if they could have done that all day either. Arabs fast workers.

There are no more notes in Mona's tiny loose-leaf book. I did not look into this diary of a mad housewife until we'd been back in the US for some time. Then I asked her if it was possible that she never put pen to paper after those last disparaging words, when we remained in Israel until the 25th, returning to Jerusalem, final words with her friend. She says she doesn't think so, but I wonder if there is some basis to my paranoia. Her revelations getting more incriminating—confessions of a former Zionist—and I don't put the lifting of some loose-leaves past the little weasel keeping tabs on the volunteers, though it is true that the more disturbing things got, the less Mona wanted to be reminded of them—and this was a hell of a time for her to be testing the literary waters.

Still, with all those young South American souls at stake (along with the faith and finances of their parents) and the heat on to keep them brainwashed, I never felt more the gold fish—in a rocking bowl. For our lively bunch of teenagers, their trip was the compromised thrill of a lifetime and a couple of colorful Americans thrown into the deal was an extra bonus. An unexpected addition to their routine like the rats (but a more welcome one) that infested their quarters. Sure, they were curious about us, complained, and we in turn asked them questions. But it seemed that whenever I stopped playing the clown the bespectacled weasel was on my tail and we were separated. I was really growing to like the South Americans and ready to break into song at the drop of a sombrero. An innocence, a joie de vivre so thoroughly Latin American that we were reminded of our younger selves harvesting le grape—and the inevitable comparison with homegrown Sabra.

Israelis like to liken their young to prickly pears, tough on the outside, sticking you, yet having a soft, sweet center. But this is part of the milk and honey myth. In any case, the desert fruit is also known for its innumerable pits that chip and lodge between teeth. It seems a child bred a Spartan will be gritty to the core. More likely to be smooth on the surface. Soon enough, the young citizens' army would show the world what stuff it was made of (There were more obvious exceptions to the rule.)

Mona was distressed that the innocence of the Latin Zionists would be corrupted by their Israeli counterparts. It's funny how we took to the South American Jews amongst the vines, the blood of the world running through their veins, when we first considered the young Zionists a noisy intrusion on our Zen meditation.

We were really getting into sculpting our vines to a comfortable shoulder height, three nodes like wickets remaining on our candelabra, a good part of the vineyard to ourselves, when a busload of the banditos descended upon us with their ceaseless chatter—teenagers weren't our favorite people before we came to Israel. But these were so winsome and some (not afraid of losing) that they became welcome counterpoint to their peers. Such a diversion from the ensuing tediousness that we wanted to adopt them—were one with them—until their young overseers stepped in.

In considering that perhaps much of the blame was ours for the developing animosity, I wonder if the die wasn't cast at that first tête-à-tête at the cowboy's house. The relaxed, intelligent atmosphere, a kind of glass menagerie, the mélange of curios, memorabilia that his psychiatrist father picked up in his travels (Yoni had a penchant for elephant figurines that his father never figured out), the booze I'd imbibed prompted me to drop a bombshell. I said how great it would have been if, instead of a dead language like Hebrew, Israeli Jews made Esperanto their official lingua franca, befitting a Holy Land, peace on earth. But promoting the internationality of a promised land when Israel was defined by war, exclusivity, and a homeland that was a Cosa Nostra was beyond the pale.

A few drinks and I function—dysfunction—on a clean slate. I mean no ill will. All I had experienced was erased by this newfound camaraderie in a civilized surrounding, only slightly modified by the reek of the cow shed that Yoni was never free of. The unsavory odor did not jibe with the clean features we did not have to take note of to know when Yoni was around. Surely, so earthy and educated a man and his apparently very tolerant woman felt some of our idealism, I thought. But what I had said were fighting words, forgiven perhaps because I was evidently senile. At least our departure was cordial, and I was, after all, a goy deep in his cups.

Unlike many of the kibbutzniks, misfits, I really think Yoni enjoyed his work and liked to be around animals, even if he milked his cows to an early death. Out of my love for animals and the chance to show my goodwill while escaping the wrath of the vineyards, not so incidentally roaming the hills without going AWOL, I volunteered to take the cattle for a walk. He was spending a fortune on feed and filling his penned-up cows with chemicals. While the hills he had not taken notice of were now rich with the nutrients of a wide variety of flowers and that rolling green ocean of grass, waves already thigh high. This walk on the wild side seemed a healthy alternative to contaminated milk. And yet, even if Yoni could break with "progress," modern practices and appearances, how could he return to the level of the Arab, be his equal and weaken the them/us syndrome that reinforced Israeli feelings of superiority. He dismissed my idea as a way of keeping out of the vineyards for a spell. A magic spell.

Trying to be penetrating but understanding, I asked Yoni if he really liked the kibbutz.

"Seven years here. I must like it."

I said I knew the meaning of his elephantine fixation.

"What?" he asked.

"When you were a child, your parents took you to a lot of Jumbo movies. As for cows, safety reasons axed a walk on the wild side, but could anything replace roaming freely?

I don't think our solitary confinement or ostracism was so much a result of anything I said or did or didn't do, as it was standard treatment. There is in the territories kibbutzim something of a brotherhood of the damned, damned if you are forced to give up West Bank Gilgal with no place to go; damned if you go down fighting, because even then nobody believed the unstable status quo could endure. There is also the camaraderie of war veteran kibbutzniks, the majority, and the antipathy of the Prussian for the Ausländer, a prejudice still prevalent in Germany and which I, passing for an Arab worker, experienced there. There were other reasons for getting the treatment, a form of brainwashing.

Compared to Sde Boker, I was really on pretty good behavior. The departure date of January 25 was not fixed in our minds. We could have extended our visas, an appealing alternative to returning to New York in the dead of winter with no place to stay but with relatives while we looked for something more permanent. And I did get satisfaction from the work, pleasure from the magic of spring in a place where it would seem impossible. I will always wonder what Melville would have made of spring. Quitting work at three in the afternoon gave me ample time to saunter in the newly sprung alpine meadows just above the back gate. I had only to follow the wadi for about a half hour, taking with me a gargantuan pear-shaped pumelo (the poor man's grapefruit I teased the members), before I was in the bosom of the rainy hills with flowers enough to be my sunshine. I thought February was the best month, with more rain and more days off to enjoy the hills now shrouded in mist and the wilderness of flora, a magic carpet that took me to Switzerland and snow-capped mountains that would appear when the wet banks of clouds lifted. Not so.

This was the first time in years I was getting into something resembling a work routine that I so badly needed, though the first half hour of work was numbing. My routine was to take the shortcut just above the swimming pool, pausing to watch the usually pink sky over the Moab fade into the palest blue. Then as Mona and the sleepy South Americans left the chow hall and piled on their paddy wagon—hauled by the perennial tractor—I would traipse through the newly sprung Goden to the gate that opened on the date grove, vineyards and pumelos. Yoni who was on the job by five to feed his cows just outside the groves, or his girlfriend, would usually open the gate, which I would swing open for whoever transported the volunteers to the vineyards. By the time the tractor had gone the length of the groves to stop outside the "tool shed' and the niños and niñas got their act together, I would be ready to go myself, working like a demon to keep warm during the first hour from seven to eight.

Mona would take one side of a vine, some with grape clusters that survived the harvest, I the other. But within the hour I would be a dozen vines down the line leaving Mona to her own delicate devices. Not only was she a perfectionist, but she was not up to wrestling the vines. Reluctantly, I backtracked to assist her, the artist working best in isolation, too many brushes spoil the canvas. I didn't know if I was farmer or artisan. I was both, gratifying my creative urge, but more important for the born creator falling into line. Temporarily, of course.

The actual pruning required skill, as well as stamina, if you were to go the distance, a satisfying counterpoint to pulling the pruned vines away from the unyielding trellis or wires that ran as high as eight feet above the ground. Forgetting my age (a way to remain young), I went at the venerable Vitis with a vengeance, as much for the sheer combative joy of it—stamping out the vineyards where the grapes of wrath are stored—the work, as well as the workout. A kind of St. Vitis dance.

To their great amusement, I had informed the niños and niñas that I was Don Quixote. Apparently, I could not look more quixotic if I were jousting with a windmill. From eight to nine, I couldn't think of more enjoyable work than pulling vines, pruning or simply tuning into the telegraph grapevine—in Spanish. With winter evaporated and spring in the air as yet free of fleas, and crisp, this was a demented man's delight. When I faced east, I looked upon the mountains of Moab, and when I was on the eastern side of the grapevine, the hills of Yehuda were my backdrop. With my Vitis touch, I was a sculptor whose craft was functional, shaping a living, breathing candelabra that would be laden with grape clusters in just a few weeks. By May, they would be ready to eat. (Now I was eating last year's grapes from the vines.) I knew the joy of partaking in this ancient occupation, though early on I did not associate grapes with Israel, Man Oh Manichevitz not withstanding. At least, not with ancient Israel, and yet, vineyards are the earliest and latest symbol of Judaism. The vine is the emblem of the nation, on the coins of the Maccabees, whose victory we celebrated a few weeks earlier, and in a colossal golden cluster grapes that overhung the porch of the second temple. In the Golan Heights we saw huge stones with grape clusters that both Arab and Jew laid claim to. The grapes of Judah still mark the tombstones of the Jews in Prague. When Noah became drunk, he cursed the vineyards of Canaan, days of wine and thorns, if not roses. "Is not the gleaning of the grapes of Ephraim better than the vintage of Abiezer?" (Judges 8:2) As in sober as a judge.

My earliest memories are of crates of grapes stacked on the sidewalk outside our house in Queens. A few days later in the "cellar," I was high on the air, rich and heavy with the fermenting grapes being pressed into wine (part of my father's early autumn ritual I partook in). Some time passed before he bottled the wine, a bottle of which nightly graced the dinner table for my judgmental father who never got drunk. He encouraged me to taste the wine.

Now, Mona and I paved the way for grapes sweet and purple that would be eaten only. I would like to think that the reason for those remaining grapes that I ate, indigenous to the land, had their roots in a commandment from the bible: "And thou shalt not glean thy vineyard, neither shalt thou gather every grape of thy vineyard; thou shalt leave them for the poor and stranger: I am the Lord your God." (Numbers 19:10) David did a number on us, saying that he saved or put aside bananas for the Arabs. Mona thought this was admirable, but with the indoctrination he was getting—we couldn't listen to Arab music without people being up in arms—he would have gotten a swift kick for being the Good Samaritan.

Mornings, I raided the banana grove and sometimes forsook lunch for the breakfast of chimpanzees. I savored this lush sliver of Tropicana, I was fond of those fronds. With or without my Wheaties, I thought there nothing more tasty than a banana—just west of where Moses crossed the Jordan. A myth to most kibbutzniks.

It was only after I questioned David's thoughtfulness—in light of the fact that less adventurous Jewish volunteers were not so fortunate—that there appeared one day a stalk of those tiny but tasty bananas hanging from the roof of the shed, up for grabs during our breaks. Dates remained hidden. I was reminded of Sde Boker where the expensive exportable fruit was very rarely on display like the other fruit or food. It was kept under wraps in the kitchen. Understandably, grapes out of season were unavailable. So that when the dentist picked at my teeth and dislodged a grape pit, I could not convince him that it was not my filling that he had loosened and I had spat out. Israel has always been the land of the grape, though there be poets who would have Tahiti as the Promised Land—where there are no vines that promise wines.

The heat transported us to Tahiti, but there was a serpent in paradise, as the sweater came off, the fleas came out. Not quite as numerous or persistent as the black flies of Labrador, they did not insist on going down your throat. But there was here something of the land God left to Cain.

By ten in the morning, we had experienced winter, spring and summer, as we know the seasons in the temperate zone—unless the mid-January day was overcast and we knew autumn the day long.

I guess it was the spraying more than anything else that hastened our departure from Gilgal. I don't know if the toxic spray from France was used to prevent the growth of fungi or one plague or another, but it was deadly stuff of a nice blue color. David was taken out of his banana grove for a few days (where he was getting a good dose of other chemicals) and went to the hospital one night, where either his heart almost stopped beating or running away with him. There were other life-threatening symptoms, and David is far from being a wimp. Without his protective mask, he had been spraying the blue death, hot on the heels of the pruners. Maybe he was anxious to prove how macho he was to the Israelis putting pressure on him to put his mouth (and body) where his mother's money was—that is, to join the army.

Come to think about it, and I haven't given it much thought this past year, he may very well have worn his mask. The grape king Isha, or Iser as Mona referred to our easygoing overseer, later told us that complications set in if the sprayer drank alcohol after work. David did drink wine that night. The vineyards' revenge, you might say. Grapes of wrath, indeed.

For a couple of days we helped the Arabs in the experimental area. Five nodes, wicks on about fifteen candles. I think the irrigation had been turned on for these barely pruned vines that would throw out shoots in just a few days, bearing miniscule clusters. The Palestinian pruners were really pros and contracted out to Gilgal. Their contractor or overseer was an Israeli who was candid about the lot of his workers, that with the weasel badgering me and David becoming omnipresent, I wondered if I was being baited or provoked to spit out where my sympathies lie—like this baloney about the bananas being put aside for the Palestinians. I had merely asked the man where the Arabs lived, what they were paid, and he went into the whole litany of Israeli abuses, the indiscriminate late night searches and seizures, etc.—the then little known history of the occupation that led to the uprising.

But I think the man was genuine, maybe feeling a little guilty about his own exploitation of the Arabs, but also wanting to see an end to an intolerable situation, for both the Jew and the Arab of conscience. Maybe this was a cry for help. The contractor had a good deal going and was comfortable in his house on the hill not far from his Arab neighbors and only needed that extra push to put his money where his mouth was. He knew the occupation was really exploitation, but how to be free of that militaristic drumming-in that this is a buffer zone. How to be free of that esprit de corps embodied by a history of pogroms, programming, Massna Saraba—the holocaust—and that overwhelming weight of monuments and memory of sacrifice that inspired the '67 victory. The apocalyptic spirit of Massada itself, this sticking to your guns no mater the cost that spoke of a Dr. Strangelovian affair with death: "We have made a covenant with death, and with hell are we at agreement." (Isaiah 28:15)

How to be free? It took great courage to break ranks like the army captain a year later who refused to serve in the occupied territories. This reservist, a sociology student, knew that Israel's leaders had failed to make peace with the Palestinians for a dead-end policy that is a cheap source of labor and a large market for its finished products. Mr. Amor, the captain, will pay a high price for advocating the Palestinian right to self-determination. Israel a higher price for discrimination.

Separate from the workers, it seemed the world were the shepherds who tramped the hills above us. Going up there almost took me back to northern Argentina eleven years earlier, when I didn't know whom to fear most—the Death Squad or the guerrillas. Ultimately, being basically democratic, I feared both equally, though it was the military that came closest to doing me in.

And so it was in the hills above Gilgal as I made my way back to the kibbutz. It was one of those glorious rain-soaked days splashed with splotches of sunshine, that threatening El Greco sky over Toledo that will produce a rainbow.

I entered a narrow gulch and quickened my step, an extra surge of adrenalin released by the appearance of a swiftly moving Arab who was apparently descending upon me. At first, he seemed to be shouting out a question and paused at the bluff directly above me. His head was loosely swathed. I could see he was elderly and that there was great urgency in his voice, words, and syllables I thought I would never forget, though I understand no Arabic. He pointed in the direction I was going in apparent warning. Though perhaps not reported in the American press, there was already great unrest in Nablus in the upper reaches of these hills, and I couldn't forget he was Palestinian. I grinned like an idiot as if we'd never gotten beyond salem and kept my mouth shut, hoping that this shepherd thought I was just another Arab—if somewhat retarded. And yet, I had more to fear from a trigger-happy Israeli.

Surely, the Arab wouldn't be shouting a warning to an Israeli. I was pretty much convinced that his carrying on was not a ruse but a way to dissuade me from returning to the kibbutz, though this was not the easiest passage to Gilgal. Had he cut me off at the pass to warn me about the possibilities of a flashflood? I thought it more likely, staying my course, smiling, now allowing for a guttural sound in simulation of the native tongue, the old-timer would think I was an Arab and merely wanted me to know that it behooved me to stay out of the way of the settlers up ahead. Whatever the danger, I could not turn back. Nearby, settlers (not likely kibbutzniks) had recently killed a Palestinian, shooting the man from their car.

A week earlier (as mentioned in chapter one), an obviously abused shepherd just outside the back gate and close enough to me to see that I was no Arab mistook me for an Israeli asking him for money.

Of course, this registered on my brain like a series of dots and dashes—an increased ringing in the ear—not entirely comprehensible to a rusty radio operator, but I felt I had little choice but to go on, the rain clouds closing in behind with perhaps Arabs. Although the kibbutzniks allowed me to wander into a minefield, I could not accept they wanted me out of the way. But I didn't know.

At any rate, when the old man had tired of trying to persuade me from going on and had returned to his flock, for the first time in forty years I thought about Psalm 23. This may seem like the most facile literary device yet, as I've picked up a Psalm here and there in this Psalm grove of a Holy Land; but it was the only one I had memorized: "The Lord is my shepherd… yea though I walk through the valley of the shadow of death, I will fear no evil."

Actually, this was the extent of my religious education. Of a very literal mind when I was a child, I'm not sure if I knew what the words were about. When an older friend told me a horse could kick me for a mile, I pictured myself flying twenty city blocks and weighed this improbability against my friend lying to me. My father, an angry atheist though baptized a Catholic, was determined to spare me the same fate and kept me out of the clutches of the church. There wasn't so much as a bible in the house. But some Christian soul took pity on me and gave me a little card with a picture of Jesus quoting the Old Testament. He told me to repeat the words every night before I went to bed—and so began my death valley days.

28

Valley of the Shadow of Death

Those words that meant nothing to me as a child permeated my very being. This Psalm grew out of this valley and spoke to my situation and sense of synchronicity. Yet another sign that all was fate and that I was on the right track. Valley or mountain, I was on the high road, and the power and glory in that certitude washed over me and spilled onto the earth around me. Rock and flower, mountain and valley were bathed in a beatific glow that only the vulnerable know—and certain sophisticated pot smokers. This was that well defined landscape that reveals itself after the smoke has lifted.

As the pass opened on a larger canyon and a ravine sloped to the very valley, a shot rang out, maybe two or three. At bottom of the ravine, maybe a third of a mile away, a man scrambled up the walls of the abyss. I could not make out a weapon, but assumed this fellow in a hurry was the pot shot perpetrator and now he was going to confront me. I was scared enough to consider turning back, little comforted by the metaphorical "rod" or "staff" of the almighty, or my father's pathetic pen knife now at the ready. More rusty than trusty, it could barely peel an apple. Nonetheless, the open knife was cupped in the palm of my hand, as a husky soldier with an Uzi slung over his shoulder met me halfway. He paused atop a knobby knoll, outside the bunker that commands a view of Jordan.

When I was near enough to Rambo to make out his features, I mistook him for one of the soldiers who was often guarding the chow hall. A smile of relief filled my face, and I called out a confident shalom. Since the dark-skinned man didn't know me from Adam, his smile was less assured. Closer inspection revealed this strapping fellow was a perfect stranger who felt ill at ease. In the shadow of Nablus, as the shepherd walks, he had confronted what was obviously in his element, though neither fish nor fowl. The momentum of my ill-gotten confidence still carried me. The soldier spoke little English and didn't know if I was an Arab, whose self-assurance could indicate he was armed.

An encounter of a kind, accordingly, his handshake was clammy, though that could have been sweat. Rambo reached for my canteen, claiming he'd been after a mountain lion or some such mythical creature. He was uneasy, coming on so strong about dangerous animals that I didn't know what to make of his chasing paper tigers. I didn't know if he was aware of my knife, but I expected anything and wondered if I'd be able to get at his throat. This may sound laughable, but I knew he was capable of anything. He had been all psyched up for an encounter with a Palestinian, and I had caught him wet-handed.

I was trying my damndest to convince him that I worked at Gilgal, but I don't think I was very persuasive. He wasn't ready for that, as implausible to this North African as my claiming to be a New Yorker. It was one thing to be a reasonably educated sabra of European descent for whom New York is familiar, but may "Orientals" did not enjoy the same opportunities.

"I would like to go to New York when I get some money and a passport."

I hoped he had no illusions about acquiring the necessary travel items now.

"New York is very expensive, no?"

"Yes."

He asked what it was like, and I wondered if this guy so intent on going to the Big Apple wasn't the shakedown artist who was making the rounds, or if he was still in doubt about my identity...but that's absurd, he would have asked for papers.

Trying to disabuse him of the idea of going to the Bad Apple, I simply told him the truth. "There's a lot of crime. It's very dangerous."

"Dangerous! You think an Israeli soldier is going to be afraid in New York?"

"You won't be allowed to take your Uzi on the subway."

Rambo versus Rimbaud. His bravado and improbable fear unnerved me. I was chilled. He wasn't thirsty but wanted to see if my canteen was a Molotov cocktail—like the police at the Ben-Gurion Centennial. If it was obvious (though not too) that I was not a Palestinian, could I not be a sympathizer? How many members of one Red Brigade or another— the IRA—had come to Israel as tourists, only to collaborate with the

Palestinians? In Rambo's eyes, was there anything else that could account for my rambling in this no-man's land (beyond the biblical shepherd)? Spring was in the air, budding, bursting through the earth, the Old Testament time for redemption, the coming of the Lord, but the grapes of wrath were ripe. A year later, he would be wearing his helmet with the words "Born to kill" scrawled on it.

It was the offspring of the shepherds who wanted to claim these hills for themselves, as well as for their sheep, who would be killed by Israelis. Again, I was struck with the fact that these Arabs came closest to being the original Jews. Whatever that really means, they belonged here, in the spirit of the people who created the Talmud. Remaining shepherds, they played their magic flutes, songs of Solomon that lured me into the hills time and again. This was the pull of roots, not unlike my encounter with the Masai, when I was drawn into the Ngorongoro crater. An African beginning that spoke of true Genesis, but this past month those now verdant hills I tramped was a journey into childhood. The wadi below was a passage to the beginnings of the Mediterranean people, if you followed it to its source.

The choice is brotherhood, the individuality beyond it, or continuing tribal warfare, brothers killing brothers because Daddy War Bucks willed it. But to get technical, the purest Jews were more Turkish than Semite, which made me more of a Semite than the average Jew—if there is such a thing. The Turkoman is still in the face of many Jews. Before leaving Anatolia, we met a young Turk who looked exactly like Tony Curtis, Hollywood's favorite Jew. When he spoke, we watched a comedy. Was there a tribe that didn't think it was chosen, not to take away from the merits of the Old Testament. The Eskimos living in the "land God left to Cain" called themselves the "people." One reason there are so many "lost tribes" is that the more imaginative tribes who evolved from the same sources and have the same collective consciousness, conjure up the same exclusivity myth. Or as Plato said: "I wonder if we could contrive some magnificent myth that would in itself carry conviction to our whole community."

One of the saddest aspects of Jewish history is the irony that, through thick and thin, mostly the world over, the Jews, some of them indeed remnants of a lost tribe, hold on to their binding customs. They did not succumb to the savagery of the host country—in many cases the alternative was denied them. There was this ennobling continuity that made for community, no matter how transient. Often the Jews had to keep their identity secret but through it all had created a kind of promised land borne of their covenant with God. This inner peace was shattered and their conviction found wanting when the God-intoxicated got drunk on power—blind drunk and oblivious to the humanity of the Palestinians. I won't try to define, divine, God beyond the signs, but even if El Supremo does not give a tinkers damn about man, you cannot go through history believing in a solemn agreement with Him or Her and not turn against yourself after you've violated the sacred pact.

Perhaps I'm reading into Rambo's discomfort the arrogance of the top down government, but the fact is that on the West Bank I may as well have been a Palestinian. My safety was nothing to the Israeli and the fact that soldiers practically acted with impunity increased my paranoia. Paranoia breeds paranoia and nowhere was it more effectively cultivated than in the Jordan Valley. As I looked for reasons for my possible dispatchment, I had to consider that I was being considered something of a sacrificial lamb. In a frame-up, my death could look like it was the Arabs' doing, some future justification for Israeli retaliation against the Palestinian. They were being driven off the land, and getting rid of a potentially troublesome writer would be killing two birds with one stone.

Since, obviously, I'm not finished with Israel, I fear Israel is not finished with me. Last night I dreamt I was Palestinian. On the West Bank, the intifada raged on. The soldier probably wanted to see if I had my bearings, maybe lost himself. As the mist closed in, he asked in what direction was Gilgal. I pointed directly below me, and then as I set out for the kibbutz, he followed behind me. I had no idea what the soldier intended, and yet I feared "no evil." He turned north on level ground, just before the grave sized holes (not freshly dug). I forget Rambo's real name, but he departed with grace and suggested we meet again, before he disappeared somewhere on his path back to his moshav where he was stationed. Not knowing where I stood had taken its toll.

Between my arm and my teeth, I was doing little work my last few days at Gilgal. Not only was I pulling vines with my left hand, but I'd also become a southpaw pruner, straining my left arm as well. Still, there was little that would interfere with my walking, and I was going into shepherd country every opportunity, if only for a couple of hours. In a few minutes I could array the most exotic bouquet and rarely returned to Mona without a bunch of flowers. Once I made up my mind to leave the country, I savored every moment of my sylvan retreats, my journey into the bible—staying clear of the approaches to the bunker. I would rather take my chances with unarmed Arabs.

I also tried to avoid the shepherds, though that wasn't always possible with men as sure-footed as goats who know every nook and niche between Gilgal and Nablus. Or if coming from the southwest, Ramallah and Gilgal. A not-so-fertile crescent of hidden valleys creased like the back of a dirt farmer's neck, and sometimes a bit hair-raising. Though a living link with the Old Testament, I never saw a Jewish settler roaming these hills, never saw a kibbutznik driving on the jeep track. They were the occupiers but also the prisoners of the Palestinians.

My contact with the shepherds was mostly non-verbal and, now far from Gilgal, I observed some deer and wanted to stay clear of them. How dear the deer were.

Tensions were building up, and it seemed that every other week a Jew was being stabbed. Maybe tourists were spared, but I think the Palestinians, unless there was a grapevine extending into the hills, still puzzled over my identity. Of course, the mad are regarded with some respect and I guess I expected to be left in peace. The kibbutznik had told me the Arabs would leave me alone, but then they didn't appear to have my best interests at heart. On the other hand, an Arab mistaking me for a Jew would assume I was armed. One guy who turned up on the kibbutz recently always packed a revolver. Rather, it always seemed to be unpacked, lying on a table or some such place and pointing at me. Was this fellow trying to tell me something?

On my last day at Gilgal, or maybe the next to last, a young Arab got close enough to me to shake my hand. This was okay, but he seemed so fascinated with my ring that I had forgotten to leave with Mona that I wondered if he wasn't above removing my finger if that's what it took to take it. It was how he stole upon me that worried me. He had no livestock, and I had to consider I was fair game, as the young do not revere enchanted people as do their parents. I suspect he thought I was a tourist or an unreasonable facsimile, and my suspicions were further aroused when this unlikely shepherd approached another fellow who had stood his ground. He seemed to be indicating to the second man that I had a noteworthy ring and maybe he was telling him that I did not appear to have a firearm. If this is worthy of mention, it's only because, lucky or not, in the three months that had passed I had only benefited from the kindness of the Arabs and, even now, may have simply met someone who admired rings and squares. I'll never know, because I was hot on the heels of the deer who'd gotten wind of these guys before I did.

A year later, I wonder if the shepherds have still pretty much remained above the fray. I wonder if the beginning will be the end, if they will be what remains of all the sons of Abraham, after the fratricide ceases. Or as this war without end continues, will they be a reminder of the way. Or will they be drawn into the civil war and experience that loss of innocence that will close the final chapter of the living bible. An Old Testament to living in harmony with the environment, a constant reminder that the Promised Land can only mean peace of mind—without which all is a no-man's land. It's easy to romanticize when I compare their peaceful life to that unnatural existence behind the barbed wire of the kibbutz.

It's easy to overlook the primitive round of the nomad—and that's what I did one day as I literally overlooked the chasm below me, the lower side of the canyon was home to maybe a dozen Arabs, their tents back from the canyon wall. Above them caves were also occupied. The females never wandered very far from an encampment, since it was the males who followed the flock. On my side of the canyon on a grassy ledge just below me, I was surprised to see three cows knee deep in flowers.

I didn't expect the Israelis to live this way, but there was a happy medium open to them before they closed the door on their past. Alas, playing the End Game of all or nothing at all, Israel has forfeited freedom for nihilistic war.

It was so easy not to see the reality of Israel, as all Jews stood tall in the shadow of the nouveau Centurion. So easy not to see the dirt for the brainwashing, the uprooted trees of the Arabs for the instant Jewish forest—some of those from seedlings bought with the pennies Mona had saved as a little girl. I try not to pass judgment, but I cannot accept genocidal occupation as God's gift.

The Jews most understanding of the Palestinian problem are the Jacobo Timermans, the writer Appleman, concentration camp victims, who are no strangers to suffering. An indirect good that can come of the uprising is a Jewish awakening to the dispossession of the Palestinians in the name of a racist dream. Jews who would like to learn what they've given their heart, soul and money to should read How Israel Lost Its Soul by Maxim Ghilan...and helped us lose ours.

29

Let the Music Begin

We have been down this road before, and we can see how far words (wars) have taken us.

If there is anything holy about the "Holy Land," it is the music. The open heart that carries us away to that promised land, peace beyond religion and regime, Israel or ISIS. Those last days in Jerusalem music may have saved my own sanity.

We were in St. Anne's church one day when materializing out of the blue like a messenger goddess, dressed in blue, was a woman sing ing. Somewhere in the Old Testament it reads "singing unto Zion," and many of the pilgrims in Jerusalem take this quite literally.

It is not unusual for the musical, mostly in choirs from the four corners, to break into song in a Jerusalem church, and St. Anne's is famous for its tricky acoustics, but never was the beautiful more beatific. This woman's notes reverberated off the walls like a rolling Jordan. The few tourists who sat in the church with my wife and me were mesmerized by the mysterious woman's voice. It was a clear voice that pierced the gathering storm clouds in the troubled Mideast and could be heard above the screech of the "yellow wind," an Arab term for a cleansing force. The woman's words were unimportant, but the message she sent was the unspoken one of transcendence—the universal language of music that takes us beyond the religions that have mostly divided man.

We didn't remain in St. Anne's very long after that because anything else that could come to pass there would be anticlimactic.

As we walked up Via Dolorosa to the Knights Palace Hotel where we were once more staying, we again came upon the singer. The woman in blue was edging her small car to the Damascus Gate. She smiled at my belated "Bravo!"

www.ingramcontent.com/pod-product-compliance
Lightning Source LLC
Chambersburg PA
CBHW031434160426
43195CB00010BB/728